PUBLIC LIBRARY OF JOHNSTON COUNTY
AND SMITHFIELD-SMITHFIELD, NC

W9-CER-115

WITHDRAWN

PUBLIC LIBRARY OF JOHNSTON COUNTY
AND SMITHFIELD-SMITHFIELD, NC

urban
DICTIONARY

FULARIOUS STREET SLANG DEFINED

COMPILED BY AARON PECKHAM,
CREATOR OF URBANDICTIONARY.COM

Andrews McMeel
Publishing, LLC
Kansas City

Urban Dictionary

Copyright © 2005 by Aaron Peckham. All rights reserved. Printed in the United States of America. No part of this book may be used or reproduced in any manner whatsoever without written permission except in the case of reprints in the context of reviews. For information, write Andrews McMeel Publishing, LLC, an Andrews McMeel Universal company, 4520 Main Street, Kansas City, Missouri 64111.

08 09 RR2 10

ISBN-13: 978-0-7407-5143-1
ISBN-10: 0-7407-5143-3

Library of Congress Cataloging-in-Publication Data

Peckham, Aaron.
    Urban dictionary: fularious street slang defined / compiled by Aaron Peckham.
    p. cm.
    ISBN 0-7407-5143-3
    1. Sociology, Urban—United States—Dictionaries 2. English
language—Slang—Dictionaries. I. Title.

HT108.5.P43 2005
307.76'0973'03—dc22

2005048223

www.andrewsmcmeel.com

Book design by Diane Marsh

ATTENTION: SCHOOLS AND BUSINESSES

Andrews McMeel books are available at quantity discounts with bulk purchase for educational, business, or sales promotional use. For information, please write to: Special Sales Department, Andrews McMeel Publishing, LLC, 4520 Main Street, Kansas City, Missouri 64111.

URBAN DICTIONARY

A dictionary of human interaction, defining slang, pop culture, and everyday urban life. A resource for parents trying to understand their kids, for language learners confused by real-world English—but most of all for your entertainment. A from-the-streets explanation of contemporary culture and language available online at www.urbandictionary.com, in the pages of this book, or from any nearby teenager.

5/12/09 Ingram (1299) 2.79

sHout outs

Big ups to the peeps who made this project possible.
To my agent, Sheila, who keeps the biz on lock; to my editor,
Lane, who kept my pages in check; to my profs, especially
Dr. Bensky, Dr. Turner, Dr. Battenburg, and Prof. Stearns,
who kept me on point; to my friends who always got my
back, especially Dave, Jordan, Mike, Russell, Scott, Barrett,
and Anna; and most of all to the 'rents, Doug and Brenda,
whose constant encouragement, advice, and support were
clutch since day one.

After six years of constant submissions, Urban
Dictionary has become the first reference for everyday
language. Dedicated and loyal users from all over the
planet took time to write creative, entertaining definitions
from their lives. Their words have now become an
invaluable resource for the world. Props.

INTRODUCTION

Urban Dictionary has always had a life of its own—and that was always the point. I started urbandictionary.com in 1999 as an online slang dictionary with user-submitted definitions. Since its inception people have written more than one million definitions for 250,000 words, and today more than two million people visit the site every month.

What started out as a site where only my dorm friends tracked their regional slang expressions has turned into an ever-evolving portrait of the language spoken by millions of everyday people, every day. Today Urban Dictionary doesn't just track the creation of new language. It's become a hip hangout for a whole community, where people get a chance to explain how they use and change existing language to express their own views of the world around them.

Urban Dictionary's users range from creatively rebellious teenagers who write openly about their lives in their definitions, to hip twentysomethings and thirtysomethings with unique and entertaining insights into the definitions of emerging words, to not quite so hip 'rents and teachers who want to know why their kids or students keep referring to them as "hella bootsy," to serious students of the English language from all over the world. The content of Urban Dictionary has become the irreverent calling card of a linguistic generation. These definitions might be funny to some and offensive to others, but that's the nature of the urban beast. To those who can't take the linguistic heat, I can only say step off and chillax. Everyone deserves the opportunity to understand and be understood.

As of this writing there are 250,000 unique words on the site, and it's the diversity and quality of opinion used to define these words that makes Urban Dictionary so popular. These are the true, funny, wry, angry, shy, intelligent, quirky, fresh, smart-ass voices of today, and they have a lot to say.

Of Urban Dictionary's one million definitions, I've chosen the funniest, wittiest, and truest submissions from the site's best authors. I chose some of these words because they reveal aspects of pop or hip-hop culture, some because they live only in the online world, and some just because they're hilarious. I couldn't make them up if I tried.

Urban Dictionary changes daily, and with every new definition it becomes a more accurate, funny, and insightful look at the world—your world. So for all of you who want to earn some *street cred*, for the urban illiterate *newbie* who confuses *skank* with *shank*, and for the slang speaker who wants to keep his *game tight*, this just might be a good book to keep handy.

*

1. Symbol used to correct a typo that was just text messaged.

Joe: Well, that was spupid.
*Joe: *stupid*

2. Something placed after a statement in advertising to say that the statement isn't true.

FREE ROOT BEER FOR LIFE!*
*only valid for 45-year-old war veterans in El Paso.

3. Symbol used to bleep out cuss words or in place of a letter when typing or writing.

Holy sh*t!

4. A nickname for President George W. Bush. It comes from the comic strip *Doonesbury,* by Garry Trudeau. Instead of actually drawing President Bush, he uses an asterisk in his place, probably to show readers his opinion of the man.

Stupid * and his War on Terror!

1+1=3
Reproduction joke. The "1+1" refers to two people having sex; the extra "1" represents a potential baby, making a total of 3 people.

Guy 1: I'm gonna get laid tonight!
Guy 2: Whatever, man, just remember that sometimes 1+1=3.

10 feet
The length of the pole that is sometimes needed to touch unsightly or repugnant objects and/or people.

Bubba: I wouldn't touch that girl with a 10-foot-pole.
Fred: You're right, Bubba. 10 feet ain't a big enough distance. Them cooties she's got can jump farther than that.

10 minutes ago

Out of style.

That hat is so 10 minutes ago.

10 on that

Phrase used to agree strongly to a statement or affirm what has been said.

Man 1: I sure do hate hangovers.
Man 2: 10 on that, brother.

10-4

Code used by police or other 10 code–using services to mean "message received," or "I understand your transmission."

Dispatch: Shooting at 3rd and California.
Patrol car: 10-4, I'm on my way!

10-9

Code used by police or other 10 code–using services meaning "repeat" or "say again."

Can you please 10-9 your last transmission?
It was a little 10-1 (distorted, broken up).

12

The ideal (or not ideal) age, depending on how you look at it.

I like girls, just don't expect me to say it out loud.
I hate 'em too—very loudly.
I didn't mean to, somebody pushed me!
School days are way too looooong.
Weekends are way too short and not enough of 'em.
Is it lunch yet?
Who taped thumbtacks to my chair seat?!
Where's the food?
Do I gotta do math today?
Who cares who was president in 1841?!
He's dead, ya know!
Oh, wow! Stephanie's bending over!
Nnnnniiiiiiiccccccce!
See? I would make a great 12-year-old. Been there, done that. Being 12 is wasted on people who will spend a whole year learning how to be 12 and when they finally get it right, they turn 13 and have to start over. Being 12 should be reserved for people who already know how.

12 rounds

To do something for a long period of time. Named for the 12 rounds in boxing matches.

I went 12 rounds with her last night.

1337

Hacker word for leet, or elite. Refers

to a skilled hacker. Written in the language of leet speak, in which letters are replaced by symbols and numbers.

He told me he hacked Paris Hilton's phone. He's so 1337.

143

Means "I love you." One letter in I, four in love, and three in you. Used in the song "143" on Musiq's album *Aijuswanaseing*.

I have to go. 143.

2-way

To have a conversation between two people via electronic means, e.g., a cell phone, an online chat, etc.

During my lunch break, I took out my cell phone and 2-wayed my friend.

20-minute rule

The rule that gives you the right to leave your place of employment 20 minutes after your boss leaves the building.

Dude, my boss just left! 20-minute rule is in effect!

$200 word

An educated or "big" word used in place of a more common word so one can try to appear smarter than they really are.

Foo: I ventured to the marketplace and purchased many consumer goods.
Dirty: Foo, all you did was go to the damn sto' and buy sum shit. That all you had to say! Quit usin' them $200 words!

24/7

24 hours a day, 7 days a week. Used as slang for something that happens often, or constantly.

That dude is stoned 24/7.

24/7/365

24 hours a day, 7 days a week, 365 days a year. Constantly, without a moment's cessation.

That dude is horny 24/7/365!

30-day trial

Time limit for doing something about a crush. Whether it be a date, going out, or sex, if no progress is made in 30 days, you have to move on to the next one.

I hope my 30-day trial with that hot senior in yearbook works.

360 flip

A skateboarding maneuver in which the skater scoops the board around with their back foot to make the board do a 360-degree spin and one flip. It's a key move that is easy for pros to do and really great to watch.

Oi, 360 flip that 10 stair!

4-banger

A vehicle with a 4-cylinder engine. They're pretty much crap without some sort of forced induction system.

You can turn your 120hp Integra 4-banger into a 250hp contender with a turbo kit, mate.

40

40 ounces of (usually low-quality) beer.

Yo, Jeff, did you pick up the 40s to kick back with?

411

Information. From dialing 411 on the phone for information.

Damn, she's fine. I'm gonna get the 411 on her.

420

1. National weed day. April 20.

It's 420 and I'm takin' a vacation day.

2. To smoke weed.

Let's go 420.

3. The weed itself. Marijuana, pot.

Did you hit that 420?

5

1. The number of fingers on one hand, or a hand slap involving the hand and this many fingers.
2. The police. Short for "five-o."
3. A number between 4 and 6.
4. Short for "five minutes."

Nice job on the 7-Eleven, man, give me 5! Now let's hit up this Dunkin' Donuts. Oh, shit, the 5 are in there! 5 of them, dawg! Better wait 5.

5 by 5

1. Loud and clear. Rating used to report the signal strength and clarity of a transmission. A 5 by 1 means a strong signal is present, but what is said cannot be understood. 1 by 5 means it can be understood, but a signal is barely coming in. 5 by 5 is ideal on both counts. Sometimes shortened to "5 by."

Command: Command to alpha2IC, do you read?
alpha2IC: Command, this is alpha2IC, I got you 5 by 5.

2. Can also be used to say one is doing well.

Guy 1: How's it going?
Guy 2: 5 by 5, man.

5 on it

1. Putting some money toward the purchase of an item or items. Usually indicates a willingness to contribute.

I've got 5 on that pizza.

2. Calling 5-minute rule on something.

Don't even try it, biotch. See that chair over there? I already got 5 on it.

5150

Crazy. California police code for "escaped lunatic." Also the name of Eddie Van Halen's home recording studio and the name of a Van Halen CD.

It's crazy in here! Everyone's gone 5150.

73

Ham radio talk for "best regards," "talk to you later," "goodbye for now." Originated during the early days of radio where abbreviations shortened messages in Morse code.

"73 de W1AW" means "talk to you again soon, from radio station call sign W1AW."

808

Loud bass. Police code for disturbing the peace.
Boom! Like an 808.

867-5309

A fake phone number given to guys from girls that essentially means "screw off" or "I already have a boyfriend, phreak." Named after the number used in the Tommy Tutone song "Jenny." Jenny is supposed to be a girl whose number was found on the wall of a bathroom. After the song came out, people nation-wide started calling the number in hopes of talking to Jenny.

Guy: Hey, what's your digits?
Girl: 867-5309. Call me!
Guy: Damn, bitch!

881

In Mandarin Chinese, the number 8 is prounounced "ba" and the number 1 is pronounced "yi." Put them together and you get "ba-ba-yi," which when spoken fast sounds like the English "bye-bye."

Luv ya, doll. 881!

8 ball
An eighth of an ounce of cocaine or meth.

Damn, that 8 ball is already gone!

9 to 5
A job (hours don't have to be 9 to 5).

I had to drop out of school and get a 9 to 5.

90% Theory
The nonscientific theory that the presence or lack of a characteristic in a population can be divided along 90% and 10% lines.

90% of people are morons; only 10% of people are worth knowing.

Only 10% of life is worth living.

90% of people who post on urbandictionary.com are complete and utter retards.

10% of the population uses 90% of our resources.

There's a 90% chance someone will find something in this example offensive.

99 problems
A lot of problems, but specifically not girl problems. From Jay-Z's song "99 Problems."

Guy 1: Hey, man, what's up with you?
Guy 2: 99 problems man, 99 problems.

uRban

a couple few

More than a few; several.

I sure would like a couple few of them possums for dinner.

a fifth

One-fifth of a liter of alcohol. Not to be confused with 750 ml, which is approximately a fifth of a gallon. There are three basic amounts: a fifth; a bottle, or seven-fifty (750 ml); and a handle (1750 ml).

I drank a fifth of bourbon by myself, but my boys and I polished off a bottle of Jäger and a handle of 151 together.

a little too Fab Five

Effeminate. Often used to describe an object or item with effeminate or homosexual overtones. Derived from the Fab Five, the five gay men who offer fashion and lifestyle advice to non-gay men on the Bravo Network series *Queer Eye for the Straight Guy*.

Tony, don't you think those low-rise bell-bottom pants and the midriff-baring shirt you're wearing are just a little too Fab Five?

a random

Someone (usually of the opposite sex, but not always) whose number you have, but whom you don't really know. May have met them once or twice (usually while intoxicated), but may have never even met them at all. You call them when you are bored and need something to do.

That guy's a random; got his number when I was wasted, but don't really know him.

aaand you're done

Expression used when someone really needs to shut up and they just don't realize it.

Chemp: And I was like, "Hells no, foo," and he was like, "Fo' real?" and I was like, "Daayum straight," and then he was like, "Listen dawg, I ain't—"
Tito: Aaand you're done.

abacadaba

To hurry up and get a multiple-choice test over with because it is so hard that it is pointless to try to take it, or you don't care about the grade. From the format of a multiple-choice test, where students fill in the lettered bubble of the correct answer.

Suze: How did you do on the test?
Regan: I just abacadaba-ed it.

abandonware

Software that is no longer sold or supported by the original publisher or developer, often found as free downloads on the Internet because it cannot be obtained elsewhere. Not legal but often seen as ethically acceptable because the company that made it is no longer selling the title or releasing it as freeware; therefore, abandonware is "keeping the game alive," so to speak.

Doom II is not abandonware because ID still sells it, while The Incredible Machine is not sold, so it's abandonware.

abc gum

Stands for "already been chewed" gum. Typically found under desks in school.

I don't want your abc gum!

abousta

About to.

I'm abousta kick yo' ass.
I'm abousta go to sleep.

above snakes

Alive and kicking.

Peter pulled a hardcore stunt, but thankfully he's still above snakes.

absofrickinlutely

1. A reinforced expression of "absolutely."

That chick is so absofrickinlutely amazing I want to jump her bones.

2. Expression of unquestionable doubt.

A: You sure that is the man in the photograph?
B: Absofrickinlutely!

absopos

To be certain, as in *abso*lutely *pos*itive.

Girl 1: Are you sure he's going to be there?
Girl 2: I'm absopos.

academic chicken

Knowingly turning in academic work of poor quality and essentially daring your professor or teacher to give you a bad grade.

I just submitted the worst paper I have ever written. It is nothing short of academic chicken.

ace

Excellent, very good.

It's ace!

acid

The drug lysergic acid diethylamide (LSD), a hallucinogen.

Dude, don't take the brown acid. You could have a bad trip.

acid jazz

A style of music that utilizes electronic and hip-hop techniques to create a somewhat sensual, psychedelic soundscape. It is often characterized by its use of loops and samples of original jazz and blues recordings but with electronic beats, scratching, and mixing.

Hey, I found the new Massive Attack album in the "acid jazz" section. I thought they were trip-hop.

ack

The sound one makes when choking on one's own words.

Ack! I didn't mean to say that. . . .

ACS

Acronym for Ancient Chinese Secret. Confidential.

When asked for the formula, I replied "ACS."

act a fool

To act like a total idiot.

It is not a good idea to act a fool around your boss.

act right

To put someone in check; to give someone a beatdown.

Yo, don't make me give you some act right.

act-right juice

An imaginary drink you give to someone who is misbehaving that makes them stop acting up.

You gotta lay off the haterade and start sippin' on some act-right juice!

action

Sexual activity.

Hey, you get any action last night?

actor

A person who commits a crime, especially murder.

Girl's been shot four times. Know who's the actor?

ad hoc

Unplanned for and done because of extenuating circumstances.

We ran out of toilet paper, so we had an ad hoc meeting to decide who would get some.

Adult Swim

Place where great cartoons like *The Family Guy* and *Futurama* and much animé hang out. Fun to watch if you like cartoons but don't want lots of the little kiddie crap that's on these days.

Futurama and The Family Guy *made nothing on Fox, but on Adult Swim they're making more money than ever.*

afaik

Acronym for "as far as I know."

A: When will the page be back?
B: Afaik in two hours.

afk

Acronym for "away from keyboard."

Yo, dudes, I'll be afk for a while.

afterparty

Party with a few intimate associates taking place after the main party, usually in a different location but peripherally related to the main party.

Eddie: 'Sup, Chavez, you know where da afterparty be?
Chavez: Yeah, when Monique be done DJing, she have it in her loft.

aggressive graffiti

Graffiti written by gang members that crosses out the preexisting graffiti of a rival. Sometimes it can include disrespectful taunts and threats against a rival gang and/or its members.

Some say aggressive graffiti is a precursor to violence.

aggro

Short for "aggravated." Crazy, wild.

The line was so long, and it was so hot, I started getting totally aggro.

agnosexual

Synonymous with "bisexual."
They call themselves agnosexuals because they think "bi" makes them sound sleazy.

aight

"All right," but in a hip and ghetto way.

My mom said, "Clean the car," and I said, "Aight."

AIM

1. An Internet text messaging program that exchanges communications between users in real time and allows college students to leave nifty online "away" messages for their buddies all day.

I used AIM to ask Sheila out on a date.

2. To AIM someone is to send them a message using the AIM program.

Sheila AIMed me back to tell me no.

ain't got no

Don't have any. Very commonly used in the southern United States.

Friend: Lend me a dollar, man.
You: You know I ain't got no money.

ain't no thang

It is no big deal.

Me: Sorry it took me so long to return your phone call.
My boss: It ain't no thang.

ain't no two bananas

The task at hand isn't going to be easy to accomplish. On Super Monkey Ball 2, the difficulty of each puzzle is rated on a 1–10 banana scale with one banana being the easiest and ten bananas being a complete pain in the ass, and damn near impossible.

Bill: My teacher wants a forty-page paper for tomorrow morning and I haven't started it yet!
Phil: That ain't no two bananas! Maybe you should drop the class.

air biscuit

A fart.

Do I smell an air biscuit?

air guitar

The act of making a guitar-playing motion with your hands, usually done while listening to music, while under the influence of alcohol, or both. What people do when they can't play guitar and want to look cool, but they just end up looking riduculous.

Jason got so drunk at the party last night that he started to air guitar along to the music and then barfed on the stereo.

air quotes

Little bunny ears made with the fingers that indicate that:
1. you're quoting someone else
2. you're being sarcastic
3. you still think the "la-sers" line from the first Austin Powers movie is funny.

Martha: Wow, it's been six years since I have seen you. Whatever happened to your (air quotes) "band"?

air time

The time a basketball player spends in the air while dunking the ball.

He had some serious air time on that last dunk.

airhead

A silly, rather unintelligent person.

Most blondes have a reputation for being airheads.

aka

Acronym for "also known as."

My name is Sammy, aka Big Sam.

alcohol

A substance found in beer (except American beer) and many other fine beverages that makes people excessively happy, sad, belligerent, or horny. It allows white men to dance and ugly men to get laid (when given to their victim).

You wanna get with that hottie? You're gonna need to buy lots of alcohol!

all about

An indication that one is enthusiastically in favor of something.

Mike: You want to go to the beach? Brady: Hell, yeah! I am all about hitting the surf!

all balled up

Depressed; having a lot of emotions knotted up inside.

After the breakup, Michelle felt all balled up.

all before lunch

A qualifying phrase intended to illustrate that someone has done a great deal in a short time (i.e., between the hours of 9 and 12, the shorter "half" of the workday). Sometimes used sarcastically.

I've researched the Abraham case on WestLaw and Lexis, ordered new office soft-

ware for the front desk, sat through three new client consultations, run to the courthouse and filed our motions, and had my oil changed on the way back, all before lunch.

Used sarcastically:
Tool: Hey, I called the office supplies place and ordered the pens you asked for.
Boss: Wow . . . and all before lunch.

all good

It's all right; don't worry. Just chill.

Kid: Waaah! Waaah! I dropped my ice cream.
Dad: It's all good, man, we can jus' buy you a new one!

all in capacity

To embarrass someone or to be embarrassed in front of a large group of people.

When she laughed in my face at the packed club, it was all in capacity.

all over it

To take care of something quickly and/or with gusto.

Boss: Did you finish the project?
Me: I'm all over it.

all over the map

Describing a situation that is

diverse or disorganized.

We can't stay in business if our finances are gonna be all over the map like this.

all talk

Describes someone who builds him- or herself up with a bunch of talk but can never back up anything he or she says.

Loser: . . . and then I surfed down the volcano on a piece of scrap metal, while shooting Indians and alligators with my bow and arrow. All of a sudden I saw this really hot girl stuck in a tree, naked, with a pack of hungry gorillas after her, so I swung from a vine and grabbed her, then I jumped onto a passing helicopter. But the helicopter landed in Iraq and Osama bin Laden started chasing us. He shot me but I deflected the bullet off the piece of scrap metal and it ricocheted back and killed him. Then I carried her across the border and all the way to France.
Me: Shut up, bitch. You're all talk.

all that

Describes a person who thinks they are the coolest, most badass person in the world even though it is usually only the opinion of that person.

Look at that fool. He thinks he's all that.

all that and a bag of chips

A superlative form of all that.

Something or someone who possesses all desired qualities, plus unimagined or unforeseen bonuses.

That bitch thinks she is all that and a bag of chips.

all the way

Used to describe having sex without being vulgar.

Yo, did you go all the way with Tina yesterday?

all the way live

Live, to an exceptional degree. Really, really cool.

Man, this shit is all the way live!

all up ons

When one person is sexually attracted to another person.

I was wearing my Autobot T-shirt and the ladies were all up ons!

all your base are belong to us

A declaration of victory or superiority. Stems from a 1991 adaptation of Toaplan's Zero Wing shoot-'em-up arcade game for the Sega Genesis game console. A brief introduction was added to the opening screen, and it has what many

consider to be the worst Japanese-to-English translation in video game history. In the introduction, a Borg-like figure named Cats says, "How are you gentlemen!! All your base are belong to us." In 2001, this amusing mistranslation spread virally through the Internet, bringing with it a slew of hacked photographs, each showing a street sign, store front, package label, etc., hacked to read "All your base are belong to us," or one of the other many supremely dopey lines from the game (such as "Somebody set us up the bomb!!!" or "What happen?"). When these phrases are used properly, the overall effect is both screamingly funny and somewhat chilling, reminiscent of a B-movie. The original has been generalized to "All your X are belong to us," where X is filled in to connote a sinister takeover of some sort.

When Joe signed up for his new job at Yoyodyne, he had to sign a draconian NDA. It basically said, "All your code are belong to us."

all-wheeling

To drive a Subaru.

I'm thinking about all-wheeling to your house, dude.

already

Short for "I already knew."
Expression of agreement.

Guy: That fool is crazy!
Girl: Already.

am I mean?

Sarcastic interjection used after saying bad words or talking shit.

He's a bitch. Am I mean?

amateur hour

Something crappy. Something that seems amateurly put together.

Junior college is the amateur hour of higher education.

ambulance chaser

Derogatory description for a personal injury lawyer who specifically seeks out clients for tripping and slipping cases against big companies. Certainly in the U.S., this is because the lawyer's fee will be a percentage of the client's damages award—therefore making it profitable to find injured former employees of big companies.

Manager: That guy who got his arm mangled up in our machine is suing.
Executive: Who's he got?
Manager: Some ambulance chaser.

amen, brother

Expression of emphatic agreement.

Tool 1: I need to go to the gym every day so I can get really diesel. Girls like that, I think.
Tool 2: Amen, brother.

amped

Fired up, stoked, ready to roll.

I was amped for the upcoming X-Games.

and a half

Added to emphasize or exaggerate a quality or characteristic.

She is a bitch and a half!

and one

While playing basketball, you get fouled while shooting the ball and still make the basket.

He takes it strong to the hole . . . (gets fouled and makes the layup) AND ONE, BABY! Yeah!

and shit

A "filler phrase" used when you become too lazy to finish a sentence or you realize you just don't want to finish the sentence.

Girlfriend: What did you do last night?
Boyfriend: Oh, you know, we went to the

bar and . . . you know, the bar and shit.
Hey, how about that chick flick you always
wanted to watch? Let's watch that.

and stuff

Term used after something totally
random or when you run of things
to say. Usually used by idiots when
speaking in front of an audience.

*Then we can, like, go sacrifice a rubber
lizard, and stuff.*

and then I found
20 dollars

Phrase often added by annoying
people to the end of a really bad
story, mocking their own story's
badness by admitting the necessity
for something interesting to happen
at the end. Also used to mock such
people.

*Person 1: So in the end I gave him back his
monkey feces and didn't invite him up when
he dropped me off. Isn't that amazing?
Person 2: (silence)
Person 1: And then I found 20 dollars!*

animé

Animé is short for "animation." The
term originated in Japan to refer to
all kinds of animation, both domestic
and foreign. In Europe and North
America, it refers only to Japanese
animation. Animé, as defined in
Europe and North America, has a
distinct art style, often featuring large
eyes, small noses, and bright colors.
Unlike Disney animated movies and
Saturday-morning cartoons in
America, Japanese animé is not
always made for and marketed to
children. Some animé has complex
storylines and characters, and some
explores mature themes, since the
Japanese have looser censorship
standards, allowing nudity, violence,
and mature themes in programming
for children and teens. This sometimes leads to a misconception that
animé is pornographic animation,
when only a relatively small percentage of animé (called hentai) is
pornographic. Every genre is repre-
sented in animé, from drama to com-
edy to romance, fantasy to horror.
Animé is sometimes also called
"Japanimation," but not as much.

She became an animé fan when she saw
Fushigi Yuugi *at a friend's house.*

animutation

A Flash animation consisting of random images often set to non-English
music. The images can include pop
culture icons, commercial products
(soft drinks, brand-name foods, etc.),
or any other image that the animator
feels like putting in the Flash.

Animutations often also contain
flashy backgrounds, lack a coherent
plot, and feature nonsensical
messages from the animator. Usually,
the lyrics of the song are translated
into disjointed English based on how
they sound. Many animutations share
common themes or images. For
example, most animutations use pictures of the Canadian improv actor
Colin Mochrie. Also known as fan-
imutation.

*"Yatta," an animutation set to a Japanese
song, features pictures of consumer goods
with labels altered to say "Yatta."*

ankle biter
A toddler. A child between the ages
of 1 and 4.

*Yeah, she's all married an' got a buncha
little ankle biters runnin' around.*

annivorcery
Anniversary of a divorce.

*My parents' annivorcery was last month.
Each of them celebrated with their new
spouses.*

anticipatience
Being patient while eagerly antici-
pating something.

She waited with anticipatience to leave

*work as her boss asked her to resubmit her
TPS report for the umpteenth time.*

antidextrous
Lacking dexterity in either hand.

*He can't throw very well with either hand;
he's antidextrous.*

antipoon
The act of not getting any.

*Last night I struck out and got nothin'
but some antipoon.*

anything that walks
Literally, any person or animal who
can move using legs or similar
appendages. Generally, though, it is
used as the epitome of low standards in the selection of a mate.

*After night after night of striking out, I'd
be happy to get lucky with anything that
walks.*

AOL
A very generous company that
sends you a free disc in the mail
every other week.

*Hey, Matt, I like your new AOL drink
coaster. Could you pass me one of your
new AOL dinner plates? These large
AOL round tortilla chips are crunchy.*

apathy

I suppose I should write a definition for apathy. I just don't really care. Maybe eventually I'll get around to doing a write-up for procrastination instead.

I don't give a shit if you need an example. Figure it out for your own damn self.

apeshit

An undignified loss of control, as in "to go apeshit."

If he had lost the election, George would have gone apeshit, trashing the Oval Office, the War Room, and the Clinton Memorial Bedroom.

apocalypse sex

Passionate but ultimately meaningless lovemaking, often with casual acquaintances, inspired by emotional bonding during or after an epic disaster.

After a few warm beers, Jessica and I groped our way through the darkness and humid heat to the ruins of her burnt-out apartment building, where, to nobody's greater surprise than ours, we ended up engaging in apocalypse sex.

apple bottom

A female who has a large, round butt.

That girl's apple bottom is looking right.

apples

Okay. All right.

Guy 1: Ay cuz, we right for smokes and beers?
Guy 2: She's apples, mate.

appz

Illegally acquired software applications.

I have a wide selection of desktop publishing and graphic design appz on my computer.

Area 51%

Area 51% is the portion of the United States composed of "Red States"—states that voted Republican in the 2004 presidential election. It is so named because it represents the percentage of the popular vote with which George W. Bush won the election. The name is strangely reminiscent of the code name of the secret U.S. military facility that supposedly hides alien activity from the American public.

It seems like the entire American South is off in its own little world—Area 51%.

argh!

1. An exclamation of annoyance, exasperation, or other negative factor.

Argh! This is taking for-freaking-EVER!

2. The sound made by a stereotypical pirate.

Arrrgggghhh, matey! Aye be sendin' ye down to Davy Jones's locker, aye be!

around the way
Nearby; local.

These are my friends who live around the way.

arse
Australian, British, and Irish word for a person's rear end.

I'm sitting on my arse.

as a friend
Used to draw the "no sex/physical intimacy" boundaries. Generally used for people who have an agreeable personality but no sex appeal.

I know we've been dating a lot, but I just like you as a friend.

as cool as the other side of the pillow
About as cool as a person can possibly be.

I was as cool as the other side of the pillow back in high school. I used to sit in the back of the class in my leather Harley-Davidson jacket and sunglasses, smoking my Marlboro Reds and drinking whiskey out of a silver flask. I'd just sit back there, all laid back across the seat, with my arms around the two hottest girls in the school. The teacher would tell me to put my cigarette out and stop drinking, and I would blow smoke in her face and say, "Make me." But she wouldn't make me because I was just too cool. No, not really, actually I was a dork who watched Star Trek *marathons and still haven't lost my virginity. No, just kidding again, I was pretty normal, but I always used to look at the other side of the pillow and wish that someday I could be that cool.*

as if
1. Expression meaning "Yeah, right! That's never going to happen." Made popular by the movie *Clueless*.

He told me he knows I'm in love with him and I was like, "As if!" He's a total loser.

2. Expression of utter repulsion, disgust, or annoyance.

The sales guy came up to me and was like, "We have the best polyester pants!" I told him loud and clear, "As if!" and then walked out the door.

asdf
Used when you can't think of an appropriate title for an e-mail, paper, etc. The a, s, d, and f keys are all in a row on American keyboards.

I wasn't feeling very creative and I didn't care about my grade, so I just called my term paper "asdf" and handed it in.

Asiaphile

A white, Western person with a pathological, often sexual obsession with Asians and Asian culture.

Asiaphiles may experience loss of interest in Western life, postcolonial angst, and in the worst cases have sexual fantasies of exotic interracial love.

asl

Acronym for age, sex, location. Used in computer chat as a question to gain basic personal information. Usually frowned upon as an impersonal and annoying introduction.

nicole: asl?
flamingo: 15/f/canada. U?
nicole: 20/f/england.
flamingo: so what time is it over there?
nicole: it's 3 a.m. and I can't sleep.

ass grind

A skateboarding term for a category of bailing that involves the skater sliding quickly across a surface on his buttocks. This usually results from a poor landing from a ramp, lip, or rail, or due to the skateboard's biting on an irregularity on the street surface.

Joe was leaning back too far when he came off that rail and ended up doing a huge ass grind.

ass out

To be out of luck; left without something.

If you get to the dinner table five minutes late you'll be ass out. Those kids are hungry!

ass rash

A fictitious condition afflicting a hot-tempered person. Used to explain their meanness.

Watch out for Ken . . . he's got an ass rash and is gonna be hard to get along with today.

asstastic

1. A complimentary statement of one's posterior. Synonym for bootylicious.

Gee, these pants make my rear end look asstastic!

2. A derogatory description for someone who excels at being an asshole. Synonym for colossus assholus.

My ex was so asstastic he left me destitute.

ate up

Obsessive or eccentric. Consumed by irrational behavior.

That dude is ate up. Every time you mention Seven of Nine he mumbles to himself in Klingon and goes to his room to fantasize about women who hang out with Borgs.

ATM space

The personal space that's allowable while waiting in line at an ATM. This space changes as you move through the line. In most of the queue, the space is as close as a foot or less, but when you are the next person in line and the person in front of you is using the ATM, it changes to as much as 6 feet to give that person some privacy.

Some people don't understand that when you get up to the machine, the person behind you needs to give proper ATM space.

attention whore

Label given to any person who craves attention (either negative or positive) to such an extent that they will do anything to receive it.

Put your shirt down. You're such an attention whore!

audiophile

One who listens to the stereo, rather than the music. An audiophile only uses high-end audio equipment and can detect very minor

differences in sound quality.

Audiophile: Those monitors sound muddy as hell.
Regular guy: What? How can you tell, good sir? I hear nothing wrong!
Audiophile: 'Cuz I'm an audiophile.

Aunt Flow

Euphemism for menstruation; checking into the "red roof inn."

Aunt Flow is in town this week. No sex for you.

autopilot

When you do something without realizing what you're doing. Usually results in making a mistake.

Dude, are you on autopilot or something? I know you're bar hopping to find a hookup, but that's Tyrone's baby mama! Watch what you're doing.

awesome

Cool, hip, exciting.

That movie was awesome!

awesomeness

The quality of being awesome.

Girl, you don't understand, he was so fine, and now he is so mine. I can't believe the awesomeness of it.

AWOL

Acronym for "absent without leave." Started as a military term but now refers to anyone who is suspiciously missing.

Mike was AWOL at the company meeting this morning. I think he's home watching the game.

awww factor

A measure of warm, fuzzy reactions to a person, product, or event.

We've got to raise the awww factor for this human-interest article in the newspaper.

ay yo trip

Phrase used to get someone's attention, like "check this out." Sometimes shortened to "ay yo."

Ay yo trip, look at this.

b school

1. Business school. Where students obtain MBAs.

I went to b school so I could get a high-paying job with a dot-com, cash out my stock at age thirty-five, and retire to Palm Beach. Oh, yeah.

2. Bride school. The School for Etiquette and Wisdom is where Korean gals go to learn how to be submissive, never give orders to the husband, and not walk around in strapless mules that clack and disturb their elders.

Part of the prenuptial agreement was that Karen attend b school and learn to bake pies, make sweaters, and gracefully open and deliver a cold one while looking demure and sexy.

ba da bing, ba da boom

Phrase used to describe something as happening easily, quickly, and smoothly. Famous users include world-renowned children's idol Bart Simpson.

You're in and out—ba da bing, ba da boom.

babe

1. Term of endearment.

Hey, babe, I missed you.

2. Term for a good-looking girl, sometimes describes guys.

All the guys think Melanie is a babe.

baby

1. Term of endearment.

When my girlfriend started calling my best

friend "baby," I knew it was over.

2. Exclamation often used during sexual intercourse.

Oh, baby! Yes!

3. The direct consequence of sexual intercourse.

How could something as good as sex have made this baby?

baby bear

Expression used when something is "just right." Not too hot or too cold, too big or too small, etc. From the story "Goldilocks and the Three Bears."

Guy 1: Are you hungry?
Guy 2: Naw, man . . . I'm baby bear.

baby daddy

Short for "baby's daddy." The father of your child/children, whom you did not marry and with whom you are not currently involved.

He isn't my boyfriend, he's my baby daddy.

baby mama

Short for "baby's mama." The mother of your child/children, whom you did not marry and with whom you are not currently involved.

Oh, her? She ain't nothing to me now, girl. She just my baby mama. So, can I get your number?

back in the day

Referring to the past. Often recalled as a better time than the present.

I remember those good times we used to have back in the day, hanging out at Lyon's.

backdoor man

The man your wife is seeing on the side. He usually comes to the back door to keep any other housewives from seeing him.

Jimmy, the pool boy, is my backdoor man.

backend

1. Booty.

That backend is a fantastic sight.

2. The part of a software product that the user does not interact with.

We've isolated that problem in the backend.

background props

Placing oneself in the background of another person's picture (could be a stranger or a friend), usually striking some strange pose or making some other gesture, unbeknownst to the subjects or the photographer.

Sometimes shortened to BGPs.

Who is that guy getting his BGPs in all of my pictures?

backne
Acne on the back.

The chick who sits in front of me in my class has hella backne.

backpacker
Term for a fashion style popular in the mid to late '90s where people involved in hip-hop wore large backpacks. Originated by graffiti writers, who kept all their cans and nozzles in the packs, the style caught on quick with the suburbanites and rock kids who didn't want to stray too far from their style but still wanted to have a hip-hop flava. People use it now as a derogatory term for nerd-rappers, hippy-hoppers, and other fringe hip-hop followers, referencing the fact that most of the listeners are suburbanites buying or co-opting into a certain style.

Every time I go to their concert it's nothing but backpackers.

backstage
Place you go to take care of personal business. In Disney theme parks, this is the area where guests are not allowed, tucked away behind nondescript doors and curtains. In reality, these areas are usually quite ugly, disgusting, and very unkempt. This is also where you see many a cast member doing what they normally are not allowed to do onstage: eat, drink, smoke, use the restroom, talk on their cell phones, talk about their personal lives, be unfriendly.

I need to go backstage for a minute to answer my phone.

backwash
Drinking something and spitting it back out into the cup or bottle.

Ew, you backwashed that. I'm not gonna drink that!

backyard
The posterior portion of the human body; bum, butt, ass.

That man has a huge backyard; his tailor must be rich!

bacon
Derogatory term for police officers, cops, pigs.

Undercover officer: You got crack?
Street hustler: Crack?! Smells like bacon up in here.

baconify

To add bacon to otherwise baconless foods.

Baconify that burger for me, Cletus.

bad

1. Opposite of good.

Jeremiah: Hey, it was pretty bad the way you beat up my mother.

2. Opposite of bad.

Methuselah: I beat up his mother! It was bad!

3. When preceded by "my," a way of taking responsibility for something you did wrong.

Jeremiah: My bad, Mom, I didn't know he'd beat you up.

4. Possessing the qualities of badness.

Methuselah is such a bad.

bad business

1. Any sort of morally ambiguous activity.

I think Bill got into some bad business with Wendy and her man last night.

2. Anything unpleasant.

That mole on her back is bad business.

badical

The conjunction of bad and radical, giving an '80s feel of extreme greatness.

Man, that Web site was badical to the extreme.

badness

Something that is not positive. Typically refers to a situation or the actions of one or more people.

Have you heard about the badness in NYC?

badong

Bad and wrong at the same time. From a line in the Steve Oedekerk movie *Kung Pow: Enter the Fist.*

Yo, man, the combination of that girl's skirt and Uggs was totally badong.

badonkadonk

An extremely curvaceous female behind. Women who possess this feature usually have a small waist that violently explodes into a round and juicy posterior. Other characteristics are moderately wide hips and a large amount of booty cleavage.

Her badonkadonk made a brotha pop mad wheelies.

bag

To crack jokes by insulting someone or their mother. Some call it "jone-ing." If you go back and forth in a competition of insults, it's called "dozens," as in "playing the dozens" or "dirty dozens."

Oh, you wanna bag? Yo momma so fat, she's on both sides of the family!

bag on that

Interjection of displeasure at something or someone, especially withregard to work or a duty of some kind.

Dude 1: The teacher assigned homework again today.
Dude 2: Bag on that!
Dude 1: Fo' shizzle my nizzle.

bagging your own groceries

When you shoot the basketball, rebound your own missed shot, and score after one or multiple rebounds.

Willis needs to either learn how to shoot or learn how to bag his own groceries.

bail

1. To leave. Short for "bail out." Synonym for "bounce."

Yo, I'm bailing on this mutha. This party is shit.

2. To ditch or pull out of something.

I'm gonna have to bail on that mission I said we would do.

3. To fall, especially in a painful, embarrassing, public way.

I was in the cafeteria with my lunch tray when I tripped and bailed in front of everyone.

bake out

Smoking marijuana in a closed area.

Let's go bake out your mom's car!

bake sale

A marijuana smoke session.

I gotta stop having those bake sales before work. I nearly ate my report.

baleedat

Believe that. Expression of agreement or approval.

Playa: I was up in my room with this girl and she gave me what I wanted.
Friend: Baleedat.

ball

To play basketball. Used only if you have some skill and play in an urban area.

I ball with my G's all day.

ball buster

1. A woman (also affectionately called a bitch) who challenges the virility and dominance of a man by utilizing verbal abuse or by controlling social situations usually controlled by men.

That ball buster of a ho didn't let me have a word in edgewise. She tore my ass up one side and down the other.

2. A woman who is so bitchin' and intelligent that most men fear opening their mouth in her presence, much less making a sexual advance.

Woowee! Look at that ball-bustin' honey!

ball in hand

In various types of pocket billiards (pool), "ball in hand" refers to a player's right to place the cue ball anywhere on the table. Getting "ball in hand" means that the opposing player (the offending player) committed a foul, such as a table scratch.

"Ball in hand," he yelled, putting the cue ball on the table after his opponent fouled.

baller

1. A person who plays basketball well.

Kobe Bryant . . . now that kid's a baller.

2. A person who finds success and wealth. Originally used to describe

ball players who made it out of the streets to make millions in the pros, but now describes any thug who is living large.

Evan's a baller now with his job downtown and a new Benz.

baller stat

Used to describe something worthy of a baller.

Blake: Yeah, I ate Chipotle three times this week.
David: Ah, that's baller stat, man.

balls

1. Courage or bravery.

He didn't have the balls to jump off a three-story platform into the water.

2. Something yelled to shock people.

The boy said to his grandmother, "Balls!" and she passed out.

3. Used to describe something that you dislike.

This math test is balls.

balls out

An extreme effort. To try extremely hard.

I decided to slack off and get a B in the

class, but Ross went *balls out* and got a
100 percent.

balls to the wall
Originally a military term for pushing maximum g force in a jet fighter, as in pushing the ball of a throttle as high as it will go (virtually touching the wall of the dashboard). Fast; hectic; pushed to the limits.

We hit the road, balls to the wall, and got there in half the time.

ballsy
Intense, manly, brave, amazing.

Did you see Jim tell off the boss? That was ballsy!

Bambi
One who is ineffectual because they are paralyzed with fear or anxiety at a time of crisis or danger. Refers to the tendency of a deer to freeze and stare at an oncoming car, resulting in death and disaster.

The president just sat there reading My Pet Goat, *a total Bambi, and the terrorists tripled the amount of time they had to attack America.*

bamboozled
To be tricked or swindled by another.

I told my wife not to go car shopping without me, but she didn't listen. So the salesman bamboozled her into buying a car she doesn't need and can't afford.

bang
1. An interjection meaning "to happen suddenly."

I was walking down the street with my lady and, bang, this guy ran by and grabbed her purse.

2. To have sex with.

Yeah, I banged her.

bang a left/right
Used while giving driving directions. Substitute "bang" for turn and then say the direction you want to go.

Right! See that light ahead? Bang a left there.

bang on
Exactly right. Also "spot on."

Jane's prediction of fourth-quarter earnings was bang on.

bangin'
1. Describing people: sexy or attractive.

*Nate: Did you check out dat ho'z dumps?
E: Fo' sheezy. Ain't they bangin', yo?*

2. Describing things: great, wonderful, awesome, sweet, nice, dope, phat, tight.

Man, that car is bangin'!

bank

1. A substantial amount of money.

Man, I got some serious bank in my wallet.

2. The condition of being rich.

Of course that fool drives that BMW — he's banked.

3. To fight.

I banked some sucker and took his wallet.

bank tank

When a small person goes to collect something of value (such as withdrawing a lot of money from the bank), they select a large family member or friend to go with them to deter theft or harassment.

Yo' mama is a bank tank—ahahahaha!

banner farm

A Web site that consists of little more than pay-per-view banner ads.

Ned was Googling and two of the links led to websites with no information, just banner adverts. He cussed those banner farms under his breath.

bare

1. A lot of.

That woman had bare cats.

2. Very.

I was bare tired.

3. An exclamation of disbelief.

Friend 1: I have a new car!
Friend 2: Bare!

barfaroni

Something that or someone who makes you so sick you feel like barfing.

That meatloaf is so barfaroni!

barge

1. To show up unexpectedly.

We straight barged his house but he wasn't home.

2. To go someplace with a group of people.

We should all barge that party.

basic training

An ordeal enlisted persons entering the military must endure, which is the systematic deconstruction of simple civilian ways to an animalistic, aggressive, killer lifestyle.

If I had known what basic training was really like I would have never, ever, ever joined the Army.

basket case

One who cannot deal with stress.

Sam is a basket case because of that bitch Heather.

bass ackwards

The art and science of hurtling blindly in the wrong direction with no sense of the impending doom about to be inflicted on one's sorry ass. Usually applied to procedures, processes, or theories based on faulty logic, or faulty personnel.

Once again, marketing wants the poor engineers to build something that will sell but doesn't have a clue what that "something" could be. Bass ackwards as usual.

bbiab

Acronym for "be back in a bit." Most often used in Internet chatting. Sometimes shortened to "biab," for "back in a bit."

I'll bbiab; g2g take the K9 for a walk.

bbiaf

Acronym for "be back in a few." Most often used in Internet chatting.

Yo, bbiaf. Going to the can.

bbl

Acronym for "be back later." Most often used in Internet chatting.

John: Hey, man, are u busy?
Bob: Yeah, but I'll bbl.

b-boy

A male who is in some way identified with hip-hop culture (as in break dancing, rapping/emceeing, graffiti, etc.).

Sean is such a b-boy. All he does is spit rhymes.

BBW

Acronym for "big beautiful woman." An empowering alternative and politically correct description for the plus-size woman, as opposed to the derogatory term "fat."

The women at this fashion club have too many issues; I heard the women at the BBW clubs are much cooler.

BCGs

Acronym for "birth control glasses," the glasses issued to new recruits in the military, so called because no girl would want to have sex with men wearing those ugly, ugly glasses.

Wow, newly shaved head and BCGs. I'll never have sex with those new recruits.

beam me up

Exclamatory ending to a controversial statement, intended to express frustration. Popularized by flamboyant Ohio senator James Traficant.

I have been fighting the political machine since the day I arrived in Congress and will do so 'til the day I die. . . . Beam me up.

beans

The club drug Ecstasy.

I was full of beans last night at the rave.

bear hug

To grab someone and hug 'em real tight, with both arms solidly holding the person immobile.

The rugby player grabbed the nerd in a tight bear hug while his teammates beat the shit outta him.

bear report

Trucker speak for a report of the location of state troopers (called smokey bears, or just bears) patrolling the road ahead, usually obtained from vehicles that have just come from the place for which you want a bear report.

Trucker 1: Breaker 1-9, Eastbound.
Trucker 2: 10-4, this is Eastbound.
Trucker 1: How about a bear report?
Trucker 2: You're looking good all the way to Guitar Town.
Trucker 1: 4-10, trucker friend.

beard

Any opposite-sex escort taken to an event to give a homosexual person the appearance of being out on a date with a person of the opposite sex.

Half of the women on the red carpet at the movie premiere were not real dates, but beards.

beat

Extremely ugly; probably derived from "beat with the ugly stick."

Man, I thought she'd have some hot friends, but, boy, were they beat!

beat box

1. To use one's mouth to create rap or techno-like sound. Often used as an accompaniment to freestyling or flowing. Beat boxing is used in the urban hip-hop scene.

To get the little campers to go to sleep,

Erik and Manuel beat boxed while Jacob busted out with mad rhymes.

2. A drum machine.

Check out this sweet old-school 808 beat box.

3. A boom box.

Yo, B! Turn that beat box down. I'm tryin' to pour one for my homies.

beat down

1. To physically rough up or convincingly administer authority over another person or thing.

I had to throw a beat down on that punk ass. He's hurtin' bad.

2. To verbally and publicly berate into submission.

Mr. Smith beat down that dude who came up on his porch asking for money. We heard him yelling at the guy all the way up the block.

3. The exercise of legitimate authority, rules, or known customs that leaves a person or persons in a poor position and often disappointed; a disappointing and unexpected result to an attempted action.

I bought my girlfriend some roses, but I got beat down when she threw them in the trash can.

beat up

Wrong or unfair.

Clubber 1: Man, I got screwed at the club on some fake beans.
Clubber 2: That's beat up, man.

beats

Pounding bass frequencies at regular or irregular intervals in a piece of music. Often timed to changes in dance motions or light-show action. Calculated frequency is expressed as beats per minute.

The pounding beats moved him to dance.

beau

Beautiful; also used for lover and boyfriend.

Me and my beau went out last night and had a fabulous time!

bed

To have sex with someone.

There's no doubt he'll bed her tonight.

bed arrest

Staying in bed for an extended period of time, only getting up to get food or go to the bathroom.

I've been on bed arrest the last few days with this amazing hottie

I met at a club last weekend!

bedroom eyes

That sensual, seductive glance you use when you are in the mood for something romantic and sexual.

When I saw my girl for the first time in a skimpy nightgown, we gave each other bed room eyes and proceeded to make some lovin'.

beef

A grudge.

50 Cent had beef with Game when he thought Game was being disloyal. Their beef's deaded now though.

beer

The reason we get up in the morning and pass out at night.

Beer so good!

beer belly

A huge gut obtained from drinking massive quantities of beer.

Look at all the old guys with their beer bellies hanging out of their tie-dye shirts and leather jackets.

beer bong

Funnel and tube used to consume large amounts of beer at one time.

Used mostly by fraternities and other lame people trying to get wasted really quickly.

Guy: Come on, do a beer bong with me. I'll teach you.
Me: No, I'm too afraid. Girls shouldn't do that.

beer goggles

Phenomenon in which one's consumption of alcohol makes physically unattractive persons appear beautiful; summed up by the phrase "there are no ugly women at closing time."

When I took her to bed, she looked like Halle Berry. But when I woke up, she looked like Keith Richards! I must've had my beer goggles on.

beer league

An amateur baseball or slow-pitch softball league. Many of the players tend to be overweight and/or of below average physical condition, probably because they consume massive quantities of beer.

After Commissioner Bud Selig contracted the New York Yankees, Rivera, Jeter, A-Rod, and the rest of the team couldn't find any other team that could afford to take on their salaries, so they ended up having to play in the beer league.

beer pong

A drinking game in which players attempt to throw ping-pong balls across a table into an opponent's half-filled cups of beer. Players are required to drink the beer from any of their cups into which the opponent throws a ball. The first player to hit all their opponent's cups wins. The loser is required to drink whatever beer is left on the table in the opponent's cups. For sanitary reasons, a cup of water is kept at either end of the table to wash the balls off after each throw, but if you've ever played you know it doesn't really help. Table size, number of players/cups, and house rules concerning bounces, misses, and crossovers vary depending on the college/fraternity/drinking club involved.

After that 20-ounce Jack and Coke and five games of beer pong, I was definitely feeling a buzz. Rock on, apartment 306.

beer shits

When you seriously need to take a dump the day after you drink a ton of beer.

Man, I have mad beer shits . . . I need to find a crapper right now! Oh, shit, there it goes!

beer taxi

Imaginary mode of transport associated with heavy drinking, when the drinker has no recollection of how they arrived back at their preferred destination.

I was so utterly trousered last night I haven't got a clue how I got home. . . . Must have been the beer taxi.

beer thirty

Time of day (usually late afternoon to early evening) at which drinking a beer becomes necessary.

Hey, looks like it's beer thirty. Better grab me a cold one.

beermuffs

An invisible article of clothing that prevents you from getting cold and appears when you've had a lot of beer. It's a figure of speech, really, and the point is just that if you're drunk enough that you don't feel the least bit cold no matter where you are, you're sporting some serious beermuffs.

When Nate was about to leave the party it dawned on him that he lived two miles away. And it was 3 a.m. And he had no car. And he was wearing shorts and a T-shirt. And it was January. And he lived in the northern part of Alaska. And there was a blizzard going on outside. He knew the only solution to this dilemma was to hop on that keg and fashion himself a good pair of beermuffs.

bee's knees
Cool.

Those new threads are the bee's knees.

befriendster
To ask someone or accept someone as your "friendster" on the Web site www.friendster.com.

We need to find a shy boy with nice hair and befriendster him.

befront
To confront or annoy.

Stop dissin' on my momma; don't befront me.

belly cleavage
Skin visible between a woman's shirt and pants. Obviously a fashion don't for men.

Belly cleavage, although often sexy, is not appropriate for a job interview.

bend a corner
To provide transportation for; to drive by and pick up.

Yo, Dave, can ya bend that corner for me, dawg?

benjamins
Hundred-dollar bills.

It's all about tha benjamins!

Bennifer
A combination consisting of 50% Benjamin Geza Affleck and 50% Jennifer Lynn Lopez, referred to as a single entity: Bennifer. Also known as Bennifer Lofleck, or Bennifer Affpez.

I got sucked into watching that Bennifer movie.

bent
1. Crooked or dishonest.

Man, don't worry 'bout that pig; he's bent.

2. Way too high.

I was sooo bent last night, I woke up still stoned.

Bermuda triangle
Two cars parked diagonally on either side of another car to form a triangle shape with the curb, thus making it difficult for the middle car to leave. Or to park cars in such a manner.

We thought it would be funny if we made a Bermuda triangle around him in the parking lot.

I couldn't leave the movies until 9 p.m. because two people decided to Bermuda triangle me in the parking lot.

bernie

Dead. From the *Weekend at Bernie's* movies, where a couple of idiots drag their dead boss all over the place and convince people he's alive.

Guy 1: Oh, yeah! This party is off the chain!
Guy 2: Shut up, man. It's bernie, and I'm gonna be ghost.

Cousin 1: So I hear your dog Fred's been circling the drain lately. Did he buy the farm yet?
Cousin 2: Yeah, dawg, he's bernie.

berry

A cop car, because the red light on top looks like a berry on top of ice cream.

I got nailed with a speeding ticket by a berry.

best

Short for "it would be best." To do something that needs to be done, lest you face unfavorable consequences.

Yo! You best back out' my face b'fo' I

bust a cap in your silly-ass face!

best be

1. You had better be.
Albert: I am a rocker. I rock out.
Ben: Best be.

2. You had better do that.

Albert: I intend to give you five dollars.
Ben: Best be.

3. Expression of satisfaction. Sometimes shortened to simply "best."

I win at Scrabble! Best!

bestest

The best of the best.

The bestest food is pizza.

bet that

Affirmative expression, such as "good deal" or "that's cool."

Mike: You want to get something to eat?
Jones: Bet that.

beta

Greek for "still doesn't work." Software undergoes beta testing shortly before it's released.

We're releasing version 0.8, our latest beta.

between the sheets

Literally, "in bed." Part of a game where you take any common sentence or title and add "between the sheets." A popular juvenile activity for which the possibilities are endless.

The Passion of Christ . . . *between the sheets!*

The Return of the King . . . *between the sheets!*

BFD

Acronym for "big friggin' deal."

Matt: Look! There's President Bush!
Sarah: BFD!

BFF

Acronym for "best friends forever."

KIT!!! Stay cool and don't skip school!!
Sincerely, Britney. P.S.: BFF!

BFFL

Acronym for "best friends for life."

After having a friendship for 40 years, Mary and Sharon consider each other BFFLs.

b-girl

A female who is in some way identified with hip-hop culture.

I never knew Emma was a b-girl until I saw her break dancing at the club last night.

b-i

Short for "business," and more specifically your personal business.

Sheila: What are you doin'?
Tajuan: Hey, stay out of my b-i.

bicoastal

Someone, often a bobo (bourgeois bohemian) or a limousine liberal, who haunts both coasts and ignores what's in between.

He was so bicoastal he'd never heard of Omaha except in ads for mail-order steak.

biff

To fall hard.

When running on Woodward, Verbeek biffed pretty bad.

big brother

Vague reference to the leader of any covert conspiracy; named for an operational body that monitored the activity of all the citizens in George Orwell's novel *1984*. Later, the name for a stupid reality TV show.

Shhhh . . . big brother might be watching and listening.

big girl's blouse

A wuss, sissy, or coward.

Kate Winslet told David Letterman about the cold water they had to shoot in while doing Titanic, *and how that big girl's blouse Leonardo DiCaprio whined and moaned about the water being too cold.*

big guy
An informal and usually friendly, complimentary greeting for a man or boy. Can be used with a sarcastic tone, implying it's time to take him down a notch.

(friendly) *Hey there, big guy, you and me gonna drink some beers or what?*

(sarcastic) *Hey, big guy, watch what you're doing.*

big help
Somebody who either isn't helpful, or somebody who can only be trusted to help you with that one menial task that would save you about 20 minutes of walking around. Invariably spoken with a slight hesitation before the term.

Johnson was a, uh, big help today as he told me when the light stopped blinking on the router.

big pimpin'
Describes a heterosexual man's ability to maintain sexual relationships with multiple simultaneous girlfriends.

Damn, you is big pimpin'! Ladies love you!

big time
Much more than usual; to the max.

That sucked big time!

big timer
Someone with lots of cars, clothes, and/or money; similar to a baller or player.

Ever since homey hit the lotto, he's more of a big timer than Snoop and Dre combined.

big up
"Up" signifies elevation. Therefore, the term "big up" literally means to elevate highly or to a superlative degree.
1. An expression of support or encouragement.

Big up on that excellent performance.

2. An expression of remembrance.

I want to big up everyone who has shown me support over the years.

big up yourself
To give yourself praise or props; to make some noise for yourself, give yourself a congratulatory handshake or a pat on the back or whatever.

Nice work, Horace. Big up yourself!

big-boned

A nice way of saying one is fat, built in an odd way, or a giant.

Bully: You're fat!
Kid: Nuh-uh, Mommy said I'm just big-boned.

bills

Dollars; specifically 100-dollar bills.

Loan me five bills, playa.

bimbo

A pretty, dumb, and usually vain and egotistic female.

Melody from Josie and the Pussycats *is such a bimbo!*

bing

Onomatopoeia used to indicate a correct answer or course of action. Used to express unequivocal approval.

Just a little farther . . . that's it! Bing!

bing bing

One United States dollar.

Man, these rims cost me 3,500 bing bings.

binge

A modifier used to indicate an excess of something.

I ate binge cookies.

That dude talks friggin' binge.

biotch

1. A woman with unsavory character traits, often a negative or belligerent attitude (i.e., a pain in the ass or a moody bitch).

Yo, dawg, that girl ain't nothin' but a biotch.

2. A man whose abilities/character/mindset/emotional responses are atypical of that which is generally associated with being a man (i.e., acting like a girl, wimp, or homosexual).

Yo, dawg, why you acting like such a biotch?

3. A nonoffensive colloquialism used to refer to a girl or a woman with whom the speaker is associated. Also: beyatch, biyatch, beyotch, biyotch, biznatch, bleyatch, bitch.

That's my biotch.

bipartisan

Political term wherein members of the Democratic and the Republican parties agree on a particular piece of legislation. Also see "mythology."

This legislation needs bipartisan support in order to pass. . . . I'll vote for your piece-of-shit pork barrel legislation that I don't believe in, if you'll vote against your morals and support my tax-wasting special-interest initiative.

bird

1. An individual who is stupid, foolish, careless, idiotic, moronic, or just plain dumb.

You are such a friggin' bird.

2. A profane hand gesture accomplished by raising only the middle finger. Called either "the bird" or "the birdie."

That mutha just flipped me the bird! Cap his ass!

3. Used to express dissatisfaction.

You want me to what?! Bird!

bird legs

Legs that are so thin they resemble legs on birds. Usually refers to female legs.

My girlfriend is skinny and has bird legs.

biscuit

A gun. Used in Outkast's song "Red Velvet."

I heard homey's got beef, so I'm packing a biscuit to the club tonight.

bit the shit

Died, expired.

Doctor: What happened to the patient in room 216?
Nurse: He bit the shit last night.

bitch

1. To whine excessively.

Stop bitching, Todd!

2. The seat in the middle of a two-seater car meant for two passengers or less. Or the seat in the middle of the back seat when there are a lot of passengers in the car.

I call not bitch!

3. Modern-day servant; a person who performs (usually degrading) tasks for another.

Bring my friend and me some vodka, bitch.

4. Hardship.

Me: I stubbed my toe real bad, sat on some gum, and got a massive paper cut from a file folder. I'm having, like, the worst day ever.
Michael Jackson: Well, ain't that a bitch!

bitch ass

Derogatory term used to describe an underachieving, undereducated loser. Synonym for "punk" or "punk ass."

Your bitch ass is tired, yo—stop trippin'.

bitchcakes

Insane with anger.

When Joan's boyfriend didn't come home for two days, she went totally bitchcakes.

bitchface

Any person whose face looks just like the face of your standard bitch. Also used to refer to someone whose face will not stop bitching or is perpetually bitchy.

Hopwil is such a bitchface! But Dark Hades is worse; he's such a big bitchface.

bitchify

To relegate someone to a subservient post; to make someone your bitch.

Man, I broke Tony's PlayStation, but I don't have the money to pay for it. Now he's bitchified me!

bite

1. To be bad or unfortunate. Synonym for "blow" or "suck."

You failed the exam? That bites.

2. To sting.

Salt from potato chips really bites if you have a paper cut.

3. To rip off another person's style, especially with respect to music or fashion. From early hip-hop culture.

Why don't you come up with your own sound instead of biting every track that hits it big in the clubs?

bite it

To die, become bernie, kick the bucket, buy the farm. Short for "bite the dust."

He thought he could jump that gorge on his skateboard, but the wind was working against him and he bit it.

bite one's head off

To overreact to something trivial another person does.

Person 1: Excuse me, where is the bathroom?
Person 2: What are you, lazy? Why don't you just look for it yourself instead of asking some random person where it is? People like you are the reason America is known as the laziest country in the world!
Person 1: Geez, what's your problem? You didn't have to bite my head off!

bizzounce

To leave. Slight variation of "bounce."

I gotta bizzounce. Peace out.

bka

Acronym for "better known as."

Marshall Mathers, bka Eminem.

black-flag

1. To put a permanent stop to something that has already been red-flagged. Derived from the practice of waving the black and red flags together at the end of a racing practice session.

It's snowing too hard to continue on, so we've black-flagged this trip and are on our way home.

2. To be punished. Derived from the use of the black flag to indicate a penalty in racing.

Pretty sure that guy's gonna get black-flagged for punching out that window.

black hat

A hacker who uses his abilities for malicious purposes. Opposite of "white hat."

He's definitely a black hat. He's on Microsoft's most-wanted list.

black out

To become mentally and physically impaired after reaching a blood alcohol level of .20, which causes you to act in an uncontrollable manner. Unfortunately, the blackout keeps you from recalling the events that occurred while acting so recklessly and almost always guarantees awakening to wounds you do not remember getting or next to a person you do not remember sleeping with.

I'm sorry, what is your name again? I blacked out.

blacklight Barbie

A woman who appears much prettier in the blacklight at a party or club than she really is.

Seeing Whitney in the daylight, I realized she was a total blacklight Barbie.

bladdered

Drunk, as in with a full bladder. Tanked, hammered, stocious.

I was in the pub yesterday from 12 p.m. to 12 a.m. By the time I left I was bladdered.

blag

To gain entrance to a restricted area or club, or some material good, through confidence, trickery, or cheekiness.

I blagged my way into the VIP area.

I blagged some free CDs off the label.

blah

Interjection used at the end of a
sentence when no one is talking,
or when a person has nothing else
to say.

*So then I told Jose that Imma find those
midgets if it's the last thing I do . . . and
blah . . .*

blast

1. Interjection expressing disappointment or anger. If a truly bad
thing happens, a "double-blast" is
in order.

*I just ran out of all my beer for the
weekend. Blast!*

I just contracted herpes. Double-blast!

2. To vomit. Usually a result of
drinking too much in one sitting.

*Dude, you're so wasted. You just blasted
all over the hood of that Caddy.*

blaze

The act of packing a bowl of
marijuana and setting fire to it with
the intent of inhaling the smoke.

Yo, you want to go blaze this?

bleakend

The two days at the end of the
week when work traditionally ceases
and drinking traditionally increases.

*Guy 1: You wanna grab a few drinks this
Saturday?*
Guy 2: What else is the bleakend for?

bleavage

Cleavage of the buttocks, often
occurring with females who wear
low-rise jeans.

*With these jeans, I'd be showin' some
serious bleavage.*

bleeder

A left-wing liberal. Comes from the
expression "bleeding heart liberal."

*That guy hasn't a conservative bone in his
body—he's a total bleeder.*

bleep

A substitute for a profane word.

*What the bleep? You need to shut the
bleep up before I bleeping bleep your bleep
off the face of the bleeping planet.*

bleh

State of mind usually caused by
boredom or a mildly annoying
situation that doesn't cause any
heavy emotional reaction.

After I flunked yet another test by a huge lack of studying, I just felt bleh.

blicka
A firearm, a gun.

I pulled my blicka on him when he started talking about my momma.

blind
In love.

Dawg's blind for that girl.

bling
Flashy or gaudy jewelry. Named for the sound it makes when worn or the imaginary sound produced by the light reflected off of it.

Look at the bling hanging around his neck—he's a baller.

bling bling
1. Expensive, often flashy jewelry sported mostly by African-American hip-hop artists and middle-class Caucasian adolescents. The real big, shiny stuff, along the lines of the crown jewels. Does not include the stuff most of us can afford. Flashier than bling.

That bling bling on her finger doesn't allow her to lift her hand above her head.

2. To sport such highly extravagant, gaudy jewelry.

Damn, Johnny, you sure be bling-blingin' tonight!

block buster
A large piece of graffiti done in block lettering, usually lacking style.

I did a block buster on your ugly grandma's garage.

block party
A party that takes over a whole block.

HAHA! That block party on Main Street was the shit! If only the cops hadn't come.

blockaway
Someone who only looks good from a block away, but when they get close you realize it was all an illusion. A variation on the ever-popular term "butter face."

That guy is a blockaway. That's a face only his momma could love.

blog
1. Short for "weblog." A meandering, blatantly uninteresting online diary that gives the author the illusion that people are interested in their stupid, pathetic life. Consists

of such riveting entries as "homework sucks" and "I slept until noon today."

June 5 blog entry: So, like, this morning Jenny called and wanted to know if I could come over, and Matt called, and Brian asked me to go to the mall with him. So I went to the mall and met up with some more of my friends and some guys started hitting on me and they were, like, so hot, too . . .

2. To post to a weblog.

Did you read what Michelle blogged yesterday? Like anyone cares.

blog class

Middle-class and upper-middle-class people who make ample use of blogs to discuss personal opinions, often of a sociopolitical nature. Also known as "blogging class."

Yo, clearly the 2004 election will come down to the blog class decision, if they get off their ass and leave their computers long enough to vote.

blogger

Short for "weblogger." Someone who keeps a weblog, or diary, on the Internet.

Adam is one of those bloggers who writes exclusively on Paris Hilton.

blogosphere

The sum total of all interactive weblog communication. It can also refer to a particular web community that allows for opinionated commentary on news stories.

Dailykos.com is a major liberal outlet in the vast blogosphere.

blograge

The expression of deep inner hatred of the world and everything in it via a blog, message board, or other "fake Internet bullshit." Inherently pathetic yet somehow deeply therapeutic in a purely superficial way.

And so today my boss reprimanded me, my brother told me I'm not invited to the wedding, and my friend Carrie backed out on the plans to go to Tahoe! Argh! My blograge is strong today.

blood from a stone

An unlikely event requiring much effort.

Trying to get you to find a job is like trying to get blood from a stone.

blootered

Intoxicated with liquor.

Had too many vodkas and got blootered pretty quickly.

blow

1. Cocaine in powder form.

Hey, dopeman, you got some blow for sale?

2. To smoke weed.

I can't wait to blow that big-ass blunt.

3. To leave.

Aight, I'm 'bout to blow.

blow chunks

To vomit.

I drank so much I thought I was going to blow chunks.

blow my buzz

When you're drunk, high, or totally messed up on something and you just want to chill out and someone tries to get all serious or emotional on you, ruining your night.

I was having a great night until I ran into my ex-girlfriend and her new boyfriend. That really blew my buzz.

blow trees

To smoke fine marijuana.

No shwag for us, G, we blowin' trees tonight.

blow up

1. To become famous, successful, and respected, usually within a small amount of time.

Quentin Tarantino worked in a video rental joint before he made Reservoir Dogs *and blew up.*

When Less Than Jake made their album Pezcore, *they blew up pretty fast.*

2. To extremely forcefully expulse feces or vomit.

I sprinted to the bathroom and hardly had sat down when I blew up.

3. To receive many calls on a portable messaging device in a short amount of time.

Damn, that girl's been blowin' up your cell ever since you broke her off a piece!

blower

A telephone.

I've got Arnie on the blower, and he wants to know if he can come over.

blue screen of death

The screen you see when your computer completely dies. Microsoft's most successful program.

At Microsoft, we are running out of money, so we will now charge you for the blue screen of death.

urban DICTIONARY

blue state

A U.S. state in which the majority of residents vote Democrat. Opposite of "red state."

In the blue states, the bobos like Howard Dean, but he'll never carry the red states.

blunt

A cigar that has been hollowed and refilled with marijuana.

I sat outside all day, sippin' on my 40 and smokin' blunts.

bmoc

Acronym for "big man on campus." A highly respected person, or someone in a position of authority.

Gotta check with the bmoc before you make that move.

b.o.

Acronym for "body odor."

Yo, you stink like b.o., dude! Take a shower.

bo selecta

Literally means "good DJ." Used to salute a DJ in a club.

Bo selecta! Kes, ya bastard! Proper bo, I tell thee!

Bob's your uncle

British slang for "all will be well" or "simple as that."

If you go and ask for the job and he remembers your name, then Bob's your uncle.

bodacious

Describes something extremely '80s, like anything fluorescent, scrunchies, leg warmers, etc.

Did you see that top that chick was wearing? It was totally bodacious.

bogart

To keep something all for oneself, thus depriving anyone else of having any. A slang term derived from the last name of famous actor Humphrey Bogart because he often kept a cigarette in the corner of his mouth, seemingly never actually drawing on it or smoking it. Often used with weed or joints but can be applied to anything.

Don't bogart that blunt, man, pass that over here!

boi

1. In the lesbian community, a young transgendered/androgynous/masculine person who is biologically female and presents themselves in a young, boyish way; a boidyke; often

also identifies as "genderqueer."

J doesn't feel like s/he fits the mold of any one gender. S/he presents hirself in a young, boyish manner, and hir appearance is quite androgynous/masculine. S/he's a boi.

2. In the gay community, a young gay man.

J is a young, masculine gay male who presents himself in a boyish manner. He's a boi.

3. An alternate spelling of boy often used by young teenage boys.

My teenage brother and his friends often refer to themselves as "skater bois."

boil down
To come down to in the end, when all the bullshit surrounding the issue is removed.

When you boil it down, my paper stack is simply bigger than yours. I win.

boink
A word that your parents use to describe sex to you, even when you are an adult.

Mom: Oh my lord, Jennifer! You're . . . you're not boinking him, are you?
Jennifer: Yes, Mom, he's my husband.

bollocks
A highly flexible term commonly used by the English.
1. Something rubbish.

That Mel Gibson movie was a load of bollocks.

2. A falsehood or series of lies.

That Tony Blair is talking bollocks.

3. When preceded by "the": something great.

That curry was the bollocks!

4. The best possible.

Your wife is the dog's bollocks when it comes to cooking!

5. Testicles.

Then she kicked him in the bollocks.

6. Exclamation used when making a error.

Bollocks!

bomb
1. When preceded by "the": cool, awesome, the shit.

Man, that's the bomb. Let's see it again.

2. Fast graffiti piece, using more than two colors and all of the artist's

signature letters. Not much detail, just enough to look good and get away before anyone sees the artist.

That bomb is the tightest shit out.

3. To create such graffiti.

I bomb like Vietnam.

bomb ass
Extremely good or cool, almost at a godly level.

That's a bomb ass album. You should buy it.

bomb diggity
Totally the awesomest.

Aw, man, Rachel is beyond the bomb diggity.

bomb.com
Awesome or cool to a high degree.

Dude, that rocking party last night was so bomb.com!

bone
1. A smokable item, such as a joint or cigarette.

Pass that bone down this way.

2. Money, usually in dollars.

Can you spot me a few bones?

3. Short for trombone (in informal speech).

Mate, can you hold my bone while I go and get some lube for the slide?

bone out
To leave.

Sarah's new digs are pimp, but the party's boring, so I'm about to bone out.

bone up
Study. Learn about.

I'm gonna go bone up on my history facts.

bonehead
Stupid, slow, stubborn person.

Those boneheads on the road really work me up!

bones
Street term for the game of dominoes.

We played bones for bones, and I won lots of chedda.

bong
A device made of clay, ceramic, plastic tubing or PVC, glass, a two-liter soda bottle, or any other item that can be filled with water in order to smoke fine and tasty nugs of marijuana.

Hey, wanna come over and hit the bong?

bong rips

A noun that refers to the action of smoking from a bong. So named for the sound that air makes when it bubbles through the bong water.

Dude, don't take bong rips while I'm on the phone with my parents; they might hear you.

boo that

Interjection used to show disapproval in a condescending fashion, often signaled by a roll of the eyes or a sour expression.

She wanted to go to that movie?! Boo that!

boob

1. A woman's breast.

Her boobs are ridiculously large.

2. A stupid person; a rural oaf.

Pat's a boob for getting all the questions wrong on his math test.

boob job

Plastic surgery done to enhance the look of a woman's breasts.

I think she feels more confident about herself since she had her boob job.

boobage

Cleavage. Refers to volume of breasts.

She lacked the proper boobage for that dress.

booger

An accumulation of human mucus removed from the nasal cavity.

Teacher: Timmy! What did you just throw at Susan?!
Timmy: Aw, gee, Mrs. Lemonbottom, it was only a booger.

book

1. A tool barely used by American society today because it is not "cool" to read.

It's a shame, really; once upon a time in America a book was a precious commodity.

2. An object used as a coaster, as a booster seat for small children, or to increase the stability of poorly built furniture.

Guest: Where do you want me to put my drink?
Host: Oh, just set it on top of that book.

book it

To travel at high speed or hurry the hell up.

When I saw the cops, Tim and I

picked up our stash and booked it.

book smart
Being able to succeed scholastically, but not necessarily in the real world.

Sure, she's book smart, but she can't even cook instant potatoes!

boom
1. To hustle.

That man's out there booming on the block.

2. Adjective used to describe a pretty girl.

Yo, guy, that girl is boom!

boomshakalaka
An onomatopoeic "in your face." The sound of a slam-dunk in basketball—the "boom" being the dunk and the "shakalaka" being the rattling of the backboard.

Pippen over to Grant . . . he shakes and bakes . . . to the basket . . . boomshakalaka!

boost
1. To steal.

I looked out my window the other day and saw this dude trying to boost my ride, so I shot him in the face.

2. To leave in a hurry.

Is he ready? C'mon then, let's boost.

boosted
1. A vehicle that has some type of forced induction.

Did you see Jimmy's boosted car?

2. A vehicle that comes stock from the factory with a turbo and has been upgraded so that it is fast as a biznitch.

Dude, did you see how boosted that Supra was?

3. A word used by ricers/tuners to describe how cool something is.

Man, your new house is boosted off its nut.

4. Excited.

No school tomorrow—I'm so boosted!

boot
To vomit.

I straight drank too much tequila, and now I have to boot!

bootsy
Bad or wretched.

That history assignment is hecka bootsy, man!

booty

1. Pirate treasure, plunder, or other ill-gotten gains.

Captain Yellowbeard: Share the booty, mates!

2. Butt, ass, specifically the female posterior.

Ike Turner: Shake dat booty, woman! I said shake it! <slap>

3. Sex.

Captain Yellowbeard: Share the booty, mates!

4. Crap.

Vanilla Ice: What does it mean that my career was "booty"? I've never heard that one.

booty call

A call for sex.

I was mad horny, so I gave my boyfriend a booty call.

bootylicious

1. Term used by rappers Dr. Dre and Snoop Dogg to mean lackluster, laughable, or just simply terrible.

Did you see that bootylicious move that chick made in the club? She must have been messed up, because she tripped on her heels and smacked her face.

2. Term used by Beyoncé Knowles in the song "Bootylicious" to mean curvaceous or voluptuous, especially in the derriere (i.e., booty).

She is so bootylicious the whole block couldn't help but check out her backside.

3. Fine.

D-d-damn, that is one bootylicious sista!

4. Sexually attractive in a way that causes males ages 18–25 to stare at the booty cheeks.

Holy coconuts, Batman! Catwoman is so bootylicious!

booyah

1. Interjection used by a winner to make a loser feel bad, equivalent to "Oh yeah! In your face! There we go!"

He won the game of Monopoly, knocked over the board, and screamed "Booyah!" at all the losers.

2. Gang terminology for the sound that a shotgun blast makes.

I pulled the trigger and, booyah, he was dead.

3. Interjection used to express

excitement and satisfaction, equivalent to "totally sweet!"

Person 1: I just baked a whole batch of cookies.
Person 2: Booyah!

bored
Lacking excitement; feeling miserably stagnant.

There is nothing to do. I'm really bored, sitting here cracked out making entries on urbandictionary.com.

bork
1. To ruin a chance at; to botch, fail, mess up.

I completely borked my interview.

2. To be irreversibly damaged.

My sound card is borked.

boss
Incredibly awesome, miraculous, great.

Dude, did you see that chick? She's boss!

bounce
1. To leave with haste. The letters "iz" are often added after the "b" to make the term even more ghettofied.

Dude, the D's are here, we need to bounce!

Aight, this shit is whack, I'ma bizounce.

2. To have an e-mail message returned because the intended recipient's mailbox is full or the message could not be delivered.

I've been trying to hit you up using the address you gave me, but the e-mails keep bouncing.

bounce like an ounce
To leave.

Yo, I'm gonna bounce like an ounce, G.

bouncebackability
Ability to turn things around unexpectedly or make a comeback. Commonly used in sports.

The boxer looked dead and buried, but with great bouncebackability came back to win.

bousta
About to. Also "abousta" and "boutsta."

I'm bousta leave.

bout
A fight.

Spike and Rampage are havin' a bout and they're both so beat up it's hard to tell who's winning.

bout it

Generally better or more "all about" whatever is being compared.

Them hoes can't front; they know J-Lo's ass is mo' bout it!

bowl

The part of a marijuana (weed, pot, ganja, etc.) pipe in which the marijuana is placed (packed) to be smoked. It may have a little hole (carb) on the side of it, which you cover while you hold the pipe and smoke the marijuana.

I wanna smoke a bowl right now sooo bad!

boxed

Laid off from a job, since they give you a box to put all your stuff in.

I can't believe John was boxed yesterday. This job will suck without him around.

boy band

An (often musical) group of males in their late teens to mid twenties who concentrate on fashion, image, and popular culture and attract an audience of around 10- to 16-year-olds (male and female). Term for groups like Hanson, Good Charlotte, Busted, and most so-called rock bands whose lyrics and style defy the opposing macho, adult styles of genuine rock bands.

Boy bands have an average shelf life of two years.

boys

Short for "boys in blue," the five-o, the fifty, cops, pigs, etc.

boys in blue

Police, the five-o, the fifty, cops, pigs or just "boys."

Be loc, we got boys comin' at six. (Translation: Be easy, the cops are right behind us.)

bozo

A clown; a very annoying silly person.

Some bozo just cut me off in traffic!

bracelets

Handcuffs.

Damn five-o got me in bracelets.

brah

A term of affection used between males with fraternal bonds; brother, comrade.

Brah, you'd better stop picking your nose in front of Mr. Neidhart.
Brahs don't shake . . . brahs gotta hug!

brain fart

A total lack of recognition. A silly mistake. Can be stress related.

I had a total brain fart when she asked for my number.

brain is in sideways

Term used to describe one who can't think straight, usually because one is in love.

Ever since I met Big Tito, I feel like my brain is in sideways.

Brazilian

A waxing in which the pubic hair is completely removed.

My girlfriend got a Brazilian.

brb

Acronym for "be right back."

I'll brb. I have to go get dolled up.

bread

Currency, money, lizard skins, greenbacks.

Hey, I think we can get some bread from my 'rents to buy beer for the party this weekend.

bread stack

A stack of money.

My bread stack's lookin' large. Time to cash out.

break

1. Short for "breakbeat." A style of dance music that uses looped beats to form a continuous rhythm. Comes in many styles, including old school, nu skool, funky, and progressive.

There's a sick breaks, hip-hop, and drum and bass party this weekend we should go to.

2. A surf spot.

You should surf some Australian breaks if you want to get any good at the sport.

break dance

A hip way of dancing that often includes spinning on the floor, sometimes on your head.

I'ma gonna break dance my way to the bathroom.

break edge

To start doing drugs or skanking again after you have been "straight edge" or "sXe."

I broke edge once on New Year's Eve, but usually I'm more sXe than your single aunt will ever be.

break out

1. To flee, like from a fight.

Break out! The teacher is coming!

2. To disperse a group in all directions in order to confuse authorities.

Hold the drugs, break out!

break the bank

To make a shitload of money.

When Joe deposited 700 Gs into his savings account at once, he broke the bank.

break the seal

The point at which you first piss after you have been drinking your favorite alcoholic beverage. After that you will have to piss a lot more often.

Damn, dude, I shouldn't have broken the seal, because now I have to piss every ten minutes.

break yourself

To submit or yield to someone else.

The armed robber told the lady, "Break yourself!" so she gave him her purse.

breakdown lane

The state you are in when a relationship ends or when you break down

and can't take something anymore. Same as heartbreak lane.

He and his girlfriend just broke up. She looks as if she just got back from breakdown lane.

breeder

Offensive term for a person who breeds with members of the opposite sex and is often of low class and intelligence. Their only purpose in life seems to be breeding others like them, and they're quite prolific at it. Sometimes a synonym for trailer trash, homophobe.

Ugh! What's that smell? Is this a breeder bar? It reeks of CK One in here.

breezy

The word "breezy" is a combination of two words that describe a woman who is easy. The word "broad" (slang for "a woman") is combined with the word "easy," creating the derogatory word "breezy."

Don't worry, you're not her baby daddy; she probably doesn't know who the daddy is. She ain't nuttin' but a breezy.

brew

1. Beer.

Can you pass me a cold brew?

2. Tea.

Would you like to come in for a hot brew?

brewski
Beer.

I'm gonna go grab a few cold brewskis out of the fridge.

brick
1. The basic unit of measure for most drugs. It's the way they're packaged after they're first processed or made. Then the brick is divided up and sold in smaller amounts. A brick is either a pound or kilogram, depending on whether you're going by American or metric measurements.

I get my dope straight off a brick—pure, clean, and untampered with.

2. A basketball shot that hits the backboard and bounces off.

She shoots the ball and—aw, it's a brick!

brill
Short for brilliant. Cool.

That was bloody brill! Let's see it again.

bring it
Interjection used as a "manly"

comeback to someone who is being challenged, or offered as a direct challenge to another. Similar to "Show me what you got"; "Do your worst"; "Bring your shit"; "Go for it!"

Basketball player 1: I'm gonna slam dunk yo' punk ass.
Basketball player 2: Aight, bring it, bitch. Let's see what you got!

bro
Close friend, bud, pal, comrade.

He's my bro. I watch his back, and he watches mine. We're like brothers, ya know?

broke down
Ugly, beat, busted, tore up. Sometimes shortened to "broke."

Bob: What seems to be the problem here, miss?
Ugly girl on the side of the road: Looks like my car's broke down. Can you help me out?
Bob: That's not the only thing that's broke down. Later.

bros before hoes
The law stating that buds always come before significant others.

Ho: Let's go bowling later.

Dude: I be goin' out skeet shootin' wit' mah bros tonight. You know how it is— bros before hoes.

broughten

Short for "that's already been brought up." We have already said (or know) everything worth saying about this subject.
Variant: brought.

Girl 1: Did anyone see the women's gold-medal soccer game? Wow, what a game.
Girl 2: Broughten. We were talking about that before you came in.

bru

Friend. Form of address equivalent to "dude." Variant of "bro."

C'mon, bru, life is meaningless, so I'm boozing it up at Navi's.

brush your shoulders off

1. Gesture you make when you feel like "it ain't no thing."

I got action from four different girls this weekend. <brushes shoulders off>

2. Also used to mean "trying to forget" or "forgotten."

Yo, I just broke up with my girlfriend last night. <brushes shoulders off>

b.s.

1. Acronym for "bullshit."
2. Acronym for "beer shits."

You: Let me use the can, I've got serious b.s.!
Your grandma: Shut up, that's total b.s. Anyway, I need to pee like a racehorse, so you'll have to wait.

b-side

The reverse side of a phonograph record, especially a single.

How many songs are you planning to record? Will all of them go on the album or will some be used as b-sides?

bucked

Shot.

Yo, man, you got bucked pretty bad, holmes.

bucket

Old car in bad shape. Short for "rust bucket."

When I was sixteen and got my license, I drove "Sparky," a bucket with over 350,000 miles on it. The ladies were all up ons.

bucket o' cluck

Huge bucket of chicken bought at a restaurant.

Let's go grab a bucket o' cluck at KFC.

bud

1. Friend, pal, chum. Shortened from "buddy."

Karen and I have been buds since elementary school.

2. The dried and cured, unpollinated flowering portion of the marijuana plant that contains the highest concentration of THC.

Let's smoke a little of this killer bud before the jazz concert.

budget

Of poor quality.

Did you see that girl Aaron hooked up with? Damn, she was budget.

buff

1. To remove graffiti or any kind of paintings or advertisements.

They buffed over my mural!

Damn, I just put those fliers up and they already got buffed.

2. Very strong or having defined muscles. Used mostly for guys.

Look at that—he's pumpin' 200 pounds! Damn, he's buff.

bug off

Interjection meaning "go away." Bluntly asking to be left alone.

Bug off, loser!

bugger

Technically means "to sodomize," but most people use the word in a variety of situations, often without realizing the true meaning. Often considered more acceptable than dropping the f-bomb (as long as you're not in the presence of anyone old enough to remember the actual meaning).

1. When something goes wrong.

Bugger! I got my nose caught in the toaster again!

2. When something surprises or impresses you, as in "Well, I'll be damned."

Bugger-me!

3. When you can't be bothered doing something.

Bugger that!

4. To refer to a person in a derogatory manner.

That bugger stole my Holden!

5. To refer to a friend or someone

you feel sorry for.

I decided to let the bugger enjoy it.

6. To mess up.

I must've buggered that question.

7. To tell someone to go away, get lost.

Bugger off!

buggin'

Freaking out, going postal.

Man, he saw his girlfriend with another guy and now he's totally buggin'.

buggy

Used to describe an item, typically a computer program, with numerous errors that may prevent or hinder it from working.

The program crashes whenever I close it; it must be buggy.

build on sand

To provide with an unstable foundation.

Having only bought high-risk stocks, I had an investment portfolio that was built on sand.

built

Large, well built, highly muscular, great presence, huge.

He is so built. He must lift weights.

bulimiate

1. To throw up.

That sausage at lunch made me wanna bulimiate.

2. A person who pukes a lot.

Quit puking, you bulimiate!

bull scare

A very strong bluff.

He's just frontin'. Ain't nothin' but a bull scare.

bullet time

A highly sophisticated slow-motion special effect technique used to show a bullet in flight. The action is slowed down to show the bullet as it passes through the air. The bullet emits tracer rings to show its path. This technique was pioneered and made popular in the science-fiction film *The Matrix*. This technique has since been used in many movies and video games, including Max Payne, Metal Gear Solid 2, and *Charlie's Angels*.

Bullet time kicks ass!

bum

To get something from someone else for free. Also used to mean "borrow," but with the understanding that repayment might not happen.

Hey, can I bum a smoke off you?

bumper check

When a lowrider hops so high the bumper hits the pavement.

I impressed a car full of hotties by bumper checking back at that last stoplight.

bumpin'

Music when played at a high volume.

Yo, dude, that new stereo system of yours is bumpin'!

bumpin' out the frame

Something really phat, like a car with a system so loud that the car is bumping out of its frame.

Yo, that new Common song is so hot, it's bumpin' out the frame.

bumps

Speakers, subs, woofers.

Hey, you guys! Check out mah bumps.

bum-rush

Attacking someone or something (usually in a group) with the reckless abandon and fervor of one who has nothing to lose.

The children bum-rushed the home-baked cookies when Mom brought them out.

bung up

To mess up while doing something. Can also mean to have an accident.

Tommy tried to fix his car, but he just bunged it up!

bunk

Nonsense, utter rubbish, bullshit.

Video games cause violence? That's all bunk.

bunny hop

To pull your bike into the air so that neither wheel is touching the ground. Used during mountain biking to avoid obstacles in the trail and similarly (with care) by road cyclists.

I was right behind Jesse when he bunny-hopped a snake. Unfortunately for the snake I didn't have enough time to avoid it.

buns

A more politically correct word used in place of "ass." Mandated by Mr. Garrison in the *South Park* movie.

If you mess with that bouncer, I reckon you'll get your buns kicked.

Kobe Bryant has signed a $50 million deal with the Los Angeles Lakers of the National Basketball Bunsociation.

What the hell?! That buns-hole just cut me off!

burn

To disrespect or diss someone; to make fun of someone. Used a lot in the ever-popular TV show *That '70s Show*.

Gabe: Hey, Tom, I heard your girlfriend tows a trailer.
Tom: What?!
Eric: Oh, damn, T! You got burned!

burn book

A book full of mean information on people. If found, can get its owner(s) in trouble—like in the movie *Mean Girls*.

Girl 1: Hey! Did you see that guy I got with last night? He was sooo fine!
Girl 2: No way! He was in someone's burn book and it said his equipment was tiny!

burn one down

To smoke a joint.

Joey, Bobby, and little Timmy sat out the kickball game and burned one down

behind the gym during recess.

burn out

1. To smoke marijuana or any other drug used with fire; to get high.

Stoner 1: Man, are we gonna burn out today?
Stoner 2: I don't know, it isn't 420.

2. To leave or go to another place.

Hey, dawg, let's burn out.

3. To disappear from common knowledge very quickly.

It's better to burn out than it is to fade away.

burning daylight

Wasting time. Literally, losing valuable daylight hours (of which there never seem to be enough).

C'mon! Get the lead out! We're burning daylight here!

burnout

1. Smoking the tires of one's car; either to heat up the tires for added stickiness or to impress the MILFs at the DQ in your swanky suburb.

I did such a smoky burnout in the Galaxie, I completely lost sight of that ricer sitting behind me!

2. A slow, often apathetic and lazy person. The guy you used to see stoned and tripping in high school every day, and 10 years later he's sitting in his parents' basement playing Final Fantasy every day.

My burnout friend: "Dude, I'm too stoned to work. Mom, can you make me a sandwich?"

bus driver

Figuratively, anyone who "takes you to school" by teaching you a lesson or showing you the proper way to do something.

After I made seven consecutive three-pointers and dunks in his face 32 times I yelled, "Call me the bus driver, because I just took yo' ass to school!"

Bushism

A statement made by George W. Bush that makes little or no sense and/or violates basic rules of grammar.

"For every fatal shooting, there were roughly three nonfatal shootings. And, folks, this is unacceptable in America. It's just unacceptable. And we're going to do something about it."
—George W. Bush in a May 2001 speech announcing the "Operation Safe Neighborhoods" plan

business class

Describes a person, especially female, who dates people for their money, is stuck up and expensive to date, can't fly coach, and is high maintenance.

Stay away from her, she's business class.

business end

The section of a tool/device directly responsible for producing the desired effect of that tool/device. Generally used in the context of a threat.

You don't wanna be on the business end of my gat, son.

business provocative

Attire intended to provoke sexual arousal or attention in the workplace.

Sara's ruffle skirt is rather business provocative.

bust a

Used to direct an action that is implied by the accompanying word. Followed by a noun or a handful of workable verbs. Sometimes implies the need for haste; however, this is not always true, as it can be used simply to complete a slang phrase.

Bust a right here on Ninth Street.

Bust a move on the dance floor.

Bust a feel on that hottie.

bust a cap
To shoot a gun.

Shut up before I bust a cap in your ass!

bust ass
1. To fart.

I just busted ass and it smells real bad.

2. If used with a possessive: to work hard.

You better be busting your ass if you want to finish the job on schedule.

bust out
1. To do something extraordinarily sick, cool, or excellent.

That dude really busts out on his skateboard.

2. To pull something out, such as a verbal call or a physical action.

He's busting out sweet nollie flips these days.

busta
1. Someone with the ability but not the desire to work; someone who depends on others to get by.

That busta is 35 years old and still living with his mother.

2. Poseur, wannabe; one who fronts.

Bitch try to perpetrate—whatta busta!

busted
1. Unattractive.

I would never date him; he was straight busted.

2. Lame.

Yo, that party was busted, so we bounced.

3. Boring.

That movie was so busted I fell asleep.

butt billboard
Blatant advertising on the rump of a pair of girl's shorts or sweatpants. Synonym for "ass billboard."

She was standing there in the mall, in plain view, wearing a butt billboard that said "Nasty."

butt dial
To accidentally call someone when your phone is in your pocket.

She heard me call her a bitch 'cause my phone butt dialed her.

butt hurt

Easily offended, taking something too personally.

Jenny tries to hide her low self-esteem by being cocky, but when Joe tells her she's ugly, Jenny gets butt hurt.

butter

Person with refined skills at a particular task, like playing basketball. Goes with the phrase "I'm on a roll!" meaning doing something so well that there is no stopping you. Later taken to the next level by saying "I must be butter, 'cause I'm on a roll!" because butter is what most people put on rolls. Finally shortened to "butter."

After draining a fourth straight three-pointer he yelled, "I must be butter, 'cause I'm on a roll!" Then some other guy replied, "Um, uh . . . yeah, whatever."

butterface

Someone with a hell of a nice body but an ugly face.

She looked real good from far away . . . but up close I realized she was a butterface.

butterfly effect

Theory that everything matters, so if you change even the smallest of life's details, you completely change its outcome.

A man traveled back in time and stepped on a bug. Thanks to the butterfly effect, the world was entirely different when he got back.

buttload

The international phrase for a large amount of anything being described.

My boss dumped a buttload of work on my desk for me to finish. After that I quit.

button man

A low-ranking member of an organized crime syndicate.

The don's territory is patrolled by hundreds of armed button men.

buzz

1. Anything that creates excitement or stimulus.

Shooting people in Vice City is my latest buzz.

2. The feeling experienced by someone in a stimulated state.

That's nothing compared to the buzz I get from speed.

3. Gossip.

So what's the buzz about Michael Jackson's new baby?

buzzkill

Something that spoils or ruins an otherwise enjoyable event, especially when in relation to ruining a drunken or drug-induced high.

We were having a great time at the party until Jim puked all over the floor. That was a major buzzkill.

buzzworthy

Worthy of attention. Should be able to be heard or known by everyone.

That's a great song—totally buzzworthy.

BYOB

Acronym for "bring your own beer," indicating a party where alcohol is not provided by the host.

Wanna come over Saturday? We're having a BYOB party.

C

cabin fever

A type of hysteria brought on by spending too much time indoors. Directly descended from long-haul journeys where you are stuck in cramped conditions for too damn long.

I'm getting cabin fever—time to get a life.

cadbury

Any individual who cannot hold their liquor (i.e., gets drunk on a glass and a half).

You stupid cadbury! A glass and a half and you passed out!

cake

1. Easy.

This is cake, yo.

2. Money.

That kid is gettin' his cake for workin' all those hours.

3. To throw game to a girl, or to try to get a number.

Look at Jerry trying to cake Lisa, and he still ain't gettin' the number.

cakin'

Well off; living the good life. Describes a person who has a good job, a flashy car, and attractive people flocking to them in admiration of the way in which they cake. If you are an intern working for peanuts and/or bubble gum, you are most definitely not cakin'. Also Cakin' McBakin'.

Taprick: I'm an intern.

Bill Gates: I'm Bill Gates. I own you.
Taprick: Wow. You're cakin', like Cakin'
McBakin'.
Bill Gates: Thanks, I do have the best job
in the world, and my success affords me
everything I want.

California stop

The act of slowing down but not
fully stopping while driving. Applies
mostly to right-hand turns at stop
signs.

Sarah got a ticket for making a California
stop when turning right at the intersection.

Californication

The spread and influence of
Western culture, especially that of
California, across the world. The
combination of the words
"California" and "fornication" hints
at the sleaziness of the process.

Californication is the number-one reason
for the corruption of Eastern religion.

Caligirl

Of or pertaining to a girl who lives
in California. Generally tan, pretty,
and a surfer, but sometimes just a
beach bunny. Generally considered
the prettiest girls in the U.S.

Neil: Whoa, check her out. Tan, hot . . .
and, dude, she surfs.

Jason: Dude, I heard she's a native
Californian—a Caligirl.

call hell

The time from when someone was
supposed to call until the point you:
1. get over it and realize you've been
blown off, or 2. actually get the
phone call.

I'm in call hell. Tyler said he'd call
Monday and it's now Wednesday.

call it

1. To call it a day, or end the current
task.

Right, I'm going to call it. That's enough
for me.

2. Medical staff term to state that an
individual has passed away.

I'm callin' it, it's 1900. Let's get the stiff
ID'd and tagged.

call me sometime

A term that young Americans use as
a goodbye phrase that the speaker
doesn't mean and the listener never
intends to do.

Ex-girlfriend: It was great seeing you.
Hey, call me sometime!
Ex-boyfriend: Yeah, sure. You too.

call someone who cares

Polite version of "call someone who gives a shit."

Teacher: Your homework is late again, Douggie.
Doug: Call someone who cares.

call waiting face-off

When you are on the phone with a friend and another friend calls you. Your two friends enter a call waiting face-off. You must choose which friend is more important.

I can't believe I lost a call waiting face-off with my girlfriend's sister.

camel toe

Crotch cleavage (especially on a woman) that is visible through tight clothing.

Did you see that girl in spandex? She had serious camel toe going on.

camgirl

A girl with an online journal and website (usually badly designed) who broadcasts her image over the Internet in exchange for wishlist items from strange, anonymous men. Usually shows less skin than a camwhore and is almost always underage.

I just bought a webcam, and once my web-site is up I think I'll become a camgirl. I'll be rakin' in the loot.

camp

Most often used to describe effeminately gay men, but one can be camp without being gay. Examples: Elton John and Jack from the TV show *Will & Grace.*

He's campier than a row of tents, and Cher is his camp icon.

campy

Overacted or exaggerated (usually on purpose); kitschy.

The Rocky Horror Picture Show is so campy, and it has a big cult following.

can

1. To give up on or desist from an activity.

Can the tickling, kids, before someone starts to cry.

2. To fire (an employee).

I thought the boss was going to give me a raise, but instead I got canned.

3. Buttocks; keister; butt; rump; gluteus maximus.

She had a can on her like the queen of Bulgaria.

4. Jail; the slammer; hoosegow; calaboose; graybar motel; the jug.

I got outta the can last week and yesterday I got busted again.

5. Bathroom.

I'll be right back. I need to go to the can.

6. Complete and on reserve, as of a film.

The network has five episodes in the can, so we'll still be able to see the show for a while even though it has been canceled.

can of whoopass

Figure of speech meaning "act of violence," generally employed as "open up a can of whoopass," meaning to cause large amounts of pain.

If I don't get my way, I'm going to open up a can of whoopass.

can of worms

A tricky situation that requires much effort to resolve.

My girlfriend caught me kissing another woman, so I think I opened up a can of worms on that one.

canceled

One who is too ugly to even date; usually refers to a woman.

Dayam! That biotch is nasty, dawg. Canceled!

candy

1. Euphemism for sex.

Hey, want some candy?

2. Something (usually flashy, like a lure) used to get sex.

Hey, want some candy?

3. Drugs, particularly cocaine, crack, or ecstasy.

Hey, want some candy?

candy shop

A place where everything in sight looks pleasing—candy for the eyes. From rapper 50 Cent's album *The Massacre*.

Damn! So many hot girls up in the club. This place is a candy shop tonight.

cankles

A pair of legs that have no defined end of the calf area as well as no defined beginning of the ankle area. Does not only refer to fatty legs, but simply all shapeless legs.

Perfect face, perfect body, smart and funny . . . but, damn . . . I can't handle them cankles.

cans

Headphones.

I recently bought a set of Koss cans, and they are more than adequate.

can't be arsed

To be seriously unmotivated, disinclined to get off one's arse, unwilling to do something.

I just can't be arsed. I'm too tired and there's nothing in it for me.

cap

1. The tip of any bullet. The tip of a bullet is just a "cap" put over the shell. The term can also be used for a shotgun cartridge, but the buckshot in a shotgun shell does not technically cap over the cartridge like a bullet does to its shell.

I'm gonna bust a cap in your ass!

2. To shoot a person with a handgun.

If I ever become a personal-injury lawyer, then cap me in the head.

3. To make fun of someone, such as by cracking jokes about them.

Stop cappin' on me! Y'all are foreva makin' fun of me.

Captain Obvious

A very slow-witted individual, usually one who states the most obvious thing.

A: Hey, water's wet!
B: Good call, Captain Obvious!

car hole

Garage, parking space, or other place to deposit one's car. Often used by Homer on the TV show *The Simpsons*.

I'm going to go park in the car hole.

card

To check people's IDs as they enter a restricted (usually overage) area, like in a club or casino.

I can't believe that security guard carded me when I was coming in!

carve

The proper technique for snowboarding. Involves descending in a relatively straight path by transitioning from toeside to heelside in a quick and fluid manner.

Yelling from the chairlift: Look at Snowflake; that fool can't carve to save his life. All he can do is the falling leaf!

case

1. To check out in advance. Usually

used in reference to a place you plan to burglarize or commit an act of mischief at.

Let's go case the house first so we know the easiest and quietest way to break in.

2. 24-pack of beer.

Can you pick up a case on the way back?

cased
Quite intoxicated by drugs or alcohol.

I was so cased last night I couldn't drive home.

cash cow
Something whose sole purpose is to bring in money, and usually loads of it.

The speed traps set up by the cops are just another cash cow to fill city hall's coffers.

cash in hand
Undeclared income that is not taxed or put through a bank.

The white-van man only takes cash in hand.

casual sex
Sex that wears trousers and a nice-looking polo shirt to work and parties.

Usually I don't care about these things, but casual sex was way underdressed at the reception on Friday.

casual undertime
Getting paid for forty hours for the week when you have worked fewer than forty hours for the week. It is best when casual undertime is achieved by legitimate means, such as leaving early for the 4th of July holiday with your boss's permission.

I work casual undertime during the work-week before a three-day weekend; I usually can leave four hours early on Friday and still be paid for them.

cat
A person, usually male and generally thought to be cool.

I haven't seen him in a while. That cat's getting fat.

catch feelings
To fall in love with someone at an inappropriate time or mistake a repeated hookup for a serious relationship.

I broke it off when she caught feelings and asked me to stop hooking up with her friends.

catch hell

To get caught and get in trouble for doing something wrong.

My boy is gonna catch hell now he done got caught with some X.

catch the vapors

To get smoked or schooled by someone.

You gonna be catching the vapors in your riced-out piece of shit while I smoke you in my Mazda RX-7.

catch you on the flip side

See you later. Talk to you soon.

I'll catch you on the flip side.

catch-22

A paradoxical, nearly impossible-to-solve problem in which a requirement cannot be met until a prerequisite is met; however, the prerequisite cannot be obtained until the original requirement is met.

So I need a key to open this door, but the key is behind that same door? Damn, this is one big catch-22.

caught up

Getting so involved with a person that one becomes oblivious to the reality of the situation.

She would snap her fingers and I would jump—damn, she got me caught up.

cell phone culture

Term used to describe the neurotic fixation with the cell phone in many countries. It describes being unconsciously attached to your cell phone—for example, habitually playing with it or holding it.

The United States is plagued by cell phone culture and latte culture. I'm moving to a third-world country.

century club

A legendary club you become a member of by drinking 100 beer shots in 100 minutes. This club doesn't have meetings or anything, you just use it to impress frat buddies, hoes, or practically anyone who admires feats of great alcohol consumption.

If you can't join the century club twice in one night, you're a pathetic lightweight.

cha-cha

1. Outdated dance where each person lines up back to front and moves around periodically yelling "cha-cha-cha" at designated intervals; somehow still used at mediocre dances.

I love the cha-cha.

2. Vagina.

I love the cha-cha.

chad

Little flap of paper created when you punch out your selection on a voting ballot. Made famous by the state of Florida in the 2000 U.S. presidential election. If you don't punch it out properly it becomes pregnant, hanging, or dimpled, or even all three!

Those damn chads delayed the election forever!

chalk it up

To attribute, credit, or sum up something.

All the people with diarrhea chalked it up to eating at Taco Bell.

cha'mon

Come on. After the sound Michael Jackson makes when he says "come on." Also said by Michael Jackass on the British TV show *Bo'Selecta!*

We're going to be late for the BBQ! Cha'mon!

chapter stealer

Someone who reads a book/ magazine at the bookstore but does not buy the book.

Aunty Beef: Just went and read four chapters of Pride and Prejudice, *pretty good stuff. Was $2 short of buying it. Will go back tomorrow. Maybe I should just sit in the bookshop and read a few chapters each lunchtime and save myself $9.90.*
Toof: You are a dirty chapter stealer.

charge it to the game

Something caused by fate that can't be altered. Similar to a party foul.

I failed that test today. Oh well, charge it to the game.

chaser

Something you drink right after taking a shot or swig of hard alcohol. Usually juice, pop, or beer.

You gotta use a chaser when drinkin' Everclear!

chaw

Chewing tobacco. Copenhagen, Grizzly, Skoal, Redman.

I need some chaw for the jaw. Gotta have a lipper in.

check 'em

1. A casual term for goodbye to mates.

Jorge: See ya later, Redmundo.
Redmundo: Check 'em!

2. A rude term for goodbye when used in certain contexts.

Teacher: Well, children, it's the last day of school. . . .
Kid: Check 'em, you crusty old hag!

check minus
Mark you get when your effort isn't quite good enough.

Cartman received a check minus on his math paper.

check out
Eyeing another's body, especially the chest, crotch, and butt regions. Usually done discreetly and often with sexual interest.

The guy at the park checked out the hot girl as she walked by.

checking the meter
Euphemism used to temporarily excuse oneself from a social gathering—presumably to see how much time is left on the (nonexistent) parking meter—in order to do drugs.

I'll be right back; I gotta check the meter.

chedda
Short for "cheddar." Cash money, scrilla.

I'm piled high in the chedda.

cheers
An interjection used throughout the day by people in the U.K. to raise their glasses and confirm mutual preference for the pub. Has come to mean many things: "okay," "cool," "thanks," "goodbye," etc. Also used throughout the day by Americans and Anglo-Canadians to indicate they've been to England or wish they could go there.

Niles: Cheers mate, how are you?
Jimmy: Cheers, brilliant, thanks a lot.
Niles: Cheers then, speak tomorrow.

cheese
Money. In the welfare program, people got free money and government cheese.

I lost my job. I need to find somewhere new to get my cheese.

cheeseball
Someone who says things or behaves in a silly, goofy, or corny way repeatedly.

Melvin is acting like a total cheeseball.

cheesin'
Walkin' around with a huge smile on

your face—like when someone is taking a picture and they tell you to "Say cheese!"

That dude's cheesin'! Wonder why he's so happy.

cherry
1. Red-hot ash at the end of a cigarette.

Knock the cherry off that cig before you throw it in the brush.

2. When the bowl of marijuana stays lit.

It's cherry, just hit it and pass.

3. When something is nice, looks new.

That car's cherry.

chew
To annoy or bother someone all the time.

I don't know if I like this brother no more 'cause he be chewing on me about that money I owe him.

chew your food
Slow down.

He was talking shit and goin' off and no one could understand him, so I told him "Yo! Chew your food."

chick
1. A girl. The term is not necessarily derogatory, but many women find it offensive because of its flippant nature.

Those chicks want me.

2. The female sex as a whole.

Chicks are confusing. I don't get them!

chick flick
A movie characteristically geared toward women. Must include: love scenes, kissing, something sad, a happy ending, Flipper.

Laura: Hey, wanna watch Bridget Jones's Diary *with me?*
Danny: That chick flick?! No way.

chicken
1. A dangerous game in which two cars drive directly at each other and the first to swerve out of the way is the "chicken." Also when two cars are driving toward a cliff or ledge and the first one to jump out of the car is the chicken.

Let's play chicken.

2. An attractive woman with thighs and breasts (like a real chicken).

That chicken was workin' her ass in the club last night.

chicken scratch

Incredibly messy handwriting that is nearly impossible to read. Usually the only person who can read it is the person who wrote it, and sometimes not even they can read it. It looks like the footprints and scratches chickens leave in the dirt.

Dude, what the hell did you write here?! I can't read this damn chicken scratch!

chief

1. To smoke weed, as in passing the peace pipe around, Native American style.

Weston Park is the place to go hang out and chief sometimes.

2. Word used to acknowledge someone's presence.

S'up, chief? Heard you threw up everywhere at the party last night.

3. A name you call someone if you forget their real name.

Yo, chief, chiefity chief, chiefy nuts, chiefinator.

chill

1. To hang out.

I'm just gonna chill with my friends at the mall today.

2. To relax.

You need to chill before you pop a vein or something.

3. To stop doing something.

If you don't chill with that annoying shit I'll beat your ass down.

4. Cool, great. An adjective used to show approval.

That kid is mad chill.

chill pill

What you need to take to relax or calm down.

Whoa, it's just a game. Don't get so upset—take a chill pill.

chillax

To relax and chill out at the same time. Having' a pimpin' day. Also "chillaxin'."

Dude, just chillax. Just because it's not your birthday doesn't mean that you won't have fun in the monkey jamboree. I'm out like a decent hurricane. Schlater.

chill in da cut

To stay at home.

Mike: Yo, cuz, what you doin' tonight?

Tony: I think I'm goin' to be chillin' in da cut, dawg!

chillin' like a villain

1. To relax in such an overtly leisurely manner that one mimics the actions of a criminal who is so removed from society because of his clandestine deeds that he has no choice but to surrender and retreat into a state of absolute serenity.

I'm so chillin' like a villain; I'm just illin'.

2. To rest like one has no care in the world.

I'm chillin' like a villain that has no chil'en (children).

3. To unwind and relax as though a major burden has been lifted.

I just finished my term paper and now I'm chillin' like a villain.

chime in

To arrive. To rock up to meet your friends, like at a club or whatevah.

I'll chime in at 10. Make sure you're there.

chimney

Someone who smokes like a fiend, generally cigarettes or weed.

Matt smokes so much that when he's sit-ting in his car people come after him with hoses and fire extinguishers. He's a disgusting chimney.

chin up

Originated from the motion of sliding the back of your hand up your throat and doing a nice little flick at the end of the whole motion. Basically means "screw you."

Man: Hey, baby, wanna come over my house and bang?
Woman: Chin up!

chin-check

Specifically, to punch someone in the chin, but can also refer to violence in general.

Show respect or get chin-checked!

chintzy

1. Cheap.

Don't be chintzy—pay for your own beer!

2. Low quality.

This is a chintzy bike. It's already falling apart!

chirp

1. To emit a short squeal from the tires when launching a car or changing gears.

Yo, bro, I just chirped third gear in my Civic.

2. To call somebody on the phone, usually when you want a booty call or just to chill with them.

Yo, I'm 'bout to chirp my slideoff, son. I'll holla at you.

3. To puke, vomit, throw up.

After a long night of drinking I gotta chirp so I don't feel all hung over the next day.

Chi-town

Nickname for Chicago. Used mostly by South Side residents and famous people from the city, giving props to their hometown.

Dawg, I went to Chi-town and rode the El into the North Side.

chixploitation

The exploitation of beautiful women (chix), commonly used as a selling point of otherwise awful movies, such as *Charlie's Angels 2: Full Throttle*. Similar to blaxploitation, the exploitation of black people in films like *Blacula*.

Sure, the chixploitation flick didn't have a plot, but that upskirt shot of Cameron Diaz ensures that video sales will be excellent.

choice

Excellent or of the best quality.

Dude, your new sneakers are choice!

choose your own adventure

A response to a question when you don't really want to be the one to make the decision. Named after the series of books where you literally "choose your own adventure."

Person 1: Should we go to the mall and buy $75 sweaters, or help the homeless? Person 2: I don't know. Choose your own adventure.

chop

1. The art of trying to get someone to go out with you or give you their digits.

Man, this kid was fully trying to chop me last night and now we're dealing.

2. A repetitive sound/word in a rap song, common among Southern rap. Often added with "screw," it makes for a unique variety of music.

Yo, DJ Michael Watts chopped that beat up!

3. In the world of hip-hop, to lose embarrassingly in a battle situation.

Damn, homie, did you see Magnillificent get chopped in that MC battle against Sicktastic?

chop and screw

When a song is screwed, that means it's slowed down a bit. "Chopping" is when you have the record on one turntable and the same record on another turntable but delayed one beat, then you cross-fade between the two for a beat to double up a half-second part. Usually you "chop" on the fourth beat to double up the first beat of the next measure. DJs often use the "flanger" effect on one of the records to make the "chops" swoop.

DJ Screw originated the chopped and screwed style.

chop shop

A garage that specializes in buying hot (recently stolen) cars and disassembling them to sell the parts individually, where they are virtually untraceable. Many parts will find themselves in west Africa, where they are then sold across the Internet with the claim that they were taken from wrecks. Since the laws regarding reporting wrecks in this part of the world are somewhat obscure, and uncooperative with the rest of the world, reclaiming the parts, even if you can prove they are yours, is very difficult.

His convertible BMW 325 was stolen in the early hours of the morning and is probably in a chop shop by now.

chopper

A Thompson submachine gun.

Hand me that chopper. I'm going to shoot anyone who gets in the way.

chops

1. Long sideburns reaching down to the jawline.

If I were really cool, I'd have me some wicked bushy chops.

2. A trumpet player's embouchure.

Al Hirt has industrial-strength chops.

3. Technical ability on the guitar.

John Petrucci has much better chops than Paul Gilbert, dumbass.

chow

1. Food.

Got any chow? My stomach is digesting itself.

2. Any one of the three meals a day, or any snack in between meals.

Often used as a means of telling time (relative to one of the three meals a day).

Private: Hey, Sarge, what time is it?
Sergeant: It's about a half-hour till dinner chow.

3. The third most important thing to a grunt.

After the good private cleaned his weapon and changed his socks, he scored some chow.

4. Acronym for "cheaper hash or weed." Mainly refers to a lesser grade of high-quality marijuana but is sometimes confused with commercial or (even worse) dirt weed or swag hash.

Man, this chow could be the bomb if Dr. Greenthumb knew how to grow it properly, but it's still a good high.

Christmas-casual

A formal yet comfortable style of dress, as for a Christmas party or when you're going to meet the parents.

Attire for the reunion is Christmas-casual, so a nice sweater and dress pants would be suitable.

chrome

A handgun.

Keep chattin' at me and I'll place my chrome to your dome and nick your mobile phone!

chron

Short for "chronic."
1. Something severe or extreme. Either severely cool or severely bad.

That was a chron 360 flip you just did.

2. High-quality weed. See "chronic" for further detail.

I've been smoking chron pretty "chron" lately.

3. Someone who smokes a lot of weed, or the process of smoking weed.

Keen to go for a chron?

chronic

Good weed, grown under good conditions to produce a lot of THC. Often covered with a distinctive layer of THC crystals. Decent chronic will smell good, but high-end chronic will smell much stronger to the point that it begins to smell like dookie. Good chron may also be recognized by red hairs, but don't be deceived because some weed will have red hairs and barely even be dank (a step below chronic) while some may have no red hairs but blaze you out of your mind.

I was about to spark a bowl of some dookie-smelling chronic, right, and as soon as that lighter got close I could see some mad crystals shining back at me. I was feeling that shit the second I inhaled.

chuck

1. To contribute, as in money for a group item.

Keen to chuck some cash for this kilo of weed?

2. To dispose of something unwanted.

I don't need this anymore. I'm gonna chuck it.

chunder

Vomit; generally chunky in nature.

He hurled in my car and now there's a lake of chunder in the backseat.

chunk it

1. To vomit or "blow chunks."

If you're gonna chunk it, please have the common decency not to do it inside the car.

2. Southern speak for "chuck it," discard it, toss it.

That hose is busted. We should just chunk it.

When you're done with the twine, chunk it over here.

chunk the deuce

1. To literally throw up the peace sign, meaning "later."

He chunked the deuce to his boys as he left the house.

2. Spoken term used to mean "leave" or say "I'm outtie." Also "throw the deuce," or "deuces."

I had to chunk the deuce early to that lame-ass party last night.

church key

Instrument used to open beer cans.

Conrad Birdie: You got a church key, man?
Mr. McAfee: We've got a church, but it's unlocked.
Conrad Birdie: A can opener, man! Man, you're from nowhere like.

cigarette

The distance it takes to walk while smoking one cigarette.

I'm not going into town; that's two cigarettes away and I only have one cigarette left.

cigaweed

A joint. A rolled marijuana cigarette.

Pass me the cigaweed and let's have toke, homie.

circle the drain

To gradually die (literally or figuratively).

When Dan started telling the girl at the bar that he lived in a barn with three sheep, two horses, and his parents, his chances of beating it up that night started circling the drain.

clam

1. Mouth.
2. A dollar.
3. Derogatory term for a Scientologist. Short for "clamhead."

I told her to shut her clam because I don't have enough clams to be a clam.

clambake

The act of smoking marijuana in an enclosed space, especially when the space is small and cramped.

All six of us had a clambake and smoked that fatty in my bathroom with the door closed, and when we came out our eyes were all glassy and bloodshot.

clap back

To return fire.

If someone shoots at you, you clap back at they ass.

classic

A term used to note that something was pure, genuine, and worth remembering. Something that will never slip your mind due to its pure humor.

Joe let out a 23-second fart. It was classic!

clean out one's closet

To put an end to the old way of living and start a new life void of all the secrets and lies from the old life and filled with mental strength.

I unfriended him on LiveJournal and removed his number from my cell phone. I'm cleaning out my closet.

click

To examine, check out.

Click the dubs on that Escalade!

clinic

A sports term usually used to describe a one-sided beating in basketball in which one player gives another player such a thrashing on the court that they look like they are

giving the losing opponent a
"clinic" in how to play basketball.

*Joe played Tom one on one and it wasn't
pretty. Joe gave Tom such a clinic, he didn't
hear the end of it for weeks afterward.*

clink

Jail. Also "cooler," "iron city,"
"lockdown," "tank," "big house."

*Spending any time in the clink has
to suck.*

clip

1. The magazine that goes in a
firearm.

*I busted down the door and emptied an
entire clip into that fool. He died eight
times before he hit the ground.*

2. To kill someone.

Jimmy got clipped 'cause he talked.

clock

1. A gauge, such as a speedometer.

These new 340 km/h AMG clocks rule!

2. To gauge, to estimate, to time.

Cop clocked me at 340 in my AMG!

3. The act of hitting a person.

Try to steal my AMG and I'll clock you.

4. To regard an act or object.

You clockin' that hot AMG?

close it out

To shut up; to stop talking or
making noise.

You better close it out!

close talker

One who leaves little space in
face-to-face chatter.

*Stay away from him. He chews garlic and
he's a real close talker!*

close the deal

The act of meeting someone and
engaging in sexual intercourse
within the same night.

*I met her at the party and before I knew it
I was closing the deal in the coatroom.*

clown

1. To laugh, make fun of, or find joy
in a person or event. Almost always
used in a derogatory or degrading
fashion.

*Ashlee Simpson got clowned when she
did a "live" performance on* Saturday
Night Live *and it was discovered she
was lip-synching to a tape.*

2. A fool or jester; someone you laugh at or "clown" at.

Ha ha, Lorenzo just dropped his sack in front of a narc. What a clown!

clownshoe

A stupid person; a dolt.

The world is full of clownshoes. You just have to deal.

club pump

The act or result of lifting weights or exercising (push-ups, pull-ups, etc.) right before going out to a bar or club with the intent of engorging your muscles with blood, or producing a pump in order to temporarily make them larger to impress the opposite sex.

I got my club pump on before I went out.

clubbing

1. Participating, individually or with a group, in the more active aspects of urban nightlife. Term encompasses both dancing and nondancing participation, sexualized and nonsex-ualized, and usually refers to large, perception- or mood-altering venues. Suggests the use of drugs or alcohol.

I was macking on some random hottie and wishing they'd play anything Calderone;

Jay was grinding to strobes in the main hall; Bess was reapplying the body glitter she'd rubbed off on everyone else; and Biff was gamely slamming Grey Goose with the DJ. It was another night clubbing.

2. When women go out to dance in circles and men go out to hunt them.

Hey, let's go out clubbing tonight.

3. Something done to seals.

Hey, let's go out clubbing tonight.

clutch

1. Great, essential, and potent rolled into a single word. Used to describe an action.

Pulling that move on Jenna was clutch.

2. Ability to perform under pressure.

In the last few seconds of a close game, only a player with clutch can lead the team to victory.

c-note

One hundred–dollar bill. "C" signifies the quantity of 100 in Roman numerals, and "note" signifies "federal reserve note."

Got change for a c-note?

co-chillin'

When you're just chillin' and
someone (like a co-captain) is with
you. Much better than just chillin'
because there are two of you.

Just co-chillin' with Skrilla, not givin' a damn.

coed

A female college student, especially
one who is young and nubile. Root
of the word is "coeducational," a
moniker applied to 20th-century
universities that educated both men
and women.

*Warm weather at the University of
Colorado meant coeds were walking
around in shorts and sunning themselves
in string bikinis.*

coffee swings

Mood swings you get from drinking
too much coffee.

*I got the coffee swings after drinkin' a
whole pot of coffee!*

coke

1. Capitalized: a short term for the
popular soft drink Coca-Cola.

Hey, pass me that Coke.

2. Uncapitalized: a short term for
the illegal drug cocaine.

Hey, pass me that coke.

cold

1. Heartless; having no emotions.

*He laughed at the crippled man who fell
down—that's cold.*

2. Plain, obviously, flat out,
straight up.

*Yo, I walked up to that guy and cold
punched him in the face.*

cold chillin'

Angry but still lounging, keeping it
in check.

*Bitch got me heated last night, but now
I'm cold chillin'. . . .*

cold lampin'

Layin' low, chillin' in the crib, not
doing much of anything, like the
cool temperature of a light in a
lamp that has not been used in
some time. Also just "lampin'."

*We was in da crib, just cold lampin' like
we do.*

college

1. A magical place where it is
rumored that learning takes place,
although those who enter it often
describe it differently afterward as a

beautiful land where beer flows in amber currents next to a golden pasture, where virgins lie naked with gentle smiles upon their calm, inviting faces; but more precisely, a Shangri-la rite of passage into adulthood that involves rampant consumption of alcoholic beverages, flagrant and promiscuous sexual behavior, and a general and fundamental disregard for any form of responsibility by its habitants. 2. The place where you enter exorbitant amounts of debt to "learn" things you will never apply to your actual occupation. Basically, an expensive four-year waiting period for a paper called "degree."

I will owe Wells Fargo my firstborn so I can pay off my college.

combobulate

To organize or pull together. Opposite of discombobulate.

I really need to combobulate my desk. Life is better now that I am combobulated.

comb-over

A thorough looking-over (from the "fine-tooth comb" expression).

Give it one last comb-over before you throw it out.

come at

To attack.

You've been talkin' trash too long, fella. Come at me!

come correct

1. To come out rightly. To speak or approach someone with respect, and not with undeniable ignorance.

That bitch better come correct next time if she wanna hang out with me!

2. To do something the right way the first time to avoid being bitched by another.

I would advise you to come correct before you start throwing out facts that are really false.

come out of the closet

1. To exit a small storage space that generally holds clothes and other items.

2. To admit the fact that one is sexually attracted to members of their own gender.

Ryan came out of the closet wearing his mom's pink dress just as his parents walked through the door. At that point he realized he might as well just come out of the closet.

come out'cha pockets

To pay someone to do something (e.g., a job, favor).

Guy 1: Hey, man! Can you help me move this weekend?
Guy 2: Okay, but you'll have to come out'cha pockets.

come up big

To come through in the clutch, succeed, come out ahead.
Also "come up huge." Opposite of "come up short."

Shaq came up big on that backward alley-oop dunk and then said, "Don't fake the funk on a nasty dunk."

come up off of

To give up an item, often personal in nature.

I had to come up off of my wallet or I would have been capped by those guys!

comptarded

A compound of "computer" and "retarded." Describes someone with limited computer knowledge, especially someone whose age or industry should indicate extensive computer skills.

Karrey doesn't even know how to send images to other people over the net; she's completely comptarded.

compunicate

To chat with someone in the same room via an instant messaging service instead of speaking to them out loud, in person.

Even though they are sitting right next to each other, Jesse and Justin compunicate when they have to tell each other something.

computer science

The study of making porn more readily available, to make it easier and faster to download, and to make what you're looking for easier to find.

condomonium

Trouble finding a condom.

It was condomonium when I looked in my wallet for protection.

conversate

To socialize.

We were drinkin' and conversatin' all night long.

cook bricks

To prepare freebase cocaine.

Last night Horace found three guys cookin' bricks downstairs. He called the five-O, but the guys were gone before the po' arrived.

cooking with gas

Working very efficiently; an elaboration on "cooking."

Once I am done procrastinating, I'll be cooking with gas.

cool

The best way to say something is neat-o, awesome, or swell. The word "cool" is very relaxed, never goes out of style, and people will never laugh at you for using it.

Homestar Runner is cool.

cool beans

Very favorable or pleasing. Great. Very nice.

Cheech: Hey, man, look at this car made out of weed!
Chong: Oh, cool beans, man!

coolio

Cool, but typically used as a one-word response and not part of a sentence.

Quaay: Hey, Inde, I just bought more RAM for my computer!
Inde: Coolio!

cooties

Highly contagious viral bacteria that breed inside young females and are released into the air via sweat glands when in the proximity of young boys. Forms of protection include sprays, suits, and name-calling.

Oh, no! Here comes Suzy—quick, guys, into our anti-cootie suits!

coozy

Insulated holder for keeping drinks (typically beer or soda) cool. Also "coozie."

Glenn was a serious NASCAR fan, and he even had a tattered coozy with Dale Earnhardt Jr.'s number on it to prove it.

cop

1. To get, receive, purchase, or have.

Yo, I'm about to cop a drink. Want one?

2. To steal, take without permission.

I went to the dealership and copped me a pimped-out Suburban.

cop a feel

To feel a woman's breasts or buttocks, usually when she is not expecting it. Often followed by a slap in the face.

Susan was looking so great that I got behind her in line and copped a feel, and she immediately turned around and slapped me.

cop it sweet

To give up or give in to something or someone. To accept an unfavorable situation. Based on the name of an Australian TV show. Has also been extended by some southern Sydney, Australia, cultures to "cop it sweet on the back foot."

They were trying to arrest him and he kept resisting until his friends told him to just cop it sweet.

copper

A policeman.

The copper was so stupid that I just doubled back on him and proceeded to drive home.

core

Short for hardcore. Cool, to the extreme.

Your look is core. I like that.

cornball

Cheesy, corny, or of an otherwise over-the-top, feel-good nature. Describes virtually any inspirational quote that makes you shudder.

The patriotic music in political ads is so cornball.

cornrows

A hairstyle that braids the hair to the scalp in a series of rows, looking like a farmer's field in symmetry. Made popular by many basketball players and actors.

They wrapped my cornrows so tight I have a headache.

cosplay

Literally "costume play." Dressing up and pretending to be a fictional character (usually a sci-fi, comic book, or animé character).

There are animé cosplay conventions around the world.

cotton slut

A man or woman who would do just about anything for a T-shirt.

I'm a cotton slut—I'm going to this event just because they're offering a T-shirt.

couch it

To be banished from your main bed to the living room/lounge couch by your spouse or your roommate for either punitive or hooking-up reasons.

Since you cheated on me with your trampy secretary, why don't you couch it, you jerk!

Man, my roommate's girlfriend is in town and he made me couch it for the weekend.

couch surfing

1. To stay on acquaintances' couches when traveling, rather than in a hotel. A cheap form of lodging used mainly by college students or recent college grads.

I'm hittin' up NYC this weekend and my boy from college just got a job and a place in Manhattan, so I'm couch surfin'.

2. What someone who can't afford rent on their own and/or can't find roommates quick enough does when they are "between places."

Joe just broke up with his girl and doesn't have a place yet, so he's couch surfin' here 'til then.

couching distance

The distance one can reach without leaving the couch or sofa.

That job is too far; it's certainly not within couching distance.

courtesy fart

A fart that is very audible but leaves absolutely no smell.
Jon let loose this massive courtesy fart. We didn't even have to clear the room!

courtesy flush

A flush in the middle of the toilet-sitting process in order to reduce the aroma. Usually performed on a "foreign throne" to be polite and not stink up the host's crapper too much.

I gave a courtesy flush at the Smiths' party because I didn't want to kill the next person to use the bathroom.

crack

Another form of cocaine: two parts cocaine to one part baking soda, with a little water, heated gently until a precipitate forms. Also "crack rock."

In my neighborhood you either slang crack rock or got a wicked jump shot.

cracked out

A physical and/or mental state of extreme exhaustion, generally coupled with any form of substance abuse (ganja, beer, or crack, of course).

I stayed up all night cracked out on Ritalin and caffeine pills.

cracker

1. One who cracks illegally into another's computer or network.

Crackers got into my computer, deleted my e-mail, changed my passwords, and replaced all my porn with family vacation pictures.

2. A racist term used against Caucasians/whites.

I heard that cracker's making moonshine in his bathtub.

cracking
Sensational, excellent, or cool.

That was a cracking pool shot!

cram
To attempt to learn large amounts of information in a short period of time, especially for a test in high school or college.

Cramming for tests is less effective than studying far in advance, but also less time consuming.

crapshoot
Something that is random, not based on skill. Refers to the dice-rolling game craps.

The stock market is a crapshoot.

craptacular
Spectacularly crappy.

Your home movies are craptacular, Chris.

crash
1. To sleep.

Dude, I'm going to go crash. See you later.

2. To stay at someone else's house

for the night.

Is it okay if I crash here?

3. To show up somewhere uninvited or unexpectedly.

Those guys crashed the party at my girl-friend's house, but they brought booze and dope, so we let them stay.

crazy
Cool; very nice. Synonym for "off the hook."

Those are some crazy shoes. Where can I get a pair?

crew
Companions; peer group.

What's the crew up to tonight?

crib
Home, domicile, or dwelling.

Dang, dude . . . your crib is phat, yo! (Translation: Your house is very pleasing to the eye; contemporary flair, yet struc-turally sound. May I have a look around, my good man?)

cromulent
Spurious, not at all legitimate. Sounds legitimate but isn't. Assumes common knowledge of the TV

show *The Simpsons.*

Yes, Professor Smith, these citations are perfectly cromulent (chuckle).

crotch rocket
Sport bike. Often derogatory.

I'd rather own a Harley than a crotch rocket.

CRS
Acronym for "can't remember shit."

I look back just a month ago and CRS.

crucial
Far beyond amazing.

Aw, shit, bro . . . that dunk was crucial!

cruisin'
1. Parading one's vehicle on city streets with or without a destination, sometimes accompanied by excessively loud music, headrest-mounted LCD monitors, or both.

All the hotties wanted to jump in the backseat when we went cruisin' in the Jaguar XJS.

2. State of unproductivity. Also "chillin'."

*Seth: Hey, Adam, what's up?
Adam: Nothin'. Just cruisin'.*

crunk
1. A state of high energy, as described by rapper Lil Jon and the East Side Boyz. Southern word for getting rowdy, out of control, having fun, partying, going crazy.

We about to get crunk up in this piece!

2. Getting a little crazy, a little drunk.

I'm planning on gettin' crunk tonight.

crunk juice
Red Bull energy drink mixed with Hennessy cognac. Made famous by the rappers of the A-Town, especially Lil Jon and the East Side Boyz.

At the party, my boy got loaded on that crunk juice. He drank so much he threw himself out the front door for bad behavior.

crush
1. A burning desire to be with someone you find very attractive and extremely special.

He has a huge crush on her.

2. To defeat in a competition, usually by a large margin.

The Rams crushed the Falcons 45-17.

cubicle farm

Monotonous office environment characterized by white-collar slaves wasting their lives in pseudo-offices with four-foot walls while slowly morphing into zombies.

After three hours in the cubicle farm, I could feel my brain turning into a mushy mass of rotten puddinglike material.

cuh

Short for "cousin" or "cuz." A friend or homie. Commonly used among Southern gangster/ghetto individuals.

Yo, what's up, cuh?

cult movie/cult film

A movie that has a significant, often independent (spread by word of mouth) following. Frequently cult movies depict controversial or distasteful people, activities, or philosophies. Examples include *Harold and Maude, The Rocky Horror Picture Show, Queen of Hearts,* and many others. Before VHS and DVD, art-film houses would frequently show these films year after year. Even after home video, many theaters make annual events of certain films.

You're such a freak. Why are you going to dress up and go see The Rocky Horror Picture Show *for the 1,500th time?*

curb serve

To sell drugs on the block.

I had to curb serve to make ends meet.

cut

Having a lot of muscle tone; ripped.

Bubba might weigh 350 pounds and bench 600 pounds, but that guy is flabby. I'm trying to be like L.L. That playa is cut.

cut and paste

To plagiarize from the Internet in order to earn an easy grade.

I cut and pasted my essay, and now I'm screwed 'cause my teacher wants to submit it to a contest.

cut ass

To make fun of someone or something. To diss something.

Kimberly's cuttin' ass on Tony, sayin' he be eatin' mad much and he's already too fat.

cut 'n' shut

A car composed of two halves from other cars welded in the center and repainted, often to sell to others. Usually structurally unsound after the process and dangerous to use.

My mate Tommy does cut 'n' shuts. Last week he welded a Ford Focus and a Rover 400 together. He made a few bob selling it to some old lady.

cut one
To fart. To expel flatulence.

Ewwwwwww! What's that smell? Who cut one?!

cut sling load
To take a dump. From the command air assault soldiers' order to the helicopter crew chief to drop the cargo load carried underneath the chopper.

Dude! I'll be back in 10 to 15 minutes— I've got to go cut sling load something fierce.

cut up
To engage in sexual activity.

Say, have you and that broad Sadie cut up yet?

cuts
The evil eye; menacing look given to someone.

Yo, you see that granny over there? She just gave you cuts.

cutter
Person who has a serious problem and cuts themselves with sharp instruments when they can't handle the emotional pain they are feeling. They think the physical pain lets out the emotional pain, too.

When she pushed up her sleeves and I saw all the scars on her arms, I figured she must have been a cutter.

cyberdump
Getting dumped by your boyfriend or girlfriend over the Internet, via e-mail or, even worse, instant messenger. A step worse than being teledumped (over the phone).

My girlfriend just dumped me over IM. What a kick in the nuts. How low can you get?

cybersex
Interchange of text in which an unsuspecting newbie describes imaginary actions of sexual intercourse to another user of the Internet who claims to be a young, good-looking woman, yet always is a fat and hairy old man who smells. Also "cyber."

So you really like her, huh? Have you two cybered yet?

D

da cheese

Something that smells really bad.

Dude, your flatulence is da cheese.

dag

1. The matted wool on a sheep's tail, but typically used to refer to people who don't have a neat, tidy, or cultured appearance. It can also refer to a person who tends to be quite informal. It is not necessarily a derogatory term.

I'm a bit of a dag today—I'm wearing my trackie-daks.

2. Expression of surprise or amazement.

Dag! I got fired from Dempsey's.

damn skippy

An assertion, usually used with "yes" or "ya" to emphasize some point made.

Person A: Didja see that fight on the corner? That chick got beat. That's brutal. Person B: Ya damn skippy that shit was brutal.

dandruff

A person who "flakes out" and ditches their friends, usually for an insufficient reason.

I think Tyler needs to get a bottle of Head & Shoulders 'cause he's been dandruff lately.

dank

Sticky, hairy, stinky, and highly potent marijuana.

I took two hits of that dank and was nearly transcendent.

dap

The knocking of fists together as a greeting, or form of respect.

He gave me a dap when we greeted.

darkout

A person who mysteriously decides not to participate in an event. They can only manage to provide justification in the form of such responses as "I don't feel like it" or "I can't be bothered." Darkouts are often a result of the subject harboring agendas that they fear would induce ridicule.

Tom's darked out on us again! He's ditched us to go with his girlfriend to see the Corrs. What a bummer!

dating

A pointless waste of time defined by massive usage of cologne and/ or perfume, awkward sweaty hand-holding, and feelings of puppy love that usually dissolve in a few weeks (or less).

Girl 1: We're dating, and, like, he, like, is picking me up in 10 minutes!
Girl 2: Wow, you, like, smell, really, like, strong!

dawg

Friend. Usually informal and often used as greeting. Also "dogg."

I heard you're so fat you have your own zip code! No offense, Santa, you know you're my dawg.

dawn patrol

The act of getting up extremely early—sometimes before sunrise—to go surfing. The term can also be used outside of surfing to refer to getting a very early start to the day.

Bob, Varno, and I are surfing a dawn patrol session at Rincon tomorrow morning.

d-boy

A drug dealer.

I fronted an 8-ball from dis d-boy yesterday.

dead-ass

Completely and honestly serious. To be truthful and not lie. A truncation of the phrase "dead-ass serious."

Guy 1: Yo, swear I saw George W. Bush jump that fence for a corndog.
Guy 2: What? Nuh-uh, you're lying.
Guy 1: No, for real! I'm dead-ass.

dead nuts on

Very accurate. Within 99% accuracy.

When I hit him with a snowball, I made sure my aim was dead nuts on.

dead presidents
U.S. currency; called so because, with the exception of the $1 coin, $10 bill, and $100 bill, portraits of deceased U.S. presidents appear on the obverse side.

I spent some mad dead presidents on my girl last night!

deaded
Blown off; rejected; deliberately singled out; abandoned for reasons unknown.

I hate the way my best people straight deaded me last night.

deal
To accept the way things are.

It doesn't seem like Avril is going to quit making music, so I'm just going to have to deal.

Death Star
A building that electronic signals (e.g., cell phone signals) cannot penetrate.

I tried to call my girl, but I was in the Death Star.

debo
To steal something.

I'm 'bout to debo all that boy's jewelry.

decency timeline
The amount of time knowing or dating someone that passes before it is considered "decent" or appropriate to do certain things with said person.

Kissing someone on a first date would be considered within the decency timeline, whereas having sex on the first date may not be, by some.

deck
1. To punch someone very hard, knocking them to the ground in some cases—hence "deck."

Johnny decked Tim, and he fell to the floor.

2. Hipster lingo for "cool."

That shirt is deck.

deck change
Wrapping a towel around oneself to change (typically into or out of a bathing suit) in a public setting.

Kyle was in the middle of a hurried deck change when he was pantsed. Hilarity ensued.

decks

"Wheels of steel," turntables, record players. Belt Driven or Direct Drive. Technics SL-1200 is acclaimed by DJs everywhere as the industry standard.

Those Numark battle decks are fly!

deep-six

To throw away, get rid of. Originally referred to death at sea, with the "six" referring to a grave, as in six feet under, and the "deep" referring to the ocean.

Deep-six that old couch. It's been on the porch long enough that animals are living in it.

deez nutz

A joke that originated from the song "Deeez Nuuuts" on Dr. Dre's original album, *The Chronic*. Since then, catching people with "deez nutz" has become one of America's favorite pastimes. The object of the game is to trick your friend into making a sexual joke. It works like a knock-knock joke: Ask someone a question, and when they respond with "What?" "Who?" "Huh?" or anything starting with one of the five "W's," you're free to get that person with "deeeeez nuuuuutz!" You may need to say the question

quickly or mumble it so people don't realize you're trying to catch them.

You: Did Dee call last night?
Victim: Who?
You: Deez nutz!

You: Do you like tapes or CDs?
Victim: CDs.
You: C (See) deez nutz!

Officer: Sir, you can't park there.
Me: Nah, it's cool, I talked to D.
Officer: D who?
Me: Deeeez nuuuutz!

def

1. Short for "definitely."

Guy 1: You drinking tonight, bro?
Guy 2: I def am, bro. I've got to get over this hangover.

2. Archaic word used to describe a person, thing, or event that is cool.

Yo, mah pizzles, I got da hookup at this def new club. It's supposed ta be off da hizzy.

dialed

Fine-tuned.

I've got that skateboarding move dialed in.

urban

dibs

The right to something. A claim of ownership.

I have dibs on that girl over there!

dice

A combination of "dope" and "nice," thus exceptionally good.

Kendall Gill is pretty dice.

dick around

To mess around; a term used when someone's doing something unproductive.

Stop dicking around! Get back to work!

dictionary attack

A hacking attempt in which the attacker tries to log in with your user name and a password. Each time the attacker tries he uses a different word in the dictionary.

My password was "password," so our corporate infrastructure fell to a dictionary attack.

diesel

Awesome or strong, as in physical power.

Did you see that guy knock out his opponent in the first round? He's diesel.

diet whoopass

A can of whoopass requiring less energy and only three calories per serving. What you open up when you're too weak to open up a regular can of whoopass on someone.

Hell, I'm tired—I only got diet whoopass left.

dig

1. To create holes in the ground.
2. To understand.
3. The infliction of pain.
4. Where you live.

C'mon you bad mama jamas, I gotta dig me a hole. You dig? So pull some weight, else you all get digs. After this we can head back to my digs for chills, holmes.

5. To like, appreciate, and understand. The word "dig" doesn't only mean "I understand" but also that "I'm a very special person who understands in a special sort of way"—in other words, you're hip.

I dig that Pac CD.

dillhole

An individual lacking intelligence, people skills, compassion, and a human soul. A dough head.

My boss, Peter, is a dillhole. Even other dillholes look at him and say, "What a dillhole!"

dime

1. A very attractive person, a perfect 10.

Damn, dat shorty be a dime.

2. $10 worth of any drug; short for "dime bag" or "dime sack." The amount varies depending on the substance, the quality, and the dealer.

Ayo, will you lemme get a dime, bro?

dime bag/sack

In the drug trade, a reference to either a small amount of pot or very small baggies (about 1 cm by 1 cm) that a rock of crystalline substance (like crack cocaine or crystal meth) can fit in. Either one is worth approximately $10.

I fell back into active addiction after I saw the dime sack and chose to smoke it.

dimensional

Totally cool, sick, ill. Describes something really good.

His new subwoofers are dimensional! They're bumpin' out the frame!

dinkum

Really, truly, honestly. Same as "fair dinkum."

Guy 1: I just got a new surfboard.
Guy 2: Dinkum?
Guy 1: Ja, want me to show it to you?

DINS

Acronym for "double income, no sex." Refers to two married, working individuals who do not engage in sexual intercourse.

Person 1: Don't Sally and Gerry have kids?
Person 2: No, they both work in the city 80-plus hours a week. They're the textbook example of DINS.

dipset

To leave a place as soon as possible to avoid trouble.

Yo, let's dipset outta here—the cops are coming.

dirt

Low-grade marijuana.

Damn, I thought I was getting chronic, but all I got is a bag of dirt.

dirty

A friend.

Yo, that's mah dirty right there.

disco nap

Sleeping when you got something goin' later on that you need to get ready for.

I was about to go to the club, but I needed a disco nap to feel refreshed.

dish

1. Something very cool, good, sweet.

I went to that new club last night and it was so dish, I loved it. We should go again tonight.

2. Big news (bigger than a scoop).

You slept with how many people last night? Gimme the dish, sistah!

diss

Also "dis."

1. To disrespect, make fun of.

He no-showed again. He can't diss me like that!

2. To fail to obey.

Don't diss me when I tell you to do something, boy.

3. To not be impressed by someone or something.

You don't like my car? Are you dissing me, man?

4. Gangsta slang for a minor, trivial insult, which need not even be intentional, yet is nonetheless grounds for homicide.

He dissed my sneakers, so I cooled his shit!

ditz

A superficially dumb Valley chick, with no common sense whatsoever. Usually white, rich, and pretty. Often uses words such as "like," "oh my gosh," "oh my goodness," "that is, like, so not cool at all," and "dude."

Heather is such a ditz! I heard she was at a party and broke her arm while drinking a beer.

diva

A bitchy woman who must have her way exactly, or no way at all. Often rude and belittles people, believes that everyone is beneath her, and thinks that she is so much more loved than she really is. Selfish, spoiled, and overly dramatic.

Celine Dion demands mint-flavored toothpicks in her dressing room at every performance. What a diva!

DL

Acronym for "down low." Secret.

Guy 1: Yo, you stepped out behind your

girl's back last night, didn't ya?
Guy 2: Yeah, but keep it on the DL, yo.

do dirt

To engage in gangsta activity, or kill for a gang.

When the OGs tell you to do dirt, you better be down.

do one's song

To keep saying something untrue or annoying, or something that's been said many times.

He did nada but doin' his old song, "I didn't rip off yo ride!"

do the math

To give someone your telephone number, or to ask someone for their telephone number.

Ho, you be fine. Do the math for me.

do time

1. To serve a prison sentence.
2. To serve a hitch in the military, especially if drafted.
3. To get grounded.

After spending most of his teen years doing time for the 'rents, the kid couldn't wait, so he did time for Uncle Sam as soon as he could. That got old, so he split before his time was up, got caught, did some time

in the big house, and still had to do the rest of his time when he got out. It was getting to be a habit.

docked

Stationary, or kept in one place. Grounded.

Man, I'm docked this weekend. My parents found some X in my room.

dodgy

1. Of questionable legality, like a scam.

Smuggling ganja out of Mendocino could get some tall dollars, but it's a dodgy scam. The cops prolly bust people for that all the time.

2. Of questionable moral or structural integrity.

Ehhh, I dunno, that piece is pretty dodgy. It's all rusty, hasn't been used in a few decades. It might fall apart.

dog it

To give something a half-assed attempt.

Joe just gave up during the run; he was doggin' it the last 100 yards.

dogs

Feet.

It feels so good to let my dogs out of my shoes.

d'oh

A Gen X interjection conveying an overall feeling of frustration. Used to express a feeling one has after realizing they have been tricked, misled, scammed, swindled, etc. Made famous by the animated sitcom character Homer Simpson on the TV show *The Simpsons*.

D'oh! Just as I was about to leave, my boss handed me a huge job that has to be done by tomorrow.

dole

Welfare or other assistance, often from the government.

Since the company he worked for went out of business and he did not quit or get fired, he was eligible to go on the dole. I don't have any money until dole day.

dollar

A general term for money—not just one dollar.

We're gonna do over some bank and get us some dollar.

dollas

Interjection used when something

good happens, such as making a three-pointer in basketball, or talking about money.

Billy hit a three and shouted out, "Dollas!"

done and done

A phrase used when one has finished something that was so involved that it was as though one had done it twice.

Finally, finals are over and it's time to hit up Cabo for spring break. Done and done.

done deal

Over, finished, no more; another way of saying "consider it done" or "good to go."

Stephanie said that it's now a done deal between her and Rob—after their 15th breakup!

done up

1. In adult culture: dressing well, as to attend a formal function.

His wife really got done up for the company dinner.

2. In youth culture, dressing in a manner that is comparable to that of a prostitute.

I still need to get done up before I go out tonight. The guys are gonna be all up on this.

3. In bad shape. Messed up or injured.

Baller 1: Yo, you playin' ball tomorrow?
Baller 2: Nah, man, I broke my leg playin' today. I'm done up.

donor machine
Motorcycle.

We've got a victim coming in to ambulance bay 2 who was riding a donor machine.

don't do me
Don't mess with me.

You tryin' to call me out? Bitch, don't do me!

don't even trip
1. Don't act like you don't understand.

Girl, don't even trip. That man is not going to call you.

2. Don't think for a minute that it's going to happen.

No, you can't use my credit card. Don't even trip.

don't get push with me
Don't bother arguing, it won't change anything, since my decision is final.

Don't get push with me; I'm not paying you any more.

doob
A nicely rolled package of weed; a joint, a doobie. Also "dube."

Let's hide out back and smoke this doob while the family's out.

doobage
Marijuana, weed, gear, grass, skunk, wacky backy, stuff.

Let's go smoke some doobage.

dooced
Losing your job for something you wrote in your online blog, journal, website, etc.

Did you hear Mary got fired yesterday for writing about her boss in her blog? Yeah, she got dooced.

dope
1. Marijuana. Often used by people who do not do drugs.

Don't you be smokin' dope!

2. Heroin. Often used by people who do marijuana.

I smoke the green, but I don't do dope.

3. Cool, good.

Man, that car is dope!

4. To take drugs to improve one's athletic performance.

China dopes up its players to enhance their performance in the Olympics.

dork

1. An individual who is keenly interested in and good at mathematics, science, and technology, and applies mathematical and scientific principles to everyday occurrences, while being lovable and very personable, often having many friends due to wittiness, and often loves video games. Not to be confused with "nerd," "geek," or "dweeb."

Dork: Wow, that light bulb that's flickering in a seemingly random fashion is actually occurring as such due to a capacitance built up on one side of the tungsten filament until it discharges, sending electrical flow through the tungsten, causing photonic emission through heated excitation, which then dissipates as you get farther from the light bulb, according to inverse square law.

Girlfriend who is also a dork: You're right, you dork. Shut up and kiss me. You're so cute.

2. Someone who is a loser, clumsy, stupid, and/or has no common sense.

You can be a total dork at times. I don't know why I hang out with you.

dot-com

Used to add emphasis to the ending of a phrase. Usually spoken with a slight pause prior to it, and with a deeper voice than normal.

Let's go get some food—I'm hungry dot-com.

dot-gone

An unsuccessful Internet company.
He made a lot of money while he worked there, but that dot-gone ruined his stock portfolio and his retirement plans.

double

A jump made of two ramps set some distance apart. One ramp is sloped up and the other down. Used by freestyle athletes in many sports.

Snowflake hit the double but didn't have enough speed going into it, so he nailed the base of the transition. Ouch.

double sweet

More than just sweet. Double the amount of enjoyment.

I'm going to the Peaches concert this weekend, and the tickets were free. Double sweet!

double-break

The act of taking a coffee break twice the length it's supposed to be. Commonly done by slackers or stupid people.

My boss is out of town, so I plan to double-break all week.

double-dare

The first counter of a dare. Can only be countered by a triple-dog-dare.

A: I dare you to dance with Noreen.
B: Oh, yeah? I double-dare you to dance with Ermalinda.

double-dip

To dip something into a sauce, take a bite, and then re-dip the half-eaten item in the sauce. Favorite behavior of crude diners.

Sign at country fair food stall: DO NOT DOUBLE-DIP!

double-fist

To hold and/or consume two drinks at once.

I was double-fisting beer at the frat house last night.

doubleplus

Very or more. From the Newspeak language in George Orwell's novel *1984*.

That bus was doubleplus speedful. I got here in half the time.

doublespeak

A form of language (most often in politics and business) used to hide the true intention of the speaker by deliberately "ambiguating" the meaning of words. Doublespeak words and phrases often have significant emotive attachments (like "axis of evil") or normally mean the complete opposite of how they are being used (like using "conservation" in the name of a bill designed to open up national parks for oil extraction).

The "Shock and Awe" plan is full of doublespeak. How can that many people be gullible enough to support it?

dough
Money.

Hey, television: Don't tell me what to buy. I'll spend my dough as I please.

douja
Weed, marijuana, ganja, pot, herb.

Dude, let's pick up some douja and get lifted before we go.

down

1. To be with it or in the know; to be knowledgeable about something, or to give respect/recognition to something.

Oh, yeah . . . I'm down with what yo talking.

2. To be keen for something.

Are you down to get a feed?

3. To be friends with someone or to spend time with them.

I'm pretty down with her.

4. To be in agreement with someone or something.

Girl 1: Wanna go for a skate?
Girl 2: Yeah, I'm down.

down ass bitch
A girl who sticks up for her man whenever he needs her. Popularized by Ja Rule in the song "Down Ass Bitch."

My girl pulled a gat on the po's last night . . . for real; she's a down ass bitch.

down pat
Well perfected.

You gotta have your kickflips down pat.

doy

Interjection used when one suddenly realizes something that should have been immediately obvious or when one does something stupid. Similar to "duh."

Doy! You have to turn the computer on before you can use it.

draft
To follow the car in front of you extremely closely at high speeds.

Damn, this guy is drafting me. Why does he want to get up on my ass?

drag ass
A lazy and/or slow person.

That dude is a drag ass. It takes him all day to do a simple thing.

drag king
A female who dresses like a male, sometimes to entertain others.

Sarah performed as a drag king in the local bar, under the name Alexander.

drag queen
A male who dresses like a female, sometimes to entertain others.

In his new leather mini and boots, he looked better as a drag queen than he did as an insurance salesman with a suit and a tie.

drama

Unnecessarily making a big deal over something.

Jenny: I hate that girl! I'm gonna kick her ass!
Taylor: Dag, Jenny, all she did was look at you. Why you gotta be so drama?

dress to impress

To wear dressy clothes to a club—something sexier than Sunday clothes, and no sneakers, jerseys, hats, jeans, or sweatpants.

Radio announcer: Tonight at Club Platinum we got Jagged Edge, so, ladies and fellas, that means dress to impress.

drift

1. To separate or not keep in touch with someone.

We drifted bad! I wish we could get back to the way we were before.

2. An insulting way to tell someone to leave.

Tool: Hey, can I bum a smoke?
Playa: No.
Tool: What about three lines?
Playa: Are you deaf? Drift.

3. To cause a vehicle to exceed its tires' limits of adhesion, exhibiting a lateral slip, resulting in an oversteer condition.

Takumi was seen speeding on Interstate 81 in his 1986 Toyota Corolla, drifting along the many curves in the road. He's going to die doing that someday.

drink the Kool-Aid

To embrace a particular philosophy or perspective, often one that is a little offbeat or just plain crazy. A reference to the 1978 Jonestown Massacre, a cult mass-suicide in Jonestown, Guyana, when Jim Jones convinced hundreds of his followers to drink Kool-Aid laced with poison.

Alice: Hey, did you hear Joe is working on the Nader campaign?
Bob: Yeah, he really drank the Kool-Aid on that one.

"Don't drink the Kool-Aid" has come to mean, "Don't trust any group you find to be a little on the kooky side," or "Whatever they tell you, don't believe it too strongly."

Chris: I'm thinking about attending a PETA rally.
Donna: Whatever you do, don't drink the Kool-Aid!

drinking bone

The imaginary bone in the body that alcoholics blame for making them drink all the time. From the Tracy Byrd song "Drinkin' Bone."

My drinking bone takes hold about once a month. Last time I got so jammered I ate a slug.

drive

A general greeting/acknowledgment to a public bus company employee when entering or exiting the vehicle.

Cheers, Drive! Running a little late today, eh?

drive by Braille

"Botts dots" are raised plastic reflectors placed on white and yellow road stripes. Driving over them makes a noise that keeps you in the lane. "Driving by Braille," or "Braille driving," is when someone is so drunk they navigate by the sound and vibration alone.

George W. Bush was so drunk when he was pulled over, he must have been driving by Braille.

drive it like you stole it

Drive fast; drive as if you stole the car and the police are after you.

If you are not here in ten minutes, I'm leaving without you. So put the pedal to the metal and drive it like you stole it.

drive-by

1. A shooting performed by a gang member in a slowly moving motor vehicle that then speeds away from the scene.

Yo, roll up here, G, I gonna do a drive-by on this muthah.

2. To suss something out, to complete a "recce," or reconnaissance.

I did a drive-by of the party and my ex's car was there, so I decided to split.

drop

1. To knock someone over, usually associated with the first hit in a fight.

I'm gonna drop that kid if he don't back off.

2. To spend (generally a lot of) money; to buy something.

Nigga, I dropped 500 Gs on these rocks.

3. To release an album.

Nelly dropped two albums at once this week and they both at the top of the charts.

4. An expensive convertible car. Short for "drop top."

We just got back from the Bentley dealership, bro. You seen the new drop?

drop a dime

To snitch on someone, often to save your own ass. Comes from the old cost for a pay phone call, 10 cents.

John got popped, so he dropped a dime on his supplier and the Ds let him go.

drop bombs

To spit flawless and unbreakable flows/lyrics on the mike.

When B-Rabbit dropped bombs on all the brothas in the freestyle battle in the movie 8 Mile, *he showed them that he could spit flames.*

drop it like it's hot

1. For women: to dance by dropping the butt to the floor and getting freaky.

She was droppin' it like it was hot on the dance flo' today.

2. In basketball: to drop shots through the hoop.

Dawg, he was droppin' it like it was hot in tha game today!

3. In rap music: to drop good lines/bars/rhymes.

Ayo, get y'verse goin' and drop it like it's hot.

drop science

To educate (or "school") someone or show off what you know, usually in rap.

Yo' rhymes are weak. Sit back and watch me drop science on yo' ass.

drop the needle

To play a vinyl record.

We dropped the needle and rocked out to Led Zeppelin.

drought

When a certain drug is in limited supply or unavailable in your city or 'hood. Prices are much higher.

Damn! I just paid $250 for an ounce! We in a drought here.

drunk shame

To humiliate an out-of-control drunkard. The victim must be a person who has passed out drunk with their shoes still on. This person is fair game for many types of "shaming," such as being written on with permanent markers, being duct-taped, and having a bunch of stuff piled on top of them. Common practice in colleges throughout America.

Joe woke up just in time for his big job

interview with a raging headache and the taste of alcohol lingering in his mouth. As he came to, he realized he had been a victim of some serious drunk shaming. He found himself under a pile of all of his clothes, his TV, his computer, his bike, about 100 beer bottles, and his two cats. He managed to get the Sharpie drawings off his face, but he missed the big drawing of a naked man on the back of his neck. Unfortunately, the interviewer didn't.

drunk-dial

To make an annoying, unwarranted phone call after having too many alcoholic drinks.

After he left the bars, he drunk-dialed me five times!

dry

1. Stupid, boring.

Insultor: Yo' momma is so fat that when she sat on the rainbow Skittles popped out! Insultee: That was dry! Like yo' upper lip.

2. When drugs become hard to get hold of in a specific area.

It's so dry here, I'm absolutely gagging for a spliff.

dry ice

Fake jewelry.

Man, that necklace isn't bling bling, it's dry ice.

drylab

To make up scientific data, especially in a science class lab.

Drylabbing will not be tolerated in this course!

Ds

1. Short for D.A. (district attorney, deputy district attorney, or their staff).

D's been giving me heat 'cause I slang bricks.

2. Short for DTs, or detectives.

Put that money away—the Ds is watching.

DTR

Acronym for "define the relationship." When two people discuss their mutual understanding of a romantic relationship (casual dating, serious boyfriend, etc.).

Friend 1: Have you DTR'ed yet? Friend 2: I dunno what we are. I guess we gotta do a little DTR'ing tonight.

dub

1. Abbreviation for the letter "W."

I drive a V. dub.

2. Twenty dollars.

That CD player costs two dubs.

3. Twenty dollars' worth of anything, especially narcotics.

Lemme get a dub; I gotta get high.

4. Plural: twenty-inch rims on tires.

I got my Escalade rollin' on dubs.

5. The art of making a remix, especially a reggae song, in which the lyrics are all or partially removed and the focus is placed on the drum track and the bass. Generally used as a name for any remix to any song.

Lee "Scratch" Perry is the master of the traditional reggae dub, especially his work with Sir Robert Nesta Marley.

duckets

Legal tender. Dinero. Cash money.

Yo, I know I got the duckets here somewhere. Bling!

duck's nuts

An expression of extreme adoration.

Man, this beer is the duck's nuts.

dude

A word that Americans (particularly stoners, surfers, and skaters) use to address each other. It can mean:
1. A man.

That dude over there is looking at me funny.

2. A friend.

Hey, dude! Long time, no see!

3. An exclamation.

Dude! Why did you do that?

dudes

Plural of "dude," but unlike the singular version, may refer to a group of guys and girls.

dudette

Any female, or a female friend.

That dudette is so hot.

dump on

To say bad things about.

I thought we were brahs, but he said you kept dumpin' on me.

dumps like a truck

A large booty. From dump truck: a vehicle with a large area for hauling things. It's just the woman-car metaphor with another twist. Similar

to "junk in the trunk," or
"badonkadonk."

That girl got dumps like a truck, yo!

Dumpster diving

Looking for treasure in someone else's
trash—either literally or figuratively.
In the world of information technology, Dumpster diving is a technique
used to retrieve information that
could be used to carry out an attack
on a computer network. Dumpster
diving isn't limited to searching
through the trash for obvious treas-
ures like access codes or passwords
written down on sticky notes.
Seemingly innocent information like
a phone list, calendar, or organiza-
tional chart can be used to assist an
attacker using social engineering techniques to gain access to the network.

*We went Dumpster diving and found his
Social Security number, phone bills, and
love notes from his girlfriend. He's pretty
much owned.*

dur

An expression showing that something someone said is obvious.
Similar to "doy" or "duh."

*Liz: Katy definitely likes Brad.
Jamie: Well, dur! She sent him three love
letters!*

dusted

1. To have bashed or beaten
someone.

*He was being smart, so I stepped up and
dusted him.*

2. To get hurt badly.

*I tried a kickflip nosegrind on the
handrail and got dusted hardcore.*

3. To catch someone doing
something they shouldn't do.

*The cops dusted me for being high while
driving.*

dutch

1. Splitting the expense, often of a
date.

We're going dutch to the movies tonight.

2. A joint, or a blunt.

I'ma finish you before I finish the dutch!

dutch oven

To fart under the covers and then
pull them over your own or someone else's head.

*Chris fainted when I gave him a dutch
oven.*

dweeb

An awkward, ineffectual person; specifically connotes physical inadequacy. A dorky or nerdy person.

That dude with the pocket protector is such a dweeb. Let's go beat on him.

dyke

A lesbian. Often considered derogatory by non-lesbians, it has been reclaimed and has a good connotation when used by lesbians themselves. It is a popular breeder misconception that all dykes are butch.

How dare you think I'm straight! I'm a dyke, you idiot!

d00d

The word "dude," in 1337 5p34k.

Hey d00d, what's up? Want to race paper airplanes in the park?

urban

ear candy
Good music.

I need to pick up that brand new CD and get me some ear candy.

ear goggles
Large earphones.

Ear goggles have better bass response than those cheap bud earphones.

ear worm
Song that is stuck in your head.

I have an ear worm. I keep hearing the Jeopardy! *tune over and over and over.*

Easter egg
A hidden item or a mistake caught by close watchers of a movie, television show, or other visual media.

Possibly from the 1975 movie *The Rocky Horror Picture Show*, when the cast had an Easter egg hunt but most of the eggs went unfound. They can be seen throughout the film in various locations (such as under Dr. Frank-N-Furter's throne).

The framed picture of Julia Roberts inside the character's home was an Easter egg inserted by the director.

easy peasy
The first half of a rhyming phrase with several alternate second halves, all of which connote an activity or a result that is, respectively, simple to perform or achieve.

As a red-stater, condemn books and films without having read or seen them? Why that's easy peasy lemon squeezy!

eat crow

When you make a mistake and are forced to acknowledge it humbly.

He claimed he was the greatest cook in the world, but when several people got food poisoning from his food, he had to eat crow.

eat it

To fall completely on your face or suffer a similar physical accident. Also "eat shit."

Man, I was runnin' from the cops last night, tripped on a stick, and completely ate it.

eatable

Something that doesn't make you throw up to think about eating it. Often confused with "edible," which refers to somthing that's physically possible to eat. Just because something is edible does not mean it is eatable.

While grass is not edible, it is eatable to some people. However, cafeteria food, while always edible, is often uneatable.

eBay

1. A large hole in the Internet, mostly lined with collector plates and *Star Wars* figurines, into which large amounts of money have fallen.

George Bush logged on to eBay and bought a George H. W. Bush action figure.

2. The yard sale of the Internet.

I was trolling around eBay today, and I found two old AMD laptops, a bootleg Blue Öyster Cult CD, some Ron Jeremy DVDs, and some livestock, all for under $60 total. I bet I get screwed on the shipping.

e-dress

Short for "e-mail address."

I tried to e-mail you a link, but your e-dress isn't working.

edumacation

Education received at a crappy school, or a lack of education altogether.

I received my edumacation at Willits High School.

Edward 40-hands

A drinking game in which partici-pants tape a 40-ounce bottle of malt liquor to each hand and can't pee until they've finished both.

Friend: I dare you to do Edward 40-hands with straight vodka in each 40. You: No way, dude.

e-famous

When one becomes famous on the Internet.

I got e-famous when a photo of me licking a frozen stop sign got out.

ego fart

Flatulence forced from one's body in a pompous, self-satisfying manner, without regard to the consideration of others.

Although his friends quickly rolled down the car windows, Shane was so full of himself, he took a big, proud whiff of his smelly ego fart.

ego search

To search for one's own name online. Also called "ego surfing" and "Googling."

She was mackin' on me until she caught me Googling our names together. Then she told me, "I don't like boys who hafta ego search; that's tired."

egonomics

The logic used to justify one's actions for personal gain; the art of being self-centered.

It was his egonomics that caused him to die a lonely man, while the geek became a millionaire.

e-gret

A message of regret sent by electronic mail.

Betty remembered to send an e-gret to Sam's secretary concerning the March 15 committee meeting she couldn't attend.

eh

An interjection Canadians use to ensure the other person is following along with the conversation. Not often used between Canadians themselves but used excessively when visiting the U.S.A. and talking to U.S. citizens.

Torontonian: Where you from, eh?
New York stater: North Tonawanda, New York.
Torontonian: Eh, you're like 10 miles from the border, eh?

e-haircut

A change in a person's online identity. Also called an "i-haircut."

Steve360: Dude, you're using a new font color.
Jane2004: Yeah, I got an e-haircut.

either and or both

A way to express indifference, a lack of caring.

Tom: Hey, Jim, do you want some ice

cream or a swift kick in the nuts?
Jim: Either and or both.

elbow

A pound of marijuana (mary jane, pot).

Dude, catch this buzz. The cat on 52nd Street sells elbows for a song.

elbow-bending

Drinking. From the arm motion that one must make in order to bring the bottle to the mouth.

What up, Jimmy? Let's go elbow-bending with good ol' Jack Daniels.

election

A lying contest between two or more very rich and powerful people.

Turn on C-SPAN to watch the election results.

eleventeen

1. Term used to convey uncertainty and ambiguity.

I can't remember when I learned to ride a bike. I must have been about eleventeen or so.

2. Term used to convey sarcasm, as when making fun of someone's age or the number of tries it took to accomplish something.

You're so smart; what are you, eleventeen?

3. Term used to describe a preteen.

John likes them young. You should have seen this eleventeen-year-old he brought to the party yesterday.

eleventy-seven

An imaginary number used when one has lost count of something and needs to verbally state a quantity.

I rang the doorbell eleventy-seven times! Where were you?

elimidate

To get rid of a disappointing date after you realize she's ugly, fat, a total bitch, or your cousin. After the Warner Bros. reality TV show *elimiDATE*.

Unfortunately, I'm going to have to elimidate you, Sally. I'm sorry. Uncle Bob doesn't want us to go out anymore. The family gene pool is already shallow enough.

e-love

Electronic love. The e-mail equivalent of a love letter. This can be just text or anything sent electronically, such as pictures or e-cards expressing love.

He sent me some e-love on our anniversary.

e-mail

Once an efficient and fast method of communication and message transferring, now a way of harassing Internet users with spam, credit card/insurance offers, porn links, and "Increase your penis size by 5 inches" advertisements.

Despite using a junk e-mail filtering program, I still have to delete 30-plus messages a day. E-mail sucks.

e-mail crossing

A phenomenon that occurs when you send an e-mail to someone at the same time they e-mail you. Each of you then answers the other's e-mail and you go out of sync, creating two separate strands of conversation that occasionally cover the same ground.

jen2jen: There's a good band playing tonight. Interested?
Rob121: I'm up for some naked chess with you later.
jen2jen: Did you get my last e-mail?
Rob121: Oh, are they?
jen2jen: Naked what?
Rob121: I think we've got an e-mail crossing.

embed

Short for "embedded journalist." A journalist embedded (i.e., deployed) with coalition forces during Operation Iraqi Freedom.

I just saw a hideous story from a British embed.

emo

Genre of soft-core punk music that integrates unenthusiastic melodramatic 17-year-olds who don't smile and high-pitched, overwrought lyrics and guitar riffs with tight wool sweaters, tighter jeans, itchy scarfs (even in the summer), ripped Chucks with favorite band's signature, black square-rimmed glasses, and ebony greasy, unwashed hair that is required to cover at least three-fifths of the face at an angle.

::sniff sniff:: "The Demise of the Siberian Traintracks of Our Rusty Forgotten Unblemished Love" sounds like it would make a great emo band name. ::cry::

emo glasses

Thick, black-rimmed glasses morose emo kids tend to wear.

Those emo glasses are so hot.

emo hair

Hair style that covers the face, usually swept at an angle.

Adam Lazzara and Tom DeLonge have sexy emo hair.

emocentric

A combination of "emo" and "egocentric." Having the feeling that nobody else is suffering quite as badly as you are.

Oh, you poor thing. You got a B on your paper. You're really suffering. Stop being so emocentric.

emoticon

A simple text depiction of what one's face would look like if an online conversation were taking place in person.

I'm happy! :) I'm unhappy! :(You're silly! :P

endo

Short for "end over end." To crash-land any wheeled vehicle on the front half of its wheeled chassis, with the rear half still in the air. Typically used in reference to the two-wheeled variety (like a bike) while completing an airborne stunt or trick, and the rider lands front wheel first with enough force that they flip over the handlebars.

Dermott: See this guy coming 'round bend #3?
Connor: Aye. He'll hit that ramp too fast and endo it.
Dermott: Hope they don't run over the poor lad!

ends

Money. What we all live and die for.

Can you hook me up with a job? I'm just trying to hold some ends.

enginerd

Engineering nerd. Mainly computer engineers or electrical engineers, but can be applied across the board if the individual is nerdy enough.

Enginerd: Hey, have you seen the new op-amp I got for my headphone amplifier? It has an amazingly high cutoff frequency.
Friend of enginerd: You are such an enginerd.

Engrish

Bad Japanese-to-English translation. Often a word-for-word, literal translation that sounds very funny to native English speakers. Most common in old video games and animé, or Japanese animation. The word "Engrish" comes from the fact that the Japanese language does not have distinct "L" and "R" sounds.

From Toaplan's game Zero Wing:
All your base are belong to us.
(Translation: Your bases are all under our control.)
A winner is you. (Translation: You win.)
Somebody set up us the bomb.
(Translation: Someone has placed a bomb on our ship!)

urban

ese

A term used to refer to any American of Hispanic descent. Ese = S.A. = Spanish American.

What up, ese? You owe me money, holmes.

evilticulate

To twiddle all one's fingers together in the fashion of Mr. Burns on the TV show *The Simpsons*.

After hatching my devious plot, I evilticulated while pondering the finer details.

exaggerationist

A person who constantly exaggerates everything they say and do, almost like it's their profession.

Lee's a full-time exaggerationist. Last night over a beer he told me he had a threesome with his girlfriend and Paris Hilton—and I know he doesn't have a girlfriend!

excardon me

A mishmash of "pardon me" and "excuse me."

Excardon me, I thought these were the gents' toilets.

exhaustia

The state of being dramatically exhausted.

(With back of hand placed to the forehead, head tilted slightly back) I am in such a state of exhaustia, I can barely conceive of continuing my life. . . .

external brain

A device one uses to record important data such as addresses and phone numbers. Typically a PDA, but can be as simple as a notepad and pen.

Hold on a second, let me put that in my external brain.

extra cheese

All the goodies. Bling, cash money, the best drugs, comp tickets, verbal praise, TLC, and all a'that!

I can't believe she dumped me even though I gave her all the extra cheese!

eye candy

Something purely aesthetically pleasing. Can be a person, a film, a sunset, a flower, or anything else you can see.

Nicole is oozing with hotness, and she's total eye candy to every man.

eye sex

The act of two people staring at each other in such a lustful way they might as well be doing it.

You so had eye sex with him! It's as good as cheating on your boyfriend.

eye tracks

Imaginary tracks left by the eyes when a person reads something. Many science-fiction fans wear glasses to keep from getting eye tracks on their fanzines, magazines, and books.

Sorry—this book is no longer mint; I got my eye tracks all over it.

ez

Informal goodbye.

Paul: Yo, Peter, gotta bounce, ez.
Peter: Ez.

e-zine

Electronic magazine or fanzine; a "publication" whose primary medium is electronic, generally presented over the Internet.

I publish an e-zine once a week on strange news stories from Germany and Florida.

faboo
Fabulous. Also "fabu."

It would be totally faboo if we got tickets to the concert!

face
Short for "in your face."
Interjection commonly used after a person has been insulted, disgraced, or humiliated.

Guy 1: Last night I got pulled over for tipping.
Guy 2: Face! I told you you'd get busted someday.

face for radio, a
A polite and indirect way of saying "ugly."

Jabba the Hutt's radio talk show is interesting and engaging, but I saw him in Return of the Jedi *and he has a total face for radio.*

face plant
A serious fall in which you land on your face. It appears as if you're trying to do an impression of a plant with your face as its roots.

Last night at Sigma Chi I was so wasted that I slipped, bounced off the ramp, and did a serious face plant onto the ground below.

face time
Direct personal interaction. Time spent talking with a client in person as opposed to via e-mail, IM, or cellular phone.

This client is important, so instead of

e-mailing him the proposal, go on over and get some face time.

fade

1. A negative term used to describe an attempt to disgrace or get rid of something or someone.

You can't fade me.

2. Gang members originally meant "murder" when they talked about fading someone. If you fade a gang member you are decreasing the number of members in his gang and effectively "fading" his color. Today the term "fade" is more flexible, sometimes simply meaning "disgrace."

Brotha's got mad caps rainin' down, but those fools can't fade me.

fade to black

1. To exit.

The crowd will still love him when he fades to black.

2. To die, especially by suicide. Used by the band Metallica in the song "Fade to Black."

Some days I feel so bad, I just want to fade to black.

faded

Stoned, drunk, all-around messed up.

Edwin sure was faded after that phat blunt.

fag

1. A cigarette.

Could I bum a fag off you?

2. A derogatory term for a homosexual.

Dude, just shut up, you fag!

fag hag

Female who enjoys the company of homosexual males.

Grace is Will's fag hag on the sitcom Will & Grace.

fag-tag

To amass a big group of gays, lesbians, and their friends and take over a traditionally straight venue.

Get ready for a big night out; we're going to fag-tag the Superclub tonight.

fair doos

Fair enough. That's acceptable. I don't care.

Bob: No, what I meant was that I think

your mum is a nice person.
Jim: Oh, right. Fair doos!

fake

"Not" or "don't." The insertion of "fake" in a sentence reverses the meaning of the sentence. Can be used like "not" is used in the movie *Wayne's World.*

I fake remember that. (I don't remember that.)

Yeah, that's a good idea . . . fake. (That's not a good idea.)

fake the deal

1. To pretend something is true or put on a front to hide the real facts.

Some believe the government lied about NASA's trips to the moon, and they have theories about how NASA faked the deal.

2. To try to dupe someone into buying or accepting something through dishonesty or questionable ethics.

I thought that 2004 Hummer was a steal at $1,000, but when they told me that the radio, steering wheel, seats, exhaust, frame, and engine were sold separately and cost a total of $70,000, I realized they had really faked the deal.

fake the funk

To assume a false ethos in an attempt to win respect from a certain influential party. Opposite of "keeping it real."

I strongly suspect he's a white boy fakin' the funk. Ain't no way he grew up in South Central.

fake-bake

To tan at a tanning salon or otherwise get artificially tan.

H.B. fake-baked to look good for the Halstead Street parade.

fall back

Chill out, relax, stop trippin'.

Fall back with that cussin'. My grandma's in the other room.

fall on the grenade

The noble act of being a wingman. A group of male buddies are at a bar flirting with a group of hotties. All of a sudden the hotties' ugly girlfriend comes out of the ladies' room. That's the grenade! It's the solemn duty of one of the men to fall on the grenade and hook up with that beastwoman so his friends can hook up with the hotties.

It's Peter's turn to fall on the grenade. I

think we should all buy him a pity round first.

fam

Short for "family." A word used to describe your people or any group you can trust or consider family.

My fam wuz mad deep up in the club the other day.

family jewels

Testicles; balls; nuts.

If he tries anything, kick 'im in the family jewels.

fanboy

A breed of human male who is obsessed with either a fictional character or an actor. Often follows various elements of geek culture (e.g., sci-fi, comics, *Star Wars,* video games, animé, hobbits, Magic: the Gathering, etc.) and lets his passion override social graces. Also see "fangirl."

At the mall I almost got mowed over by some Dragon Ball Z fanboy on his skateboard.

fanfic

Short for "fanfiction." A story written by a fan of a particular art (movie, book, TV show, video game, etc.) about the characters and world in that series, usually without the original creator's permission. Plural: "fanfics."

By the very nature of fanfic, there're a lot of really terrible fics out there. But it's great when you find a good one!

fangirl

A breed of human female who is obsessed with either a fictional character or an actor. Fangirls tend to congregate at animé conventions and on fan blogs. Have been known to emit high-pitched sounds, as well as glomp, grope, and tackle when encountering their particular obsessions. Often claim that "I'm really gonna marry him cuz we R ment 2 b!!!!!!!11111!!!!!!@#$347903458134!@!@!" Also uses excessive amounts of punctuation.

Hugh Jackman: 'ello.
Fangirl: Squeeeeee! (Immediately attaches to Jackman's leg.)
Jackman: Security!

fanny

1. An idiot.

Shut the hell up, you fanny!

2. British term for messing around or assing around.

Stop fannying around and get back to work.

fanservice

When a character or celebrity does something shocking or exciting just to stand out or to please their fans. Usually seen in reference to Japanese pop culture, and often of a sexual nature.

Some episodes of the animé Ranma 1/2 contain fanservice.

fanzine

Often a low-budget or amateur publication devoted to the fan appreciation of a particular celebrity or musical act.

My cousin makes an Elvis fanzine that she hands out at record swaps.

far out

Expression of disbelief or surprise.

Your full-time job is beer taster? That's far out!

fart cannon

A disproportionately large muffler or exhaust pipe, mounted on an automobile with a small displacement engine. Named for the flatulence-like sound the vehicle's exhaust makes.

A six-inch fart cannon attached to a one-inch tailpipe? Don't tell me. You've seen The Fast and the Furious *at least once, right?*

farting terms

A milestone in a new relationship when both parties feel at ease when breaking wind in front of each other.

You've been with that bird for a long time and you're not even on farting terms yet? Do you have to go to the bathroom every time you need to rasp?

fashion roadkill

An item of clothing that is tacky, cheap, and just plain wrong.

What is she wearing? The color is crap and it's three sizes too small. It's fashion roadkill.

fat as a tick

Bloated and obese. Derived from the state of a tick (parasitic insect) after it has gorged itself on a host mammal's blood. Not complimentary.

Christ! All that beer you've been guzzling lately has made you fat as a tick!

fat cat

Smug, selfish, and greedy businessman/woman who exploits their position for their own personal gain at the cost of others.

Those fat cats at city hall don't realize the need for Feng Shui classes at the junior high level. All they want are their kick-backs for commercial building permits.

fatty

A large joint.

Yo, G, light up a fatty.

fauxhawk

Like a mohawk, but instead of shaving the sides of your head, you just glue up the middle part in the style of a mohawk.

Ladies want me because I got a fauxhawk.

fauxlationship

A temporary relationship to relieve emptiness caused by the lack of a real relationship. Also used to describe relationships with no commitment. Not a very responsible idea.

I don't trust her, man. It looks like a fauxlationship to me.

f-bomb

1. A euphemism for the f-word. (Also known as "effinheimer.")

DC was droppin f-bombs all over, yo, until his grandma heard him and washed his mouth out.

2. A euphemism for the word "friend" when used in the breakup conversation. Usually only used by the dumpee.

Her: I think we should just be friends, Jim. Him: Why you droppin' the f-bomb on me? That's cold.

feck

1. Alternative to the f-bomb. Used not just by do-gooders who want to avoid the foulest four-letter word but also by those who find it humorous.

Who the feck are you kidding?

2. A mess.

My hair's a feck. I'll just wear a hat.

feel

Inappropriate touch; Grope.

Janet deflected Justin's feel with her solar areola medallion.

feel it

To like or enjoy something.

You heard that new Gang Starr song? I'm feelin' it fo' sho.

feel it hard

When you have just finished insulting or angering someone with something you said. Can be attached to the end of the insult in order to tell them to "take it hard," adding more strength and power to the insult.

The gap in your teeth is so big, I don't know whether to smile back or kick a field goal! Feel it hard!

fell off the truck

Stolen goods. Articles whose origin is not strictly legal.
Also "fell off the back of a lorry" in the U.K.

Gotta deal on a nice telly. Fell off the back of a truck.

femullet

The female version of the mullet. Commonly paired with cancer-spotted skin, way too much blue eyeshadow, Hooter's shirts, and farm equipment.

That trashy lady's femullet looks like she got hit with her husband's sheepshearing blade.

fetch

Cool, awesome, or good. From the movie *Mean Girls,* where one of the popular girls was trying to coin it.

OMG, that's so fetch!

fiend

1. To crave something or someone when it is unavailable. Also "feen."

I'm fiendin' for a cig right now.

2. One who craves a certain substance, usually a drug. Various types of fiends include the tweaker, the crack fiend, the pothead, the cokehead, etc.

The Dopium Tribe? I heard dey be jus' sum local fiends who run aroun' smokin' dat Golden Poppy all day.

filthy

Rich, as in filthy rich.

You know I stay filthy like Bill Gates.

fine

Good-looking or hot.

Juan is fine.

fink

1. An informant.
2. Followed by "out": quit, give up, let down.
3. Followed by "on": inform against.

You're such a fink—I can't believe you finked out by finking on me!

F

finna

1. The state of being about to do something.
2. One who always says they are going to do something.

You know what you finna do, finna? You finna get out—now!

first base

To kiss, make out, French kiss.

I only got to first base last night.

fish

1. A woman. Used primarily by gay men, either in a positive or derogatory way, depending on the context.

Ugh! Why are there so many fish in the club tonight?

2. Feminine. Mostly used by gay men to compliment feminine-looking drag queens or transgender women who appear too convincing to be able to tell they're not biologically female.

Hey, girl, look at you! You're looking fish tonight!

3. A new inmate at a prison.

The lights went out and the whole jail started to chant "Fish, fish, fish," at the fish they just brought in.

fish market

A gathering with an overabundance of females in attendance.
Opposite of a sausage fest, a party with too many males.

This party is a total fish market. The only guy here is gay. I'm going home.

fishbowl

1. To fill a vehicle with marijuana smoke by closing all the windows and doors and shutting off all air vents while smoking inside the vehicle. Can be extremely dangerous while driving, and may cause asphyxiation if one stays in a fishbowl too long.

Holla, we gonna go fishbowl the Tahoe. Peace.

2. The inside of a fishbowled vehicle.

Look at that fishbowl, dawg. I wanna get in on some of that.

fishwrap

Newspaper, or any type of publication on newsprint.

So I fire open the fishwrap yesterday, and what do I see? The Paris Hilton skin flick's for sale . . . now on DVD!

fit

1. British slang for "hot" or "fine."

Dude, that girl is fit! I'm gonna get her number.

2. Clothes. Short for "outfit."

That fit is off the hook! Where'd you get that dress?

fit as

Stunning in appearance. Hot. Fine.

That girl is fit as. She can have any bloke she wants.

fit wicked

Pretty cool.

Dat show was fit wicked, innit?

fitted

Short for "well-outfitted." Describes someone who dresses well and has good fashion sense.

Chris came up to tha club fitted!

five-finger discount

Stealing.

Girl 1: How much was that?
Girl 2: Dunno. I got it for a five-finger discount.

five-O

Slang for police officers and/or a warning that police are approaching. Derived from the television show *Hawaii Five-O.* Also "pig," "piglet."

Look out, man, five-O!

fives

Defines a claim to or ownership of a certain item. Originally used to define such a claim for five minutes but is now commonly interchanged with the word "dibs."

Fives on that seat!

five-second rule

The rule by which one determines whether food is safe after falling on the floor. If one is able to retrieve said item within five seconds, it is not dirty and is safe to eat. Note: In fraternity houses, this rule is the 1.5-second rule. Rule is invalid in restrooms.

Person 1: Oh no, my chicken wing fell on the floor!
Person 2: 5 . . . 4 . . . 3 . . . 2 . . .
Person 1: Got it!
Person 2: 5-second rule. It's yours, dude.

fix

1. Temporary satisfaction of a craving or addiction.

Man, I really need to get a fix. I'm shaking.

2. To kick one's ass, typically as revenge for something they did.

So Johnny broke your windows, eh? We'll fix him good then.

flake

To decide not to go at the last second; to ditch or bail out. Often followed by the word "out."

It's been an hour since we were supposed to meet. I bet she flaked on me.

You said we were gonna see the movie! Don't change your mind and flake out!

flame

To unleash a tirade.

Jon Stewart flamed the guys on Crossfire *for neglecting their duties as journalists.*

flame war

On the Internet, a heated argument between two individuals in which they post personal attacks on each other instead of debating the topic at hand.

I can't come to work today because I'm busy having a flame war over which band is better.

flaming

Overtly homosexual.

Adrian, you're wearing your mom's lingerie. That is so flaming, man.

flash

Showy, ostentatious.

He think he flash as a rat with a gold tooth.

flat

1. Apartment.

Wanna come back to my flat?

2. Describes someone who is dull and boring.

Stop being so flat; come to the party!

flat leaver

A friend who doesn't show up or come through for another friend.

He told me he was coming with us and then flaked out. He's such a flat leaver.

flat tire

Stepping on the back of someone's shoe to make it come off or make them trip.

When I gave him a flat tire everyone laughed.

flava

Style. From "flavor."

What's yo' flava?

flex

To make a statement, clearly express yourself, or threaten verbally, more than physically.

Oh, you wanna flex? Okay, step outside—I'll show you what's up! No? That's what I thought.

flex nuts

To dominate an individual or group of people.

Jason tried to flex nuts and got beat down.

flexitarian

Someone who essentially eats just vegetables (as well as fish, eggs, and milk) but is okay with eating meat occasionally as a matter of convenience; a lenient vegetarian.

Rather than offend his hosts, he ate a good-sized portion of the spaghetti carbonara they offered rather than making a meal out of salad, bread, and dessert. Why go hungry? He's a flexitarian.

flick

1. To get rid of, drop, or discontinue something.

I'll probably flick this business degree before second semester.

2. Proceeded by "the": the brush-off. The pink slip. Notice that something is over.

I gave my work the flick.
You should give your woman the flick.

flicks

Photographs. Often used in graffiti culture.

Did you get flicks of that train you painted last night?

flip

To cruise around in a car.

Me and Tré were flippin', lookin' for some leg.

flip a bitch

To make an illegal U-turn, usually in the middle of a street or over a double line. Often results in passengers' freaking out.

Just flip a bitch here. There's no cops around.

flip mode

An unexpected reversal.

He thought I was coming with rock when I went flip mode and went all scissors on him.

flip off

Giving the middle finger.

I got really mad at Steve and flipped him off!

flipside

Tomorrow.

Later, G. Catch you on the flipside.

floor

To thoroughly beat and/or mutilate someone or something; this generally leaves the recipient on the ground in pain.

Son, you best thro' down right now befo' I floor yo' ass.

floor juice

The invisible layer of scum found on all floors and items that have come in contact with a floor. Often contains multiple germs, diseases, and other infectious organisms.

To lick one's shoes is to taste the floor juice, innit.

floor sweepin's

Detritus, debris, worthless junk.

Back to the drawing board, bucko. Your first draft was floor sweepin's.

floss

1. To show off. To flaunt expensive merchandise such as iced-out Rollies, Jaguars on triple golds, gem-encrusted pimp goblets, huge amounts of dank hydro, etc.
2. To stick dental floss between your teeth.

You better quit yo' flossin' before I bust you so hard in the teeth you'll be flossin' with a tow rope.

flow

1. A rapper's ability to rhyme to phat beats in a skillful manner.

My flows are hot. I put the hurt on whack-ass MCs.

2. Money. Short for "cash flow."

I be mad bling'n 'cause I gots much flow.

flush

To beat someone severely or to kill them.

You better watch your mouth or you gonna get flushed.

fly

Cool.

He was drivin' some fly-ass car he just dropped 50 Gs on.

urban

fly the bird

Extending the middle finger in a show of disapproval.

Some jackhole cut me off in traffic this morning, so I rolled down the window and flew him the bird.

fo' rizzle

For real. That is correct, my good sir.

That shizzle be off the hizzle fo' rizzle.

fo' shizzle, my nizzle

Affirmative response. A bastardization of "fo' sheezy, mah neezy," which is a bastardization of "for sure, mah nigga," which is a bastardization of "I concur with you wholeheartedly, my African-American brother."

Kid 1: It's late. I'm heading back to the hizzouse. You stayin'?
Kid 2: Fo' shizzle, my nizzle.

fo' sho'

For sure. Yes. Okay.

Damon: Are you going to the Kid Rock concert tonight, Mike?
Mike: Like, fo' sho' I am!

fob

Short for "fresh off the boat." Usually derogatory. Most often used for first-generation immigrants, especially Asian immigrants, but sometimes applied to all, even if they did not come by boat.

Is that fob trying to eat Jell-O with chopsticks?

fobby

Term used to describe fashion, accessories, and other products (e.g., Hello Kitty and Sanrio products) from Eastern Asia. Originally from fob, or "fresh off the boat," but has lost a lot of its negative connotation.

That fobby notebook is sooo cute! Get me some more fobby gifts when you go back to Taiwan!

fokk

Variant of the f-bomb. Best served for moments of surprise or utter astonishment.

I don't fokkin' b'lieve it, man . . . !

foo'

A contracted version of "fool." Made famous by Mr. T on the TV show *The A-Team*. Possibly due to the extended contact with cheap substitute gold, he could no longer tell the difference between the people he met. In order to save himself the humiliation of asking who he was talking to, he simply referred to anyone and everyone as "foo'" or "sucka."

You crazy foo'!

food coma
The feeling of listlessness, bordering on sleep, that one feels after eating a large meal, often caused by a rush of blood to the stomach and intestines during food digestion.

Man, we ate the whole pu pu platter and now I'm slipping into a food coma.

foodie
One who appreciates good cuisine, or just eats too damn much.

I'm a big foodie; I like Italian food, Chinese food, food food . . .

foolio
Variation of "fool."

Hey, foolio, let's go catch a movie tonight.

for real
Expression of agreement.

Kitty: Crystal is a real bitch.
Kimmy: For real.

for serious
1. Expression of doubt/surprise, asking for confirmation.

Yo' girl is preggers with triplets?! For serious?!

2. Exclamation/statement issuing confirmation.

For serious, that chick wants me!

3. Expression of agreement.

Jake: That teacher is dumb.
Dan: For serious, man.

foreploy
Misrepresenting oneself for the sole purpose of getting laid.

The whole evening was foreploy; the jerk only wanted to hit it.

four on the floor
Indicates that a car has a four-speed transmission where the shifter is "on the floor" rather than on the steering column.

That old Camaro had a 454 with four on the floor.

four to the floor
Especially common in techno, an unaccented 4/4 time pattern in which each beat is marked with a heavy kick drum. This is desperately boring at normal volume but at club levels takes over your entire body.

We were driving 'round town in his Corsa,
playing four to the floor German house
music.

fourth wall

The thin line that exists between a
story and reality. When a character
in a story tells the reader in some
way that they know that they are a
character in a story, it is called
"breaking the fourth wall."

Character 1: The screenwriter is a jackass
who can't write me properly.
(Crashing noise)
Character 2: Well, there goes the fourth
wall.

frag

To kill an enemy in a single-person
shooter computer game.

Dude . . . my frag count just hit 250.
Yeah, man! Unreal Tournament rules!

freak

1. To make out or have sexual
intercourse.

She likes to freak on a regular basis.

2. To dance as if simulating sex.

Freaking isn't allowed at some dances
anymore because it offends the chaperones.

freak show

A person who is always putting on a
great variety of freaky displays.

You were dancing on the bar last night,
freak show.

freeballin'

For males: not wearing underwear.

I'm freeballin' right now.

freebase

To inhale drugs by cooking them,
often in a metal spoon with a flame
underneath. One holds a flame
under the spoon and collects the
fumes from the crushed pills in an
empty bottle, then inhales the fumes
by taking a hit off the bottle.

Sketchy Alex freebases epileptic drugs with
my spoon.

freedom fries

New word for "French fries."
An expression made up by ubercon-
servatives to eradicate any mention
of France in the U.S.

If Congress is stupid enough to turn
French fries into freedom fries, it is stupid
enough to make these transformations:
Turkey = independence bird
Peking duck = democracy duck
Guinea pig = freedom pig

Hamburgers = liberty meat
World = America
Inspections = war
Statesmanship = war
Diplomacy = war
Peace = war

freeper

Right-wing political activist. So called because it is the nickname of the denizens of the ultra-right-wing website FreeRepublic.com. Similar to "ditto-head." Also spelled "FReeper."

Bill thinks that anyone who opposes President Bush should be thrown in jail. He's a total Freeper.

freeride

1. A more adventurous and challenging form of mountain biking involving jumps, drops, berms, etc.

Hey, Gaz, you sick freerider, you wanna go freeride some?

2. In snowboarding, riding down a mountain with all types of terrain (trees, dropoffs, etc.) but not doing tricks like jumps, rails, and other things, which are part of freestyling.

I want a snowboard for freeriding.

freestyle

1. In music (usually rap and techno): where everything is made up as you go along. In rap, people make up lyrics as they go along; in techno, the DJ improvises beats and mixes songs on the spot.

I sit here spittin' weird on this teen-geared urban dictionary/
Hopin' the votes of my definition hit high notes like a canary/
So don't lose your skill and become sick and senile/
And as long as it ain't prewritten it's kickin' a freestyle.

2. In sports (especially extreme sports): where someone improvises a stunt or series of stunts.

I'd like to see more of those freestyle moves.

freestyle loafing

A sport in which the only goal is to sit around in the most comfortable position possible. Well complemented by smoking weed.

After work, I'm gonna go home and do some freestyle loafing. It's gonna be tight.

freeze

Cocaine.

Steve got himself out of a sticky situation by telling the cop that his bag of freeze was actually a bag of flour he was bringing to his grandma to help her bake some cookies.

frequent flier

Anyone who repeatedly does something. Takes its meaning from the context in which it is used, such as individuals who repeatedly call 911 for minor issues or mental patients who frequently get admitted to the psychiatric ward.

Betty knows her way around the floor because she is a frequent flier.

fresh

Acceptable and highly approved.

Lets go to Darrell's Shop—they got fresher records there.

freshman 20

The 20 pounds a freshman generally gains the first year away from home at college, where no one watches over their eating habits. Used to be the "freshman 15," but people just keep getting fatter.

Sheila came home from school with the freshman 20 showing in the way her clothes fit.

friend of Bill W.

A member of Alcoholics Anonymous (AA) and, therefore (usually), a recovering alcoholic. Derived from the name of Bill Wilson, one of the founding members of AA.

I was at an airport and was tempted to head to one of the bars, so instead I had "Bill W." paged as a code to have someone from the program come for a "meeting" with me.

friend with benefits

A friend with whom you may occasionally "hook up" or make out without commitment.

Friend: I heard you made out with Josh . . . do you like him? Are you going out? Because I thought you were just friends. You: Nope. We're just friends with benefits, is all. We're not together or anything.

friend-flirt

To flirt with a friend as if you are just being funny, when in fact you are hot for this person. Commonly used to break out of the "just-friends" relationship.

I'm friend-flirting with Jessica over IM, but I don't think she thinks it's for real.

front

To act like you are someone you're not. More specifically, to think and act like you are a badass when you are not. To fake something, often by acting in an opposite fashion.

Don't be frontin' like you don't know what the hell is goin' on!

froshmore

1. A freshman who only has upperclassman friends. Has a positive connotation.

Devon is a froshmore. He's too cool for the rest of us.

2. A sophomore who is still treated like a freshman. Has a negative connotation.

Joe is a froshmore. What a loser.

frottage

To induce sexual pleasure by applying one's body to another's. The process is especially popular at music concerts and nightclubs. Also "dry-humping."

I went to the club last night and was over-whelmed by all the frottage.

frozen

Wearing lots of diamonds (ice).

Jacob the jeweler keeps my arms so frozen.

frumpy

Showing a lack of concern for appearance. Often characterized by sweatpants, frizzy hair, grandma panties, and a pasty complexion.

I don't pay you to dress all frumpy. Now go put on some heels and do something with that hair.

FUD

Acronym for "fear, uncertainty, and doubt." Also known as scare tactics, either accomplished by threat or by making the opponent doubt his standpoint. Used not only in lawsuits but also in politics and military propaganda.

The company's FUD-spreading caused many supporters to abandon their cause, except for the few who could see through its scaremongering propaganda.

fugazi

Fake.

Hey, baby, that ice you got is fugazi! I hope you didn't pay much for that.

fugly

Combination of "funny" and "ugly" or "fucking" and "ugly."

She's so fugly no one will date her.

fularious

Combination of "funny" and "hilarious" or "fucking" and "hilarious."

That joke was fularious!

full of shit

1. Totally unfounded, not credible, or ridiculous . . . usually refers to something somebody just said.

Eric: . . . So I told the Olsen twins I wasn't in the mood, because, you know, I can do better. Then a couple minutes later I ran into the Hilton sisters and scored a threesome. It was just like in the video, dude, I swear.
Stan: Man, you're so full of shit, your eyes are brown.

full on

Holding nothing back. Intense. Relentless.

No way, mate, that was so full on it's doing my head in!

full-court press

To aggressively put the moves on, or to hit on, someone. To not give up on trying to get someone to go out with you. Named after the play in basketball.

Could you see if Mike likes me? I don't want to put the full-court press on him if

he doesn't, because then I'll look like an idiot.

fully sick

Great. Of high quality.

Guy: Check out my fully sick ride!
Chick: Fully sick!

fun police

Person or group of people who make others stop having fun for whatever reason, usually out of jealousy or spite, but sometimes because said fun is against the law. Also, another name for one's wife, instructor, parent(s), or the legitimate authorities. Also "fun assassin."

We were having fun hurling dog shit over the house into the yard across the street with my homemade trebuchet when the effing fun police made us stop.

fundamental

Radical or awesome.

Did you see those dubs? They're fundamental!

funk button

Metaphorical button that, when pressed, releases a euphoric feeling when one is engaged in a pleasurable activity.

*I can't take any more; I've busted my
funk button.*

funky cold medina

A drink that drives ladies crazy and
makes them want the man who buys
it for them. After the title of a
1980s song by rapper Tone-Loc.

*Bartender, how about a funky cold medina
for the lady?*

fuzz

Synonym for police, detectives, FBI,
ATF, DEA, IRS, INS, EPA, DOE,
DOI, NSA, FSA, NSC, DOJ, CID,
OSI, USM, FPS, BIA, UMP, USDA,
and any other organization that
holds authority.

*Hey, man, watch yourself. The fuzz are
right around the corner.*

fuzzbuster

A radar detector.

*I laugh at the pigs hiding out on the side of
the highway now that I got my fuzzbuster.
Better stick to Dunkin' Donuts.*

fuzzy math

A poorly thought-out solution.

*Guy 1: I bet we can jump the gap if we're
goin' at least 70 mph.
Guy 2: That's fuzzy-ass math.*

uRBan

G

G

1. A gangster.

That's a real G. Don't piss him off.

2. A thousand dollars.

Let me borrow a G.

3. A term of endearment.

What up, G?

g2g

Texting abbreviation for "got to go."

g2g. Boss just came in.

gaffle

To be taken advantage of, tricked, bamboozled, swindled.

Dude, you got gaffled at the club when you spent $50 to get in and I spent $20.
Uncle Sam gaffles me every time I have to pay my taxes.

gah

An interjection denoting frustration and/or excitement.

Gah! I scored only 95 on my last science exam. They'll never let me back into the science club again.

gain

Volume or amplification.

We need more gain!

game

1. Something you play, usually a competitive activity.

"Drinking checkers" is a shitty drinking game. "Beirut" is better.

2. To play a game.

I went gaming in Vegas and lost all my wealth to a slot machine.

3. Skill or ability in any game.

Shaq lost to Aaron Carter in one-on-one? Damn, that fool must have no game at all.

4. An animal that is hunted.

Yo' honor, I didn't mean to shoot that mutha in that gang war. . . . I thought he was game, you know, like a deer or some shit.

5. Short for "game over!"

Three-pointer at the buzzer . . . and it's good! That's game!

6. A measure of smoothness with the opposite sex.

You couldn't even get some from Line-em-up Liz? You must have no game.

7. Lines or moves used to get the opposite sex into bed.

I broke out the old "You must be from Tennessee" game on her and it worked like a charm.

8. Willing to do something.

Guy 1: You want to go to the ball game, game at the casino, shoot some game, then work game on some women?
Guy 2: I'm game.

game over

1. When something doesn't go your way.

You found out that your ho is pregnant? Game over.

2. When a girl is not attractive.

No way, dude, that girl is game over.

game recognize game

An esoteric catchphrase of the urban male pimp, playa, rapper, or wannabe that carries the weighty implication that only someone who has their game tight can have the appropriate respect and admiration for someone else's doubtlessly tight game.

Guy 1: It was tight how you played Shaniqua and Latisha off each other like that . . . playa, playa!
Guy 2: Game recognize game, homie, you know how I do.

game tight

To be well informed, have your priorities in order, and make ends meet. To be at the top of your game.

I hope my lawyer got his game tight. I don't want to go to jail.

gangbanger
A person who is either a member of or heavily affiliated with a local gang.

I ain't cruisin' till tomorrow—mad gangbangers out tonight.

gangbusters
1. Energetic or intense.

Check out my gangbusters new CD.

2. Preceded by "like": a lot, to the extreme.

It's raining like gangbusters.

gangsta
Tight, ill, cool.

Girl 1: I got that boy buyin' me clothes, cars, and jewelz.
Girl 2: Dat's gangsta.

gangsta grip
To hold an object sideways. Often associated with firearms.

I got my cap to the back and my AK-47 in a gangsta grip.

gangsta lean
A common driving position in which the driver holds the wheel with his left hand while leaning to his right toward the passenger seat, usually bobbing his head or bumpin' with the beat. It's a pretty badass way to drive. This move works best in a Chevy Caprice or any pimp-style car with a three-person front seat.

Sammy was gangsta leanin' so hard yesterday that his head was partially out the passenger window. What a pimp.

gangsta style
The style of doing things with a sense of professionalism, style, and a little violence.

I have to pee gangsta style.

ganja
Marijuana, pot, cannabis, weed.

At 4:20 everybody's burnin' ganja.

gank
1. To steal in a surreptitious or underhanded manner.

People always gank my damn lighters!

2. To gang up on and frag an opponent in an online game.

The Blood Brotherhood ganked that guy hardcore!

3. To do a character assassination.

P. Diddy ain't got no street cred since J.Lo ganked him in Vibe.

gaper

Person who gazes stupidly or in openmouthed surprise or wonder. An idiot.

Traffic was backed up because of all the gapers trying to view the accident.

garage-sale

In skiing, to wipe out big time. Usually classified by the uncontrolled flailing and loss of poles and skis.

The skier who thought he was hot shit garage-saled big time in the middle of the trail.

garmz

"Garments," clothing.

I need to buy some new garmz.

gas (up)

To fill another's head with false notions, or having one's head filled with false notions.

She was all gassed up, so when she wasn't voted prom queen she was salty.

gat

1. Gangsta firearm. Short for "Gatling."

Just get that gat out of my face and everything will be jake.

2. To shoot someone with a gun.

Yo, I be gattin' yo' ass if you don't shut up 'bout mah momma.

gauge

Slang for a shotgun. Comes from the caliber of the shotgun, which is measured by gauge.

I blasted him with my gauge!

gay

Term often used to describe something stupid or unfortunate. Originating among homophobes and quite often used by teenage males in an attempt to buff up their "masculinity."

Man, these seats are gay. I can't even see what's going on!

gay buffer

When you sit down somewhere (usually in a movie theater) and purposely leave an extra seat between you and a person of the same sex so as not to appear gay.

Dude, leave me a gay buffer! You're so close to me we're practically making out.

gaydar
The ability/gift of being able to detect homosexuality in other people.

Whoa! Look at that guy. My gaydar is going crazy!

g'day, mate
An Australian greeting between males.

G'day, mate, hopinta me V8 an ell tell ya aaaall about Oz.

gear
Drug of choice. Varies according to context.

Bring some gear with you when you come over.

gearhead
1. Someone who is totally into cars and is very knowledgeable about how to modify and fix them.

Eric is such a gearhead he has a seatbelt buckle for a belt buckle.

2. Someone who collects the latest, coolest, most efficient, and techno-logically advanced gadgets for their sport, interest, or hobby.

Did you know Jeff can track our hike's distance, route, and elevation gain with his new GPS unit? He is such a gearhead.

geek
Previously a four-letter word, now a six-figure salary.

Bill Gates is a geek, yet he is the richest man in the world.

geek out
To engage in a conversation of a highly technical nature, typically with other members of the party you are with, completely (and usually inadvertently) alienating others in the process.

We were having a great conversation about how bad Windows was, when suddenly Bill started geeking out about assembler code on a PDP-10.

geeked
Stimulated or energized; stirred up, fired up.

Dude, I am so geeked about US Youth Soccer's national championships.

geekstress
A female geek.

He and his girlfriend geek out all the time about Linux. She's a geekstress.

gellin'

Totally relaxed. Not caring.

Susan: Hey, Tonya, what are you doing?
Tonya: I'm gellin'.

geocaching

A great game where people hide boxes (or caches) of goodies all over the world and register the geographic coordinates on the Internet. Using a GPS unit, others are then able to go hunting for these boxes, take or leave items for others, and/or transfer a Travel Bug to another location.

Sorry I missed the wedding, but I did rack up ten more geocaching finds!

get a room

Derisive or humorous comment said to couples engaged in heavy-duty public displays of affection (PDAs), such as swapping spit in the middle of a party. Usually indicates discomfort or jealousy on the part of the speaker. The implication is you should get a motel room because you're practically doing it here.

Get a room! We're trying to watch the game here.

get busy

1. To dance.

I love this music. I wanna get busy!

2. To have sex.

I love this music. I wanna get busy!

get fitted

Short for "get outfitted." To get dressed or change clothes.

I'm gonna go home, take a shower, and get fitted.

get hot

Get to work, get busy.

You guys haven't started the project yet? Better get hot, biotches!

get involved

To be part of the noble sport of drinking.

Come on, mate, it's been [insert number less than ten here] hours since you kicked it home—get involved!

get it

To achieve intimacy with someone after minimal effort.

Hey, Jimmie, did you get it last night at the club?

get it on

1. Get something started.

I got my popcorn, I got my candy, I got my baby; let's get this movie on.

2. Euphemism for having sex, popularized by Marvin Gaye in his classic song "Let's Get It On."

I think my roommate's getting it on with his girlfriend. He left a sock on the doorknob, so I've been sexiled.

get it twisted
To take something the wrong way or twist what someone has said.

Don't get this twisted, dawg, but Nikki, she's my girl, so you best back off.

get me
Term meaning, "I acknowledge what you said."

Me: Goin' for a snout.
You: Get me! I need a break too.

get off
1. To orgasm.

Excuse me, but I need to get off.

2. To enjoy tremendously. Typically followed by "on."

Louis really gets off on adding definitions to urbandictionary.com.

get on my level
To compete with or get on the same page as me.

The player dunked the basketball and screamed, "Get on my level!"

get on the good foot
Southernism: to begin a task pronto. To get moving, get crackin'.

I'd better get on the good foot—I was supposed to be at work an hour ago!

get one's swerve on
To drink alcohol in order to get drunk.

I gots to get my swerve on tonight!

get out
Term used sarcastically to mean "really?"

Get out! I didn't know a chickenhead was a crankster.

get paid
Obtaining cash through other than commonly respectable means, such as by pawning items, selling stolen items, or illegal activity. Generally not in reference to gainful employment.

Punk 1: Yo, I jacked this car stereo from

a Hyundai last night.
Punk 2: Straight up! Whatcha gon do
wit it?
Punk 1: Whatcha think? I'm gonna
pawn it and get paid.

get right

To get high on some badass sativa
(marijuana). To get in the proper
headspace.

We should get right and then play some
music.

get served

To be completely owned or shown
up by someone.

Ray: Check this shot out. Money! (bricks it)
Darryl: I've seen you put up so many
bricks today that for a while I couldn't tell
if you were trying to play basketball or
undertaking a major construction project.
Tony: Oooooh, you just got served!
Ray: No, I didn't, I just got unlucky.
Tony: Yeah, you just got served more than
the daily special at a diner.

get silly

To drink, to get wasted.

Hey, guys, I stole a 12-pack of Natty
from my dad's fridge. Wanna get silly
tonight?

get stupid

To have a good time. More
specifically, to become drug- or
alcohol-intoxicated.

They did nothing but get stupid during
their Christmas vacation.

get the plates

"Get the plates" is a phrase used to
imply that someone or something
has just been "served," or shown
up. Commonly used in high schools
with many variations such as "Start
handing the plates out" and "Get the
plates 'cause you just got served."

Whoa, get the plates 'cause that was
embarrassing. He got served.

get with

To engage in sexual acts with.
Usually refers to two people who
are not dating or have just started
dating.

Nikki got with Brendt at the skatium
and then two days later he asked her out.

get with the program

Get your act together, get with it,
get a clue.

We always spot you guys two points at
game start and you still lose every time.
Get with the program already!

get your [verb] on

Can be used as a substitute phrase for performing or completing a certain action.

I'm tired, so I'm gonna get my sit on. Yo, Rosco! I got the juice, time to get our drink on.

get your finger out

Hurry up. Most often said to slackers. Implies that the person has their finger in their bum or is sitting on their thumbs.

If you don't get your finger out and finish this job the boss will be furious.

gg

Abbreviation for "good going" or "good game."

After the race, the hare reluctantly gave the tortoise props and said "gg."

ghetto

Unappealing, run-down, nasty. Opposite of "pimp."

Man, datz ghetto. Let's bounce.

ghetto bird

A police helicopter.

At least two ghetto birds were chasing Lorenzo down the I-10 last night after he jacked that car.

ghetto blaster

1. A small stereo, sometimes containing a tape deck or CD player and normally somewhat lacking in sound quality and appearance.

Let's roll to tha partay, man. I got tha ghetto blaster and some 40s.

2. Any broken-down or distorted stereo.

Man, that ghetto blaster is whack.

ghetto fabulous

Referring to the style of nouveau riche people who have grown up in ghetto or urban areas with a combination of bad taste, an urban aesthetic, and a desire to wear one's wealth. Basically, high-priced but tacky clothing and accessories.

People with million-dollar homes decked out all in black, gold, and black glass—ghetto fabulous, man.

ghetto level

How ghetto, gangsta, hard, and/or urban you happen to be. Ghetto levels are between 10 and 1, with 10 being most gangsta and 1 being least gangsta.

A man who lived in the ghetto, slang rocks, and worked his way out only to be brought down by old beef has a ghetto level of 10.

Your pizza guy has a ghetto level of 3.

GHI

Acronym for "gotta have it." Used as a modifier, as in "GHI culture," or "in GHI mode."

We live in a GHI-obsessed society where impulse buying is the norm, especially with the advent of Internet commerce.

ghost

1. To steal something. Possibly named for the ghost Boo from the game Mario Kart 64, who would steal your item when activated.

I'ma ghost that Ferrari!

2. To hold smoke in your lungs for so long that nothing comes out when you exhale.

I hit that joint hard and ghosted that shit.

3. To put to death, deprive of life, kill, murder, put an end to, extinguish, cause death or extinction.

Riddick just ghosted those two!

4. Preceded by "get": to get out of somewhere fast.

Damn, dawg! When the cops showed up he got ghost real fast.

GIGO

Acronym for "garbage in, garbage out."

Office manager: I heard Microsoft is coming out with another update.
Techie: Pfft! GIGO.

ginormous

The combination of "gigantic" and "enormous."

He's only five foot three, but he drives around in this ginormous car.

girly man

1. Male who is weak, pathetic, soft, and consequently possesses no upper body strength. After the "Hans and Franz" skits on the TV show *Saturday Night Live*.

You are just a bunch of little girly men.

2. Democratic state legislator in California. Insult hurled by movie actor and California Governor Arnold Schwarzenegger in a speech.

If you've got a problem with the law, tell it to the girly men in Sacramento!

give it up

A request for praise that can be issued either by the receiving party or a third party.

Give it up for my man DJ Mike!

give lip

To lip off, contradict, or argue with someone.

Stop giving me lip!

glass

Slang term for high-purity methamphetamine. According to the U.S. Drug Enforcement Agency (DEA), it refers to any product with 85 percent or higher purity. In real street usage refers to any product with a clear, crystalline appearance.

Yo, G, you holding any glass?

GLBT

Acronym for "gay, lesbian, bisexual, transsexual."

GLBT people deserve to have the right to marry.

gleek

To build up saliva in the salivary glands using some stimulus, like sour food or yawning, and then pressing the tongue upon the glands, causing the saliva to shoot out, usually at an impressive distance.

Yuck! Eric just gleeked all over my food!

glomp

To hug with enthusiasm. To pretty much tackle someone in greeting. When used online, often surrounded by "action stars"—asterisks denoting an action.

Girl A: *Glomps B* Welcome back! We missed you! How was your vacation?
Girl B: *Glomps A back* I missed you too! My vacation was great!

go career

1. To make a career out of a temporary job. To become a lifer.

I didn't think I'd like sitting at a desk all day in front of a computer, but after this, I might just go career.

2. To voluntarily extend one's military tour of duty into long-term employment.

The sergeant decided to apply to OCS and possibly go career.

go commando

To dress without underpants or a bra but be otherwise normally attired.

I'm afraid I can't lower my trousers, Your Honor, as I have gone commando today.

go gold

A term used to describe when a piece of software (or music) is completed and written to a master disk (such as a CD-R or a DVD-R) ready to be shipped off for manufacturing.

According to Todd, the computer game Doom 3 went gold on July 14th, 2004.

go green

To succumb to violent rage. Similar to "hulk out" or "go aggro."

Man, I hate it when people steal my parking spot! It makes me go green!

go hard

To be tight or quite remarkable.

That shirt go hard with them shoes.

go juice

Coffee. Term usually used in the morning. "Go-go juice" is appropriate as well.

I need some go juice to get through the morning.

go you

Interjection meaning "way to go"

or "good job."

You won the spelling bee with "sycophant"? Go you.

G.O.A.T.

Acronym for "greatest of all time." Tight, the best.

Those shoes are G.O.A.T.

gobshite

Loudmouthed person who talks a lot but says nothing of any value; shite comes out of their gob.

Shut it, you little gobshite!

go-code

An order issued, often between armed personnel, that basically means "go!"

Okay, be ready. I'm gonna give the go-code.

God squad

Derisive name given to various religious organizations that aggressively and proactively campaign for new members to spread their faith.

Don't answer the door. The God squad is out there.

going down

A statement used to express that

you will destroy, bring down, beat up, or otherwise eliminate someone or something.

Man 1: Your momma is an ugly ho!
Man 2 (just before he punches Man 1): Dude, you're going down!

going out
A relationship in which a person becomes so romantically entwined with another person that, in the course of several months, the male companion often loses all ability or desire to reason.

Sarah and I have been going out for four whole months. I haven't made a decision in three months. Last week I had the urge to have an opinion, but my soul mate came in and we talked about it until the feeling went away.

gold digger
A person who goes out with you fo' yo' money.

I knew she was low, but I didn't know she was a gold digger. The other night she traded her phone number for some stock options.

gold on a roll
Fake gold or something that is a cheap kind of metal like steel or tin that is only plated with gold. Some people will try to pass off items made with this material as being real gold.

I floss my gold on a roll. I bought it for $16, but it looks real.

golden
Complete, good to go, all right!

Once we get this test finished, we'll be golden.

golds
Gold teeth. A gold grill. From rapper Master P's song "Where U From?"

Flava Flav and Rakim were among the first rappers to rock golds.

gone pear-shaped
British slang for events taking an unexpected turn for the worse.

I was hoping this would be a great party, but it's all gone pear-shaped now that the police have turned up.

goober
Term of endearment for a kind-hearted, rather oblivious goofball.

"That John is such a goober," said Jane as John vector-danced his junior prom away.

good
Content.

Mom: Do you want some juice?
Kid: Nah, I'm good.

good looking out

To let someone know you are thankful for their watching out for you or helping you out with something.

Guy 1: Wut up, son? Seen yo' ex at da club just now.
Guy 2: Good lookin' out, whoadie. Let's hit a different place, fo' sho'.

good Lord

An expression of surprise or astonishment. Originally British, it now has a slightly sarcastic or ironic connotation.

Butler: Excuse me, but Madame appears to have been swept out to sea by a tidal wave.
Duke: Good Lord, Jeeves, that's appalling. Well, tell the maid to remove one place setting from the dining table.

good times

Phrase popularized by a *Saturday Night Live* sketch in which Ana Gasteyer (who played "Margaret Jo McCullen") and Molly Shannon (who played "Teri Rialto") acted as the two monotone hosts of a radio cooking show, "Delicious Dish," which mocked National Public Radio. The two would repeat the phrase "good times" at certain intervals. Now a phrase used by many when expressing or reflecting on a fun, exciting, unique, or crazy moment in the past or present.

Friend 1: Remember those endless summer days we had when we were younger?
Friend 2: Yeah, good times.

good to go

Ready.

We're good to go. Lock and load.

goof

A person acting in a stupid manner.

He got drunk and hurt himself trying to climb a tree. What a goof!

goof juice

Alcohol. Usually cheap wine.

Todd only has to have a few glasses of goof juice to get the same effect as drinking a case of beer.

gooftard

Combination of "goofy" and "retard."

That guy is such a gooftard; he put his underwear on over his pants.

Google

A popular Internet search engine, or to use the Google search engine.

Hang on, I'll see if I can Google it and get an answer.

Google bomb

1. A collaborative effort among webpage authors to exploit a weakness in the Google search engine and make the address of another webpage appear at the top of the search results list when a particular phrase is typed into the search engine.
2. To conspire with other webpage authors to create a Google bomb by agreeing on the search phrase and victim site.

The most famous Google bomb can be triggered by searching for "miserable failure." As of 8/1/05, the White House biography of George W. Bush was still at top of the list. Some counterstrikes have been made on Jimmy Carter's bio and Michael Moore's website.

Google hand

The measure of one's ability to rapidly locate information on the Internet using Google.

I just asked Jim about a rare breed of Guinean banana slug. He had some links for me in a couple of minutes.

Damn, is his Google hand strong!

Google-fu

The ability to quickly answer any given question using Internet resources, especially the Google search engine.

My Google-fu is strong this morning. I've saved so much time I think I'll take a long lunch.

Googlewhack

When you type a search term into the Google search engine and only get one result.

I found a new Googlewhack today— smooshed acidheads!

goon

A person with poor social skills and a limited ability to interact with other people. Someone you would rather not have to spend any length of time with.

Are the goons coming to the pub tonight? If so, I'm out.

goose

To grab someone's butt cheeks and squeeze. Most often done in a playful manner between friends.

He goosed me so hard it bruised me!

goose egg
Zero. To be left with nothing. The way the number is shaped is similar to a goose's egg.

I played a tennis match and was goose-egged. I lost 6–0, 6–0, 6–0.

gorp
A general term for trail mix. Acronym for "good old raisins and peanuts."

Hey, pass the gorp! I'm starving over here!

got next
Phrase used to procure the right to play a game once the current player has departed. Most often used in arcades. Can be used in conjunction with placing your quarter next to the coin slot.

You: Sweet, it's a Ms. Pac-Man machine. Guy in line: Hey, I got next.

got your back
An expression used to assure someone that you are watching out for them.

Don't trip, son. I got your back.

got your shit together
To be successful, organized, mature.

Mike and Jenny down the street have a new car, and good careers—they really have got their shit together.

gotcha
I understand.

Caller: Do you understand what I am saying?
Receiver: Yeah, gotcha.

gotsta
A Vanilla Ice–style way of saying "must" or "have to."

I gotsta get me some of those crispy Air Force Ones.

governator
A machine sent back in time to terminate Gray Davis and become governor of California.

Arnold Schwarzenegger is . . .
the governator.

government sneeze
Mistake made by the government.

Nixon's Watergate scandal is a well-known government sneeze.

goya
Military acronym for "get off your ass."

Hey, you've been sitting on the couch all afternoon. GOYA!

grab a wheel
To draft off of. To ride behind someone and let them break the wind resistance for you. Often used by cyclers.

Dude, if you're hurting, grab a wheel before we hit this hill.

grabass
An informal game in which the participants attempt to grab the posteriors of one another. Usually associated with horseplay.

I'm up here in the condo trying to call these little bastard teenagers in for lunch, but they're down on the beach playing grabass with each other.

granny panties
Underwear that is big and ugly.

Granny panties won't get you any action.

granola
Earthy, hippieish.

That chick doesn't shave her armpits; she's hella granola.

grass
Marijuana. Pot.

Lemme smoke some grass, yo.

gravy
A state of complacency or happiness. Stable goodness.

It's all gravy. Life is good.

gray market
Halfway between the white market (completely legal) and black market (completely illegal). The gray market sells products that are legal to own but can be used illegally or are illegal to use altogether.

In Virginia, police radar detectors are gray market items because it is legal to own one but illegal to actually use it.

graybar hotel
Jail; hoosegow; the can; the jug; the calaboose; the slammer. A school of crime where you can get free medical care from quacks, work out, watch TV, and sleep a lot. Also "graybar motel."

I kited some checks, so they sent me on a three-month vacation at the graybar hotel.

Greek
A person involved in a fraternity

or sorority system.

Did you rush? Yeah, I'm Greek now.

green

1. Inexperienced.

You're so not green. You know exactly what you're doing.

2. Marijuana. Weed.

The five-o busted me with some green.

3. Money.

Man, I wish I could buy that shirt, but I'm outta green.

grills

Removable gold or platinum teeth that go over the top of your real teeth. Also "golds" or "fronts."

I'm from tha Dirty South. Best believe you gonna see a gold grill when you look in my mouth!

grind

1. The same old stuff you do every day.

Bob: What up, dawg?
John Gotti: You know, the same old grind. Put a couple hits on people, organized some drug deals. Set up a coup d'état of a third-world country that's now under

Mafia rule. Nothing exciting.

2. Dance move that involves rubbing one's crotch or butt against someone else's crotch or butt.

Yo, man, we was doin' the grind out there, and she can really shake dat ass of hers.

3. To sell drugs. Comes from what you do to cocaine to prepare it for use, but has been bastardized to mean drug dealing in general.

If you need a lift, I know someone who's grindin' tonight.

4. To perform a skateboarding move in which a part of the skateboard is slid off a rail or edge.

That rail's one of the best for grinding.

5. To work or try hard to accomplish something.

Yo, after I got fired from Mickey D's, I was out there straight grindin', lookin' for another job.

grip

1. An abundant amount of something.

Yo! I got a grip of cash today. Let's go spend it.

There's no need to buy more beer; I have a grip at home.

uRbaN

2. An undefined unit of time, usually to express a long period as opposed to a short period.

What up, man? I haven't seen you for a grip.

grody

Disgusting, dirty, or just plain unappealing. Possibly the Americanized pronunciation of the British "grotty," which means "of poor quality."

Those are the grodiest restrooms in the state!

groggy

Drunk or tired.

I felt so groggy after ten hours of hard work.

groupie

A young woman, often underage, who seeks to achieve status by having sex with rock musicians, roadies, security, and other band-related guys.

She was a groupie for Nirvana, but she never got past the roadies.

grow a set

A request for someone to grow a set of testicles, to stiffen up their spine, to get tough, to stand up for themselves, etc.

Your GF will not let you come over for a beer?!?! Dude, grow a set!

grub

1. Food.

You hungry? Let's get some grub.

2. Descriptor for delightfully tasty food.

This pizza is friggin' grub, dude.

3. To eat. To masticate and digest food to please the hunger that dwells within.

Hey, Sam, where do you wanna grub?

grunge

A form of rock that began in Seattle in the late '80s and early '90s. Although derived from punk, grunge is slightly more refined and melodic (though not much), and is characterized by rough, heavy guitar riffs and a generally dirty, muddy sound.

For newbies, grunge can be thought of as "anti-pop." While pop is very concerned with its image, grunge really doesn't give a shit and is very anti-commercial and anti-mainstream. This attitude is often mistaken for arrogance, which is why many people don't like Pearl Jam, and Eddie Vedder in particular.

Grunge was also characterized by torn, faded jeans, ratty T-shirts, flannel shirts, and long, unkempt hair.

Many people feel that Kurt Cobain, the front man and lead singer of Nirvana, was the "spokesman for Generation X." Cobain's masterpiece "Smells Like Teen Spirit" was hailed by many at the time as perfectly describing Generation X's feelings toward the world. "Smells Like Teen Spirit" is the most popular grunge song of all time, and it catapulted Nirvana's popularity through the stratosphere and put grunge on the map.

Cobain became the symbol for grunge because of the popularity of "Smells Like Teen Spirit," and so when he committed suicide in 1994, many felt that grunge died with him.

My favorite grunge bands are Nirvana, Pearl Jam, Soundgarden, Alice in Chains, and Stone Temple Pilots.

GSBI

Acronym for "good-sounding bad idea." An idea that sounds exciting or plausible but upon further thought or execution is revealed to be astoundingly dumb and/or dangerous.

Cat decided to ride her bike to school as exercise, disregarding the fact it was

10-plus miles away and she needed to be there in 30 minutes. It was a GSBI.

gtg

1. Shorthand for "got to go."

Shoot, it's almost midnight—gtg.

2. Shorthand for "good to go."

Girl 1: Say, I'm heading out. You coming?
Girl 2: Yeah—gtg.

guff

To break wind, let it rip, fart.

Phewwww! Can you smell that? I just guffed!

guh

An exclamation of disgust, repulsion, or sickness.

Guh! Why did you send me to that website?! Gouge my eyes out now!

guitarded

Having little to no musical skill on the guitar.

He can't even make an Em chord; he must be guitarded.

gully

1. Rough and rugged; unpolished and hardcore.

That hotel we laid up in was so gully. No TV, no towels, just a bed and a lightbulb.

2. Something from the streets. Gutter and/or gangsta. Similar to "hood" ("I'm so hood") or "street" ("I'm so street").

I'm so damn gully.

gumby

Someone with little or no coordination or common sense and who lacks any talent or potential to do anything but mess everything up.

I can't believe you just destroyed all life on Earth. All I asked you to do was flush the toilet! You're such a gumby!

gun

Someone who excels at something. A metaphor that translates the power and effectiveness of the weapon into a compliment.

That basketball player is a gun.

gun show

The showing off of one's biceps. Plays off of the slang term for arms—"guns."

Billy: Have you got your tickets yet?
Sarah: To what?
Billy: To the gun show! (pulls back his right sleeve, flexing his muscles, and points with his left hand)

guns

The bicep muscles. Could also refer to the whole arm, but this is normally not the case. Also spelled "gunz."

Check out those guns of German giant Markus Rühl.

hack

1. To program a computer in a clever, virtuosic, and wizardly manner. Ordinary computer jockeys merely write programs; hacking is the domain of digital poets. Hacking is a subtle and arguably mystical art, equal parts wit and technical ability, that is rarely appreciated by nonhackers.

I stayed up all night hacking, and when I finally looked out the window, it was 8 a.m.

2. To break into computer systems with malicious intent. This sense of the term is the one that is most commonly heard in the media, although sense 1 is much more faithful to its original meaning. Contrary to popular misconception, this sort of hacking rarely requires cleverness or exceptional technical

ability; most so-called "black hat" hackers rely on brute force techniques or exploit known weaknesses and the incompetence of system administrators.

Some script kiddie hacked into the web server and trashed the database.

3. To jury-rig or improvise something inelegant but effective, usually as a temporary solution to a problem.

I didn't have time to do things properly, so I just hacked together something that worked.

4. A clever or elegant technical accomplishment, especially one with a playful or prankish bent. A clever routine in a computer program, especially one that uses tools for purposes other than those for which

they were intended, might be considered a hack. Students at technical universities, such as MIT, are famous for performing elaborate hacks, such as disassembling the dean's car and then reassembling it inside his house, or turning a 14-story building into a giant Tetris game by placing computer-controlled lighting panels in its windows.

A computerized bartender that automatically mixes your drinks and debits your account? Now that's a hack.

5. A temporary, jury-rigged solution, especially in the fields of computer programming and engineering: the technical equivalent of chewing gum and duct tape. Short for "hack job."

This subroutine is just a hack; I'm going to go back and put some real code in later.

6. A cheap, mediocre, or second-rate practitioner, especially in the fields of journalism and literature; a charlatan or incompetent.

That two-bit pulp writer? Ah, he's nothing but a hack.

hacker

One who enjoys or is proficient at using a computer and may occasionally circumvent security measures out of curiosity, but

becomes a cracker when he starts destroying data or causing trouble.

I am a computer hacker, not a cracker. I use my powers for good.

hair band

A group of men in a rock band, each with an obscenely large mane that is typically wavy and always past the shoulders. The men in the band (most formed in or around 1980) bang their heads so their hair flies all over. In addition, it is customary to wear either extremely tight pants or similarly tight stonewashed cutoff jeans when part of a hair band.

Def Leppard, Spinal Tap, Poison, and Twisted Sister were superior hair bands in the '80s.

hairy eyeball

When someone looks you up and down in a judgmental way.

I ran into my boyfriend's ex-girlfriend at the party and she gave me the hairy eyeball.

half-step

1. To act tough but back down when confronted. A person who does this is called a "half-stepper."

If a person gives you the finger while out

driving, and then when you stop at the
lights they pretend they can't see you and
act like nothing is happening, they're
half-stepping.

2. To not do a complete job.
To bullshit. Opposite of "come
correct."

*He was half-steppin' how he treats his
girl. She deserves better.*

hammer down

Trucker-speak for hurry up, give it
more gas. To put the pedal to the
metal.

We're late, so hammer down.

hammer lane

A trucker term referring to the
passing lane on the highway. The
fast lane.

*Move into the hammer lane so we can get
past these four-wheelers.*

hammer pants

A style of pegged baggy pants, with
a huge billowing crotch that goes
down below the knees.

*Can you believe people actually wore
hammer pants in the '90s? What the hell
was Gen X thinking?*

hamster-wheel brain

When your brain runs around some
issue over and over again and won't
stop, just like a hamster running in
its exercise wheel. It keeps running,
but doesn't get anywhere.

*I'm having such hamster-wheel brain
about whether to take this job offer.*

hand

Control in a relationship.

*Ramone has hand in his relationship.
That girl does whatever he says.*

hand sandwich

When you have all of the
ingredients for a sandwich
except bread, so you just eat the
components out of your hand.

*I just took a giant hit from the bong and
got the munchies, but the bread was moldy,
so I had to eat a hand sandwich.*

handle

1. One's online name. Often, a
hacker will use a handle and be
referred to by this handle by all his
associates to help lessen the chances
of getting caught. Often also a
privacy measure.

*My handles are Shinji, Cryo-man, and
Saihenjin. But you can call me Bob.*

2. A half-gallon of liquor. It gets its name from the little handle that's always on half-gallons.

Grab the handle and let's get crunk!

3. A new steady hookup.

Guy 1: Is that Doug's new handle?
Guy 2: Yeah, her name is Jen.

handles

In streetball, dribbling ability. How well you can dribble the basketball and perform tricks determines your handles.

That player just shook 'em wit' his crazy handles!

hand-waving

Attempt to get past a moment when a difficult explanation is required.

His project was late and all he could offer was some hand-waving.

hang

Chill. Short for "hang out."

I'm just gonna hang at Lolita's place today.

hang out

To chill with friends. Sometimes used as code in front of one's parents to mean "get messed up."

Hey, you wanna hang out or just chill?

hangover

The body ache experienced after heavy drinking. Commonly accompanied by vomiting, shaking, headache, short-term amnesia, and diarrhea.

I got drunk watching the game last night. My hangover was so bad that I awoke this morning with puke all over my shirt and no idea how I got home.

haps

Short for "happenings." What's going on.

Hey, brother, what's the haps on the craps? Who's winning?

hard

1. Extremely good, really nice, expensive.

That new Escalade is so hard!

2. Tough, mostly because of poverty and surviving (or not) public schools or a bad family life. Something often said of poor, urban American youth. Marked by resourcefulness, pragmatism, and coldness. Also "hardcore."

Yeah, Darius is so hard. His dad beat him and his Mom had to work triple shifts.

hardcore

1. Awesome. Severe. At the top of one's game.

He is the most hardcore biker I have ever seen.

2. Tough. Diehard. Having no fear of the consequences of one's actions.

That skateboarder wears no helmet or pads—he is so hardcore.

hard up

Broke. Not having enough money. Between a rock and a hard place. A difficult situation.

I was hard up for cash after my trip to Vegas.

hard-drive manifest destiny

An excuse for downloading stuff (such as songs or movies) from the Internet because you have the space and/or you were meant to.

My mom looked at me inquisitively and asked, "Why do you need a new hard drive?" I replied, "Hard-drive manifest destiny."

harsh one's mellow

To interfere with someone's drug buzz, or to bother someone who is either stoned or just relaxing.

Dude, can you turn off The Montel Williams Show? It's totally harshing my mellow.

harvester

An automatic website scanner that searches Internet sites for e-mail addresses. The reason spammers know your e-mail address.

I set a trap for the harvesters by putting hundreds of bogus e-mail addresses on my website.

hasbian

A former lesbian who is now in a heterosexual relationship.

Mona is a hasbian. She used to date chicks, but now she wants to date men.

hash

Hashish, an extract from the resin of marijuana plants. This resin is usually many times more potent than the plant material acquired from such plants.

Coach gets mad at me when I smoke his hash.

hash brownies

Brownies baked with marijuana with the intention of getting high.

Suburban mom 1: You want some of these

hash brownies?
Suburban mom 2: Yeah, I need to get stoned.

hater

A person who feels anger or jealousy toward someone who has succeeded in something they have worked hard for. The hater speaks badly and/or takes negative actions in an attempt to create problems for the successful person.

T-Bo dropped a dime on Big Mike just because Big Mike was makin' some change! T-Bo a hater!

hateration

The act or process of hating on someone/something.

Stop the hateration because it will get you nowhere.

have kittens

To be excited or surprised.

Troy, you got me flowers? I'm simply having kittens!

hawk

To sell something aggressively, like the street vendors who sell their stuff on a blanket on the sidewalk or from a booth or table.

I bought a South Park *T-shirt from a hawker's booth in D.C.*

head change

The point at which one feels a change in his or her behavior and equilibrium from the effects of a drug.

Nah, he's a heavyweight; he can blaze mad and not even get a head change.

heads are gonna roll

Used by higher-ups in a company to sound like a threat to a person's employment. Anyone who actually uses this phrase is insecure and probably incapable of firing anyone.

Those TPS reports still aren't done. Heads are going to roll at the 2 P.M. meeting.

heart-on

A warm feeling in one's heart. A feeling of awe, astonishment, surprise, or admiration.

The way Vicki Valerie sings gives me a major heart-on!

heat

A firearm. Most often a gun.

Bob: I've had about enough of you guys. (pulls out a pistol)
Sherman: Whoa! Big Bob's packing heat! Take it easy, Bob.

heatbag

A person who attracts attention from the authorities. Contrast with "heatscore," which is a place that attracts attention.

Don't be so loud, you heatbag. The cops will hear us.

heater

1. A fastball in baseball. In the major leagues, the heater generally travels to the batter at speeds of 95 mph or more.

The pitcher struck him out with a heater.

2. A gun, usually a handgun.

He blasted his heater out the window at the fools on the corner.

heatscore

A place or activity that draws the attention of police or other authorities.

Driving a car without license plates is heatscore.

heaving

1. When referring to a place: uncomfortably busy.
2. Vomiting, or being within seconds of doing so.

The dance floor was heaving, but some guy started heaving and a space opened up.

heavy

1. Really good.

That tune is heavy.

2. Carrying a gun or other type of firearm.

Don't mess with him; he came heavy.

heavy in the game

Phrase used to describe a prime-time playa.

Pharrell is heavy in the game—he's so successful!

heebie-jeebies

A sensation one feels when they enter a scary situation with unknown consequences.

The kids all got the heebie-jeebies as they entered the old haunted mansion on a Halloween dare.

heel

In professional wrestling, a "bad" guy.

Stone Cold Steve Austin turned heel after joining forces with Mr. McMahon.

heh

A half laugh used when you don't wanna make someone feel bad about something they said that wasn't funny. Can be used to great effect in electronic communication.

Person A: A man walks into a bar. Ouch!
Person B: heh

Heisman

1 In American football, when an offensive player pushes a defensive player away with one arm in order to flee and/or incapacitate the defensive player, emulating the pose on the Heisman Trophy.

Wow, did you see Ricky Williams Heisman that linebacker?

2. A direct and impersonal rejection of a sexual overture, pass, or advance.

She gave him the Heisman when he smiled at her over his martini.

3. A skillful dodging of an impending and usually negative engagement or interaction.

I Heismanned my boss yesterday when he approached me about those TPS coversheets and reports.

hell, yeah

Expression of either great joy or agreement.

Announcer: If you want to see Stone Cold open a can of whoopass, gimme a "hell, yeah"!
Response: Hell, yeah!

hella

1. Very, totally.
2. Lots of. Short for "a hell of a lot of."

Guy 1: That party was hella sketch. What was with all those skanky-ass girls?
Guy 2: There was hella weed, tho!

hellified

Extreme. A large amount.

You missed one hellified party at T-Bone's last night.

helluva

Very. Extremely.

You got a helluva lot of hotties in the car!

hellza

Very. Extremely. Totally.

That concert was hellza cool!

herb

Marijuana.

Kent is smokin' the herb again.

herbal refreshment

Weed, pot, chronic, kill, KB, marijuana, dope. When you say this instead, it's more subtle and adds some much-needed variety to your pathetic stoner life.

Everyone meet at my house at exactly 4:20 P.M. on the 20th day of April. Drinks are on the house and so is the herbal refreshment.

hexa

Very. Totally. Word substituted for "hella." Also "hecka."

That's hexa cool.

HG

Short for "homegirl."

That's my HG, Yvette.

hickey

A form of love bite. A bruise raised on the body of a sexual partner by very hard kissing, biting, or sucking.

You've got a hickey on your neck. Who you been with, you little tart?

high

The state of mind achieved by

smoking a moderate amount of marijuana. The stage just before getting stoned.

Dude, I barely smoked any. I'm only high.

high and dry

What one is when they smoke a significant amount of marijuana but do not drink alcoholic beverages.

Cop: So . . . you were swerving all over the road. How much have you had to drink tonight?
Pat: Nothing, sir. It's just hard to hold the wheel while you're lighting your bowl. I don't drink. I'm high and dry.

high five

Symbol of celebration when something good is said/done. The causes for the call of "high five" can vary from anything as small as finding something cool on the floor to something as big as saving the world from almost certain destruction.

Dude, look at what I just found on the floor—an uneaten cookie! High five!

high five for friendship

A posh way of breaking up with one's significant other, or a way to let someone know that you don't want to be involved. Involves giving them a high five and inquiring

"High five for friendship?"

Amy, I don't know if this is working out. How about a high five for friendship?

high on life
Living life to its fullest.

Yeah, I'm high on life.

high roller
Rich guy who has a nice car, nice clothes, and buys everything he likes.

Yo, that guy with that Benz is a high roller, yeah.

high-maintenance
Requiring a lot of attention. Emotionally needy or prone to over-dramatizing.

Although he was a nice boy, his low self-esteem made him high-maintenance.

himbo
The male version of a bimbo, whore, or slut.

He's such a himbo that he'd sleep with anything that has, or had, a pulse.

himplants
1. Pectoral implants for men.

Brad is so vain, he's had a nose job, Botox, and liposuction, and those awesome pecs of his are just himplants.

2. Penile implants.

He finally gave in and answered one of those e-mails that sells himplants that would help him please the ladies.

hip
Cooler than cool, the pinnacle of what is "it." Beyond all trends and conventional coolness.

Stay away from the tacky velvet-rope MTV frat-boy clubs on the beach. Check out this party downtown instead; it's gonna be hip.

hip-hop
The expression of the relationship between urban youth and their environment. Hip-hop is the art of the streets and consists of four key elements: break dancing, emceeing, graffiti, and turntablism.

Hip-hop is my life.

hippie Christmas
The morning after hippies have made tie-dyed T-shirts, candles, or prayer flags.

Our neighbors were sharing another hippie

Christmas on their driveway with twenty of their closest friends, unwrapping tie-dyed T-shirts and prayer flags to dry in the sun.

hippiecrite

A fake hippie who complains about every polluting object known to man but uses the same products that they complain about.

Hippiecrite: Oh, those awful cars! (one week later) Hey, I just bought a Suburban! Check it out—it has a V8!

hissy fit

An unreasonable emotional outburst.

Just because I forgot your birthday, there's no reason to throw a hissy fit.

hit

1. Ugly. Similar to "beat."

He acted like he'd get some good-lookin' women to come to the party, but all the chicks he brought were hit!

2. The inhalation of marijuana smoke.

I'll take a hit off that joint.

3. To kill somebody as part of a financed murder contract; such a contract.

Tony was very upset when he found out his mother and uncle had attempted to orchestrate a hit on him.

hit back

To return a favor.

Let me borrow some ends. I'll hit you back on the 1st, my brotha.

hit fo' it

Usually used immediately prior to a fight, a challenge to throw the first punch.

When Pookie saw Ray-Ray in the hallway he told him to hit fo' it if he was so serious about their dispute.

hit it

1. Can be used by either sex in reference to anything you desire (e.g., a beautiful woman, a handsome man, a nice car, etc.).

Person 1: Did you see that girl/guy/car? Person 2: Yeah, I'd hit it!

2. More specifically, vernacular commonly used by males to mean "I would like to have sexual relations with that person."

Wow, she's stacked! I'd hit it!

3. To acquire a desired item before

supplies run out. To take advantage of a beneficial situation.

Girl, that fried chicken is good. You better hit it!

hit me back

A way to ask for a reply.

Guy 1: Yo, punk, hit me back wit' yo' digits, fo' shizzle.
Guy 2: Okay.

hit me up

1. To connect someone with something they desire.

You got a bag you can hit me up with?

2. To demand something.

Hit me up with that shit.

3. To call someone.

Hit me up later tonight.

hit the block

To send men to surround a block with dozens of cars and fire weapons all over the block. Most often done in Mafia and gang wars.

Hymie Weiss's gang hit the block where Al Capone was dining with a friend, but no one was hurt.

hit the books

To study really hard, avoiding other distractions.

I haven't studied for today's test yet. Time to hit the books!

hit the sheets

To go to bed/have sex with someone.

I couldn't believe how hot he was. We hit the sheets that night.

hit up

1. To contact someone.

You should hit up Tommy to see if he stole your Buddha.

2. To go somewhere.

Let's hit up this drum and bass party tonight.

3. To connect someone with something they desire.

You got a bag you can hit me up with?

4. To graffiti.

You, we headin' out tonight to hit up the hood.

ho

A prostitute. Short for "whore,"

which can sound like "ho," depending on how you pronounce it. Sometimes equated with the term "slut," but hoes get paid for what they do.

Look at that ho. She made about $500 the other day.

ho card
Calling someone's bluff.

I challenged him but he didn't do nothin', so I pulled his ho card.

hobag
A slutty person.

That girl was an über-hobag.

hobo power
A measure of the degree of offense of an odor. One would have to reach the stench of 10 hobos in order to gain a measurement of 10 hobo power (or HP). 8–10 hobo power may describe the exhaust fumes from the bus that just pulled out in front of you. A good broccoli fart might reach 25 hobo power. At 50 hobo power there is projectile vomiting. 100 hobo power has never been documented in nature. It is theoretical at this point in science, much like absolute zero. It is widely assumed that if one were to experi-

ence 100 hobo power, its effects would surely be fatal.

I swear when Jimmy pulled that Yokozuna on my face, I almost puked. His ass must be about 45 hobo power.

hold it down
1. To maintain in a state of coolness/smoothness.

Person 1: I'ma hit that party tonight.
Person 2: Aight, hold it down.

2. To take care of or do something.

Person 1: Yo, money! Are you seein' that shorty?
Person 2: Naw, dawg! You can hold it down!

hold up
Wait a minute. Postpone plans.

Hold up! Let me grab some munchies before we get goin'.

hold your horses
Wait. Don't be impatient.

Whoa, hold your horses there, big guy. We're not leaving yet.

holding
Possessing drugs that are available for sale.

I'm holding if you wanna give me a call sometime.

hole
The drug spot. A house or apartment where drugs are bought and sold.

Tow me to the hole so I can get a bag.

hole in the lip
National leading cause of a beverage running out of the mouth and down your shirt due to poor aim (the mouth of your can was tilted to your nose) or poor control (tilted the coffee cup too far back).

Dude, you spilled coffee all down the front of your shirt. You have a hole in your lip or something?

holla
1. A way for a brotha to say he wants to get in your pants.

Ay, my boy right here wanna holla atcha.

2. A pimp-ass way of saying "What up?"

Holla! What you be doin'?

3. May be used to end a conversation.

I gotta go. Holla.

holla back
After farewells have been made, you say this to the other person if you want them to stay in touch.

Guy 1: Yo, dawg, peace.
Guy 2: Aight, man. Holla back.

holmes
Gangster slang. What you would call a good friend, a stranger, or even mockery against an adversary. Also "homes" or "homey."

You got a problem with it, holmes?

home skillet
Friend.

Word up, my home skillet.

home slice
Good friend or buddy. Someone who seems like a little slice of home.

Hey, whassup, home slice?

homeboy
A good friend or a person from your gang.

David's my homeboy.

honcho
A person in charge of some group

or of some function, usually a male.

He quickly got promoted to be the head marketing honcho in that dot-com startup.

honey shot

During sporting events, when the cameraman zooms in on the pretty girl in the stands, usually when she's bending over showing cleavage.

Voice of control-room supervisor: Camera three! The chick in row 18, section F! Quick, zoom in tight! Ah, that's it! That's our honey shot for tonight!

honey wagon

A tanker truck used to suck up the waste matter from portable toilets and other sources.

The honey wagon arrived to clean up the washroom areas.

hooah

Phonetic spelling of the military acronym HUA, "heard, understood, acknowledged." An affirmative or pleased response.

Sergeant: Y'all ready for chow?
Private(s): Hooah, sergeant!

hooch

1. Moonshine or bootleg alcohol.

That mob boss got arrested for running hooch.

2. Marijuana. Rarely used nowadays, but popular during the late '60s and early '70s.

Let's roll up some hooch before this concert!

hoochie

A female who appears trashy, often wearing inappropriately tight clothing (with or without pudge overflowing the waistband); eyebrows shaved and penciled back on in dramatic fashion; heavy makeup with dark lipstick; and large, gaudy, costume-grade jewelry. Frequently accompanied by multiple children from different fathers.

Damn, did you see Estela's sister at the sideshow last night? Sportin' a camel toe through her jeans, cornrows—you know she's a straight-up hoochie.

hood

1. Short for "neighborhood."

I need to raise up out my hood.

2. The ghetto. A particularly rough area of a city.

Some fools got capped last night in the hood for lookin' at someone the wrong way.

3. Someone who is street-smart and from the ghetto.

Brian is hood; he got jumped last night by two dudes, but when it was over he walked away with their wallets and his.

hood slide
An alternative to walking/running around a vehicle, in which a running jump is taken onto the hood of a vehicle (preferably yours), landing body first, and letting yourself slide across the hood to the other side of the vehicle, where you land on your feet. Made easier by a good wax job. Not recomended on full-size vans, Hyundais, or basically any cheap car that caves easily.

Did you see that hood slide Bo Duke just did on The Dukes of Hazzard? *I wish I could be that cool.*

hoodie
A sweatshirt with a hood on the back. Usually has a large pocket on the stomach.

I own so many hoodies I've lost count.

hoodlum
1. A criminal.

Check that crew of hoodlums over there. They've all done time for something or other.

2. Young troublemakers who wear hooded sweatshirts and/or large puffy jackets, baseball caps, and shiny pants and may sport chains. Often seen loitering in front of drug stores and on stoops and fences, harassing passersby.

Little Timmy ran into a group of hoods the other night. They rolled him for everything he owned—shoes, socks, and underwear included.

hood-rich
Burberry gear and a Benzo, but no cheddar.

My homey from the projects with the Benz on 22 spinners is hood-rich.

hook
The chorus of a song.

Yo, I love the hook on this song.

hook up
1. To make something happen. To connect people with the goods or services they want.

About the goods for the party—my f riend who works the streets said he could hook it up.

2. Goods or services received as a favor.

Jerry gave me the hook-up with those backstage passes.

3. To make out with someone.

Sandra and I hooked up last night and I noticed that her Adam's apple was kinda big.

4. To have sex with someone.

Hooking up with Derrick last night was the biggest mistake of my life.

5. Informal agreement between people to meet up later.

Why don't we each do what we need to do now; we'll hook up later.

hooker boots

Tall leather or pleather boots with large heels. They generally extend at least to, but often above, the knee. Fake hooker boots are often constructed with high-heeled shoes and matching tube socks.

All of the girls at school wear hooker boots.

hooligan

Young, foolish person who gallivants and roams the streets causing trouble. Same as a punk or hoodlum.

You little hooligans stay off my lawn and out of my neighborhood!

hooptie

An old piece of crap car. Features include a peeling do-it-yourself tint job; chain links around the license plate; plastic hubcaps; driver's entry on the passenger side; windows that don't roll down; and an overly aggressive aftermarket spoiler.

Hey man, you have the phattest hooptie in town!

hoosegow

Jail. Prison.

I ain't got time for the piggies or the hoosegow.

hork

To steal something small, usually from another person, rather than from a store.

I turned around for five minutes and someone horked my Pepsi from the fridge at work.

hosed

In a bad situation; screwed.

I bought a car on eBay, but it won't start and I can't contact the seller. I think I got hosed.

hoss

A Southern colloquial term for a friend.

You betta' get that grass mowed, hoss.

hot
1. Attractive.

Man, that girl is hot. You think she'd go out with me?

2. Stolen.

I've got some hot phones at the moment if you want to buy one cheap.

3. A phone that might be tapped.

I'm getting a new number tomorrow. This one is getting way too hot!

4. Suspicious situation or improper place for conducting illegal business. The police might be nearby, or the neighbors might call them if they saw anything suss going down.

This chop spot is red hot! Let's roll.

hot and bothered
Sexually aroused to the point where you are unable to think clearly.

I got the mad flow that makes all the ladies get hot and bothered.

hot damn
Expression of pleasure or excitement. As opposed to "cold damn," which isn't quite as expressive.

Hot damn! I thought those laxatives would never work!

hot sex
Good or cool.

Dude, that new car is hot sex!

hot shit
Banging, off the chain, cool.

Yo, those jeans are hot shit!

hotbox
A vehicle or room filled with marijuana smoke; to fill a vehicle or room with said smoke.

We smoked a blunt in the S500 and it was hotboxed in five minutes.

Hotlanta
Nickname of Atlanta, Georgia. "Hot" refers to both weather and social climate.

We drove to Hotlanta to party last summer.

hottie
A very attractive person.

John and Ruth are two major hotties at our school.

house

1. Anywhere you are right now, usually used to announce one's arrival. Also "hizzouse."

Give it up! Give it up! DJ Screw is in the house!

2. A type of electronic-based music, similar to trance or rave.

What kind of music do I like? I like house.

Hov

Nickname of rap artist Jay-Z. He is also referred to as "J-Hova," as he considers himself to be the messiah of hip-hop music.

I just copped that new Hov CD!

how many beans make five

A British expression meaning "one knows one's stuff" or referring to one who's good at mathematical puzzles.

He's a clever bloke—he knows how many beans make five.

HoYay

Short for "homoeroticism yay!" Homoerotic subtext (and obvious text) in film, books, television shows, or movies.

Clark and Lex are staring into each other's eyes again! HoYay!

huck

To jump in freeride mountain biking.

He hucked a 20-foot drop off the trail.

huff

To inhale chemical fumes, such as nitrous oxide or non-water-soluble ether, in order to become intoxicated.

That moron likes to huff paint thinner.

hulk out

To become enraged; to lose one's temper, clothing, and power of coherent speech before embarking on a spree of violence and wanton destruction. After the comic book character The Incredible Hulk, who turned from a geek to a thundering green mass of unstoppable fury.

It all happened so fast . . . the Broncos ran in their fifth touchdown and he just hulked out. I hope he's going to pay for a new TV. And the window.

hulled out

Raggedy. Stomped. Ugly as hell. Beatdown. Tore up from the floor up.

That car is hulled out. Are you sure it's drivable?

hump

To grind one's crotch in a press-and-release pattern against a particular object or surface.

My dog keeps humping my leg.

hump day

The middle of a workweek (usually Wednesday); used in the context of climbing a proverbial hill to get through a tough week.

After hump day, the work seems to go faster.

hung up

Stuck on someone.

Man, Alexa's got it going on—I'm really hung up!

hunny

Woman usually seen in the company of rappers, pimps, or gang members. Usually implies that said woman is attractive, but results may vary.

Sir Mix-A-Lot definitely would've dedicated "Baby Got Back" to his hunny.

hunt for green October

A search for marijuana, usually involving making phone calls and asking random people on the street.

Has absolutely nothing to do with nuclear submarine warfare or Commies.

Tommy went out on a hunt for green October about four hours ago and no one's heard from him since.

hurt

Ugly, extremely unattractive, dilapidated.

Your school is hurt! They need to tear it down and start all over.

hustla

Someone who is skilled at turning a profit.

That hustla Master P turns a profit in many different businesses.

hustle

To screw people over for profit.

I lost $500 today getting hustled on a fixed game.

hyphy

Stupid, silly, drunk, high, and just generally out of hand.

We got hyphy in da parking lot after the club let out!

I

I ain't trippin'

Interjection meaning "No shit!" "I swear to God!" or "I'm not kidding!"

Guy 1: Son, you are straight trippin' if you think you're gonna hit that.
Guy 2: I ain't trippin'! Watch me work my magic, fool!

I and I

Used in the Rastafarian culture in place of "you and me" to show that all people are equal under Jah.

Your parents are coming to see I and I.

I rule you

I win. I beat you. I'm better than you. I own you.

I rule you at stuff all the time, baby.

IANAL

Acronym for "I am not a lawyer." Often used on the Internet.

IANAL, but it seems to me that the lawsuit was doomed to fail.

ice

1. Diamonds.

I keep my girlfriend flooded with ice.

2. To shoot and kill someone.

Ay, yo! Homeboy just got iced!

iced up

Wearing diamonds from your dome to your kicks.

Jay-Z's all iced up, baby!

ice-grill

A particularly dirty look; a mean, hard, cold, or otherwise uncaring facial expression. To give someone such a look.

Yo, man, why you ice-grillin' me?

idiot box

Television (negative connotation).

Hmm. I can't find any cultural events for us to attend tonight. I guess we'll just have to watch the idiot box.

idjit

Variation of "idiot."

Don't be an idjit; quit licking that frozen flagpole.

idk

Shorthand form for "I don't know."

Person 1: what do you want to do today?
Person 2: idk—you pick.

ill

Dope, cool, tight, raw, phat.

Yo, that beat was so ill!

I'll pencil you in

When somebody wants to schedule something with you, but you don't want to use a pen to finalize it in your calendar because that person is a loser. If something better comes along you can erase it.

Sure, I'd love to watch slides from your trip to the Grand Canyon—I'll pencil you in.

I'll tell you that shit for free

When something is so obvious to one person that he would not even charge someone for that information.

Tom: What do you think of Tim's mam?
Muthar: She's a propa slag—I'll tell you that shit for free!

I'm allergic to bullshit

Just another way to say that you don't believe what someone says.

Guy 1: I did that hot girl last night!
*Guy 2: *sneezes* Oh, sorry, dude, I'm allergic to bullshit.*

I'm friends with that

I'm okay with that. Also often used in the negative, as in "I'm so not friends with that" to express distaste for the subject. Similar to being "down with that."

Stay home and smoke a blunt with you instead of going to school? I'm hella good friends with that.

I'm over it

1. The expression of a loss of interest in something or someone.

I thought that Bud Light was great beer when I started drinking, but now I'm over it.

2. The indication that a negative event no longer bothers someone.

I suffered for days after she broke up with me, but now I'm over it.

I'ma

short for "I'm going to."

I'ma get my ass out of here before she starts screaming.

imbo

Imbecile. A person stupider than a moron but not as stupid as an idiot.

Rachel? Don't worry about her—she's a real imbo.

IMO

Acronym for "in my opinion."

This game sucks, IMO.

in bed together

In business together.

Okay, you can go tell Jack that we're back in bed together. I'm sure he'll be very happy.

in like

The stage of infatuation where one is enchanted by another but not yet "in love."

She is so amazing—I am completely in like with her!

in the cut

Secluded or hard to find.

Guy 1: Trey's party was off the hook!
Guy 2: Really, where was it? I couldn't find the place.
Guy 1: It's back in the cut, on Bent Street.

in the zone

Expression used to describe a state of consciousness where actual skills match the perceived performance requirements perfectly. Being "in the zone" implies increased focus and attention, which allow for higher levels of performance.

Good Charlotte gets in the zone by warming up before a show.

in there like swimwear

A sure thing; a lock; goal attainment is assured; prospects are brilliant. All over it; about to take care of with gusto. From the tendency of thongs and other tight-fitting swimwear to become wedged where the sun never shines. "In there like swimwear" is "in like Flynn" for a new millennium. Can you name a single Errol Flynn movie? But everyone knows (and loves) Sisqo's "Thong Song."

Make friends with her friends and you'll be in there like swimwear.

indie

Short for "independent." Commonly associated with bands who are not signed to a major label, but can also refer to indie movies.

Music by The Streets is an example of indie music. In America *is a good indie movie.*

indie rock

A genre of music and the cult following of a younger generation that strives to be different from pop music followers. Indie rock is often "underground," not known to popular audiences because of independent record labels. The musical style combines British punk, rock and roll, and heavy metal.

Thank God most people haven't discovered indie rock. When they do, it will be ruined.

inf

Totally. Extremely. Short for "infinitely."

That attempt at humor was inf lame, Joey.

ink

Tattoos.

Okay, let me see your ink.

innit

Contraction of "isn't it," "isn't he/she," "aren't they," and "isn't there."

Hey dere's some pigs in dat cop car over there, innit?
Yo, look at my new car, innit!
Raj: The Matrix *is to'ally cool!*
Nisha: Innit!

interceptor

An interceptor is a person who tries (and sometimes succeeds) to steal a girl (or guy) from up under you while you're trying to run game. They'll come in trying to talk for themselves while you're trying to handle your business, or they may try to do it when you turn your back.

I was trying to holla at Jennifer, but Craig, ol' punk ass, was trying to intercept me. And he's supposed to be my boy!

Internet

A vast array of pornography and advertisements.

I took the initiative in creating the Internet.

Internet anytime minutes

What office workers use when they are being the "most productive" at their jobs.

T-roy looked at the clock and said, "Well, boys, I have two hours left to do absolutely nothing! The Web don't surf itself! It's time to use up some of my Internet anytime minutes to look busy!"

Inter-robbed

Alleged losses from people downloading or sharing product over the Internet.

Metallica was Inter-robbed by Napster users.

Interweb

A sarcastic term for the Internet. Often used in the context of parody regarding an inexperienced, unskilled, or incoherent user.

Hey, guys, I'm using the Interweb!

intoximicated

That point in the evening when your alchohol consumption has reached the level where you are ambitiously telling a story but can't seem to get the words exactly right. This is a happy state of drunkenness, not to be confused with the ugly states of "shitfaced" or "blackout."

I was so intoximicated I told him about this great "trap I took to the Crammed Cannedyon."

Irish breakfast

A pint of the black stuff, to start the day right.

Seamus: I can't think straight before I've had my Irish breakfast.
Kieran: You can't think straight after it!

IRL

Abbreviation for "in real life." Often used in Internet chat rooms.

Reese Witherspoon does not live in Alabama IRL.

ish

Term often used to replace "shit." Derived from the process of editing the vocals of rap-songs by reversing the curse words so said song can be played on radio or television.

That's some dope ish.

itch

Cloth seats in a car. Used in the song "Get Your Roll On" by Big Tymers.

Jimmy is cheap. He refused to spend an extra $50 to outfit his new Ferrari with leather seats. He got itch and we're always scratching.

it's all good

Despite any possible doubt, everything's cool.

Oh, you slept with my girl? It's all good, homey!

it's all gravy

It's all right; it's all good; everything is cool.

Gangsta 1: Damn, you spilled yo' 40 on yo' Timbs!
Gangsta 2: It's all gravy! Chill, son!

it's all love

Everything's fine and understood. It's all good.

No, I understand now. It's all love, girl!

it's my birthday

An expression of delight, accompanied by dancing around. Basically saying that the person in question is great, skilled, lucky, etc. Usually said in a kind of singsong way.

Ooooh, yeah! I just won that race! It's my birthday! It's my birthday!

it's not you, it's me

It's you. Oh yes, it's very definitely you.

Guy: What have I done? Why are you leaving me?
Girl: It's not you, it's me.

on

What you say when the battle/showdown is about to begin, or when you want to fight someone.

It's on, mother trucker!

it's on the right

Road-rage expression yelled when someone is going slow and you want to go faster. Meant to inform them that the gas pedal is on the right, so that they may feel free to use it at any time. Use this expression only if you are quite certain that their gas pedal is actually on the right.

Yo, dump truck/cement mixer/old lady in the Buick—it's on the right!

-izz-

An infix used to sanitize foul words. You can say "shizzit" on the radio, but not "shit." It is inserted into any word immediately after a syllable–initial consonant (1), or in monosyllabic vowel–initial words, at the beginning of the word (2). This infix contributes no meaning to the word but is a part of a series of hip-hop word games, starting with -iz- and developing to include -izz and –izzle, which truncate the remaining part of the word.

I put throw ups on almost every train in the station that said "I'm the shizzit."

-izzle

A suffix used to replace the end of words to make them rhyme. Commonly used by rapper Snoop Dogg. Best when preceded by a consonant sound.

fo' shizzle/for sure
Neptizzle/Neptune
Valentizzle/Valentine

J

1. A jump shot in basketball.

Diggity damn! Julio is short and can't dribble for shit, but that fool sure can stroke the J.

2. A joint of marijuana.

Roll that J up, cuz.

jabroni
Loser. Dumbass.

Hey, you freakin' jabroni! What's the matter with you?

jack
To hijack or steal. Commonly refers to robbery, theft, misuse, seizure, possession.

Yo, I got up to go to the bathroom and some jerk jacked my seat.

Yesterday I jacked a pack of gum from the mall.

jack in
To gain entry; to connect, as to a computer network. To enter or connect by deceptive or unscrupulous means, especially with malicious intent.

He tried to jack in and take down their group from the inside after he heard what they were saying about him behind his back.

jack shit
Absolutely nothing. Can be shortened to just "jack."

Your wife: Hi, honey . . . my, you're home late. What did you do today?
You: Jack shit.

jack squat

1. Nothing, zero, zilch, nada, shit all, jack shit. Can be shortened to just "jack."

I came out of that deal with jack squat.

2. Possibly a short, fat man.

Here comes that jerk, Jack Squat.

jack with

To mess with.

The used-car salesman jacked with the ignorant teenager.

jackass

A stupid person who has no common sense.

People like Tony Blair who condemn us to war are total jackasses.

jacked

Well-muscled, iron-bound, pumped.

That weight lifter sure is jacked. Too bad he's on steroids.

jacked up

Messed up. Screwed up.

That's jacked up, man. I can't believe your girlfriend is cheating on you.

I got in a wreck last night. My car got totally jacked up.

jag

A jagoff. A jerk. Someone who is goofy, worthless, and weak.

Get that jag outta here! I won't have him messing up my night.

jagbag

A jerk. Variant of "jagoff" or "jag."

I was drivin' down the road when this jagbag cut me off.

jagoff

A jerk. Used by Joe Pesci in the film *Casino*.

That lazy jagoff just stole my toast from the breakfast table.

jailbait

1. An underage girl. Named for the punishment for statutory rape.

The rule with jailbait is that 16 will get you 20.

2. A juvenile delinquent or repeat offender, from their taste for getting into trouble, their constant trips to prison, and the fate of the silly bastards when they get there.

Jake got sent up for dealing crack to schoolkids again? Man, that dumbass jailbait thrustbucket must like prison food and free orange jumpsuits.

jakes

Cops, narcs, FBI, or other authorities who can arrest suspects.

Yo, keep an eye out for the jakes 'fore you have to do time.

jammered

So intoxicated that you pull out your tie through your zipper and piss in your pants.

Tryce got so jammered at Blake's that he hooked up with a mailbox.

jammin'

Very busy, with lots of people around.

On opening day, the theater was jammin'.

janky

Of inferior quality; held in low social regard; old and dilapidated; refers almost exclusively to inanimate material objects, not to people.

We tried to pick up on these girls waiting for the bus, but I was driving my sister's janky 1989 Geo Metro, so we just got clowned instead.

Japanimation

Japanese animated cartoons made in the 1980s or earlier. Usually television series made on small budgets result-ing in Bullwinkle-style art and as much story as possible crammed into a half-hour. Generally replaced with the word "animé" since the 1990s.

Kyojin no Hoshi is a well-known Japanimation title in Japan.

jawn

Thing. Item. Object.

Yo, hand me that jawn right there.

jawsome

Awesome; used by the Street Sharks on their cartoon show and action figures.

I did jawsome on that test.

Jeebus

A less offensive version of "Jesus," often used in place of saying the Lamb of God's name in vain. Used by Homer Simpson on the TV show *The Simpsons.*

Help! Save me, Jeebus!

jeet jet?

In Pittsburghese, a smashed-up version of "Did you eat yet?"
Joe: Jeet jet?
Tourist: What? Say that slower.

jet
To leave a place quickly.

Let's jet before we miss the train.

jib
To maneuver a bicycle, skateboard, snowboard, or skis in a tricky manner on top of and around a structure such as a stump, rocks, stairs, railings, rooftops, etc. To play around, show off, jump, flip, and hop.

Let's go jib on the steps at the library.

jibber-jabber
Incoherent or unintelligible speech; has its origins from the word "gibberish"; to speak incoherently.

I don't understand quantum mechanics. It all sounds like jibber-jabber to me.

jiggy
1. Preceded by "get": to have sex or mess around with someone.

I got jiggy with her last night.

2. As an interjection: "sweet!" or "tiiiiiight!"

Gator boots with a pimped-out Gucci suit—jiggy!

3. Aight. All is well.

You aight? Everything jiggy over here?

jive
1. To irritate or annoy someone.

Quit jivin' me! Go find someone else to bug.

2. Pointless or deceptive talk or rhetoric.

Don't give me that jive. I'm smarter than that.

j/k
Just kidding.

I was j/k when I said you look like a whale in your hotornot.com photo.

jo' mama
Your mom. Yo' mama.

Yo, deez, tell jo' mama to move her fat ass so there's room for my bike in your three-car garage.

jock
1. To engage in flirtatious behavior with another; to crush on someone; to hit on someone.

Brandon, constantly laughing, smiling, lightly touching, and generally talking up a storm, was jocking Amanda.

2. To attempt to imitate someone's

style, especially in music. Derived from the term "being on someone's jock" (as in jock strap).

I see you wearing all that blue FUBU. Don't jock my style, get your own!

joint

1. When preceded by "the": jail.

Is your honey doing time in the joint right now?

2. A rolled marijuana cigarette.

Pass that joint over here. I'll take a hit.

3. A place. Can be anyplace—doesn't have to be jail or a crack house.

Delonte: Ayyo, let's hit up dat science museum tomorrow.
James: Hell, yeah, dawg, that joint is off da heezy fo' sheezy.
Delonte: Yeah, that joint sho' is better than the joint.

jone

To make fun of somebody or something.

I know you ain't tryna jone!

jones

A state in which one experiences strong desire or attraction. Same as "fancy," "crush on," "want." Can be

used as a verb (jonesing) or a noun (a jones).

She's been jonesin' him for months.

He's got a major jones for her.

josh

To joke.

Man, chill! I was just joshin' wif ya.

jota

A marijuana joint.

That's why you take a jota to a hotel, because it's illegal and the cops will see you elsewhere.

jugs

Breasts.

Look at those jugs.

juice

1. Respect and credibility on the street. Also called "sauce."

I can't be seen with them—they don't have juice.

2. Steroids.

I shot up with some juice today.

3. The percent a bookie takes from one's winnings.

My bookie takes 5 percent juice.

4. An intrinsically rewarding aspect of something or of life in general.

There's no juice left for me in getting stoned anymore.

jump

Dangerously good, ill, hot, bangin', off the chain, etc.

Dag, yo, Emmaleigh is one jump playa, fo' real.

jump off

1. A casual sexual partner or girlfriend.

Cassandra is Tye's main jump off.

2. Anything new or hot, especially a party or a material item.

I saw Kill Bill *last night, and, damn, it was the jump off!*

jump on it

To do something immediately.

That class is almost full. Jump on it!

jump the couch

A defining moment when you know someone has gone off the deep end. Inspired by Tom Cruise's behavior on *The Oprah Winfrey Show* when he announced his love for Katie Holmes.

My new boyfriend Benny seemed totally normal until he jumped the couch and started rubbing spicy brown mustard on his body at my family reunion.

jump the gun

To do something prematurely.

I think I jumped the gun on calling her "bitch." She won't talk to me anymore. I guess it was too early.

jump the shark

The beginning of the end; the turning point when things go downhill. Often used in reference to TV shows because it comes from a *Happy Days* episode in which Fonzie overcomes his fear of sharks by jumping over a tank of sharks on a motorcycle. That was the clear turning point in the series.

My girlfriend and I jumped the shark a month ago when we got into an argument over painting the living room yellow.

junk in the trunk

A big butt; a little more than "badonkadonk" but less extreme than "having an SUV in the pants."

I don't mind a woman with a little meat on her bones, a little junk in her trunk.

K

1. A short version of "okay" (used mostly online).

Let's go to the park, K?

2. Slang name for an AK-47.

Pull that K out, homey.

keep it real

To not be fake. Be yourself.

I'm keeping it real.

keep on the down low

To keep quiet about something. To not divulge information to people who should not know it. Also "keep on the hush."

Keep this shit on the down low for now.

keg

A small barrel containing up to 30 gallons of alcohol.

Man, that keg we downed last night was a bitch!

kegerator

A refrigerator modified to contain a keg and to dispense beer. A quality home improvement for the weekend warrior.

I have a kegerator in the garage.

kegstand

A common party activity in which two people hold the drinker's feet while the person's hands hold on to the keg. A fourth person holds the tap in the drinker's mouth until they give the signal to stop, and everyone else counts. The object of this activity is to chug beer from the keg upside down for as long as possible.

Colin Powell: Mr. President, I strongly suggest you look at these files reporting a possible imminent terrorist threat on American soil.
W: Uh, just a second, I'm in the middle of some important business. All right, Dick, get my left foot . . . Laura, get my right foot, and Jenna, you get the tap. I'm gonna suck this baby dry! Woowee!
Janet Reno (opens the door) (in a low, bellowing voice): Did somebody say "kegstands"? Let me at it!

keister
Your butt. What you need to get up off of.

Get off your damn keister and get in the game!

key
Just perfect. Describes something that would make you a whole lot happier.

A Big Mac would be key right now.

key up
Expression of affirmation or agreement.

Chase: Yo, Mikey, you gonna go smoke?
Mike: Key up.

kick it
1. To get your game on. To try to get with a person.

I was trying to kick it with that girl.

2. To chill, hang out.

Let's kick it sometime.

kick it up a notch
To make things more intense, exciting, or interesting. Trademark phrase of chef Emeril Lagasse.

Guest: Dude, this party sucks!
Host: Let's kick it up a notch! (brings out strippers and beer)

kick off
To start a fight.

When I called them wankers they kicked off.

kick rocks
Rude expression used to tell someone to leave. Derived from the lonely gesture of kicking rocks when one is bored or depressed.

You said what?! Kick rocks before I stomp yo' punk ass!

kick to the curb
To break up with someone in a negative manner.

After she cheated on Mike, she got kicked to the curb.

kickin'
Offensively pungent; emitting smelly and disgusting odor.

Take a breath mint; your breath is kickin'.

kickin' rad
Cool. Very good. Favorable. More than "radical."

That wife beater is kickin' rad!

kicks
Sneakers. Running shoes.

Fo' sheezy, mah neezy! You gots some fly-ass kicks!

kiff
Cool.

Dude, that wave was kiff! Check out my kiff board.

kill
1. To finish something, usually food or drink.

Hey, can I kill that sandwich?

2. Marijuana that is very physically dense and extremely potent.

Even a 10 sack of that kill is enough to pass around and get you faded.

kill clouds
To shoot your gun in the air.

Fake gangsters don't shoot straight to take body shots, they point it up in the sky and kill clouds.

kill it
1. To do something very well.

John was killin' it all day long in the competition.

2. To do your own thing, in a sort of funny or offbeat way.

Max is killin' it in his overalls.

killer
Very cool.

That laser light show was killer!

killographic
Containing graphic violent content. Term coined by the National Institute on Media and the Family to describe media, specifically video games, that make use of "graphic depiction of brutal violence."

The National Institute on Media and the

Family says the game Manhunt is
killographic.

kinky

Weird or cool, usually with respect
to sexual preferences.

Jared: We had kinky sex on the patio last
night!
Ryan: Really? What's a patio?

kip

1. A bed.

After working that double shift, we were
all ready for the kip.

2. To sleep. Sometimes followed by
"down," as in "bed down." Used in
Beautiful South's song "From
Under the Covers."

You take the bed, and I'll kip down on
the sofa.

kipe/kype

To steal, pilfer, or swipe something of
small value, like a candy bar or some
other commonly shoplifted item.

Jesse kiped some Pabst from the store
while we distracted the clerk.

kiss my grits

A saying that means something like
"kiss my ass."

Amanda: You're a dork.
Jason: Kiss my grits.

KIT

Acronym for "keep in touch."

It's been great getting to know you better
this year! Stay cool! KIT!

kite

Correspondence received while
incarcerated.

My cuz sent me a kite . . . told me to hold
it down while I'm doin' my bid.

knife around

To not do anything of particular
significance. Can range from
running miscellaneous errands
around town, to doing household
chores, to freestyle loafing.

Jess: Hey, what are you up to?
Ben: Oh, just knifin' around.

knob

A complete moron. Synonym for
"tool."

Dude, you're such a friggin' knob!

knock off

1. An item that looks exactly like an
original product but lacks the

expensive designer label, which is replaced with a fake one. Usually costs half the price with half the style appeal.

I hate those Coach knock-off purses with the little "Gs" on them instead of little "Cs."

2. To end the day's work; to clock out.
3. To steal.

I knocked off work, mate, and seen some bastard knocked off me car stereo.

knock over
To hold up or rob.

In New Orleans, every week someone tries to knock over a Popeye's Chicken store.

knock up
1. In North America: to get pregnant.

Amanda got knocked up because she and Jimmy didn't use protection.

2. In Great Britain: to wake someone up.

Billy, go and knock up your sleepyhead brother.

knockin' over tables
To hit on women while intoxicated.

Sometimes, when drunkenly talking to a woman and resting your arm on her table, the table will get knocked over.

Greg went to talk to that chick. Look at him over there, knockin' over tables.

knuck if you buck
A phrase used to express the intent of violence, literally translated as "knuckle up if you're buck wild." As popularized by Crime Mob in the song "Knuck if You Buck."

Rowdy clubgoer #1: You just stepped on my Timbs!
Rowdy clubgoer #2: Well, whatcha gonna do 'bout it?! Knuck if you buck!

knuckle up
Expression of encouragement meaning "muster your courage, intestinal fortitude, and love for the American way in preparation for a challenge of epic proportions!" Uttered many times during battle against the electromechanical foe by one of the dudes in the movie *The Matrix: Revolutions*.

Here they come, boys . . . knuckle up!

knucklehead
A dunce. A dummy. A very stubborn person or animal.

I told him how to do it, but he would not listen, the knucklehead!

Kodak's Law

When you most need a camera, you will inevitably not have one.

When the aliens finally arrive, you can be sure that Kodak's Law will keep you from being able to prove it happened.

kook

Someone posing very hard as a surfer or skateboarder. Someone who goes to every surfing or skateboarding event to hang out, compile pictures, start conversations, and generally be seen with real surfers or skateboarders.

Dude, did you see that kook trying to drop in on me the other day?

kthxbye

Okay, thanks, and bye. Quick, informal expression of politeness after one has done something for another.

Nerd: I just uploaded that paper you asked me to write. It took me about four days. I hope you'll like it.
Lindsey: kthxbye.

uRbaN

La La Land
Los Angeles.

La La Land is no place to be at night.

lab
1. Studio for recording music.

Dawg, them're some great lyrics. Let's take 'em back to the lab.

2. One's home base, like a household.

Let's take it to the lab so I can meditate.

label whore
Someone who only wears brand-name clothes, with the name of the brand usually placed somewhere for all to see. A walking advertisement for a clothing store or brand.

Look at that spaz wearing all Abercrombie—what a label whore.

lace the track
To add lyrics to an instrumental track.

The way Boomer laced the track, you'd think he was straight from Compton.

laced
1. One drug mixed into another, often without the consumer's knowledge.

Man, that weed I smoked last night was laced with cocaine.

2. Something nice or done-up right. Someone who is very put together, has their game on tight, looks good, wears nice clothes and jewelry, has a nice car, money, fancy bling bling, etc.

My college professor asked us, "Why do people always want to make more money in their jobs?" My answer to his question: "To stay laced, dumbass!" What an idiot!

laced up

1. Ready for a fight.

You best get laced up, sucka!

2. Beat or knocked out in a fight.

He got laced up on Broadway by some fool he didn't even know.

laid-back

Easygoing. Going with the flow. Gets along with most people and usually causes no problems. Fine with whatever.

My professor is so laid-back that no matter how badly I bomb the test I'll still pass the class.

lame-o

A person who acts incredibly stupid.

Just come with us. Don't be a lame-o!

lampin'

Chillin'. Marinatin'. Short for "cold lampin'."

I'm just lampin', takin' it easy.

land clam

A mass of phlegm expelled from the esophagus onto a surface such as asphalt or concrete. It is the only nonshelled mollusk known to man.

While hacking outside Lincoln Center, Charles fathered a land clam on 65th Street.

land yacht

A very large luxury car.

My Lincoln Town Car is not a boat, it's a land yacht!

large time

1. A lot of fun.

We met Airman Smith at the squadron banquet, and a large time was had by all.

2. Very big event of much size.

The concert next Saturday is going to be a large time.

last month

A fad that's no longer cool or interesting. As the Internet makes life faster, fads don't last as long as they did before. Fad seasons are trending closer to one month.

Trucker hats are so last month.

urban

late

To proclaim that one is vacating the premises. Short for "later," as in "see you later." Also "lates."

I'll see you at the club. Late, man.

lava lamp

A person who is very attractive but very unintelligent. Named after the novelty light fixture that is fun to look at but not that bright.

You're actually considering going out with Alicia? She may be pretty and all, but she's a total lava lamp.

lawn job

Deep ruts left across someone's lawn by a car backing up into the yard and then peeling out; to leave such ruts.

Check out all this grass that's under my fender from lawn-jobbing that guy's yard last night.

lax

A total lack of stress. Short for "relax."

Ahh . . . this is lax . . .

lay rap

To hit on, flirt, or throw out pickup lines to a member of the opposite sex.

That girl was so hot, everyone was trying to lay rap on her.

layup

An easy score, in a sexual sense.

He saw Betty across the room and he knew it was going to be a layup.

league skimmer

A person who goes out with people who are way out of their league.

Look at Harry going out with Jen. He's a league skimmer.

lean back

A type of dance you do in which you shrug your shoulders to the beat of the song and progressively lean back. Popularized by Terror Squad's song "Lean Back."

Oooh, I love this song featuring Fat Joe! Let me get my dance on while I lean back.

leet

Elite. Often used to describe someone with good computer skills.

Dude, I just hacked microsoft.com. I'm leet.

left coast

A slightly derogatory word for

America's west coast, used by Republicans to refer to the primarily Democratic California, Oregon, and Washington.

Arnie must feel very alone on the left coast.

less than three

Love. Refers to the common text-icon "<3," which looks like a heart when rotated counterclock-wise.

Goodbye, my less than three.

let's be friends

In a dating relationship, this is where one of the parties involved means one or more of the following:
"I don't want to date you anymore."
"I am interested in dating someone else."
"I am already dating someone else, and I need to lose your sorry ass."

I really like you and all that crap, but let's be friends.

let's blow this Popsicle stand

A pretty lame way to say "Let's get out of here."

This place is bernie. Let's blow this Popsicle stand!

let's go there

I'm more than willing to engage you on this topic.

Although I'm a little uncomfortable with this subject, hell, let's go there!

level 4

California prison code for the most serious criminal offenses. Maximum security: cells, fenced or walled perimeters, electronic security, armed officers inside and out. Used by rappers Snoop Dogg and 50 Cent, among others.

I'm level 4, so I walk the yard with lifers.

level up

To achieve a higher level of consciousness, usually through drugs or alcohol. To reach the first heavy daze of the day.

Before going downtown to hit the bars, we leveled up with some shots.

lid

1. One ounce of marijuana.

I knew she could smoke a quarter in an hour but not a lid!

2. A man's toupee or really bad haircut.

Nice lid, buddy. That hairpiece doesn't quite work.

lifer

One who has remained at a location for an extended amount of time so as to be considered a permanent resident. Often has no hope or desire to leave their current environment.

Dennis has been a helper for five years. He is definitely a lifer.

lift

1. To take that which is not yours. Gank, steal, boost, heist.

If you leave your doors unlocked, yo' shit's gon' get lifted.

2. To fit a vehicle with hydraulics. Also "juiced."

That fool just got his Caprice lifted.

lifted

High; under the influence.

School's out! C'mon, let's go get lifted!

light up

To smoke.

Fifteen-minute break, man. Time to light up.

lightweight

1. So-so, kind of, a little bit.

That party was lightweight tight.

2. One who can't handle their alcohol/weed.

Look at that lightweight, puking after two cups!

like

1. Means "said" or "spoke" when preceded by "am," "are," "is," "was," "were."

I'm like, "Gag me with a spoon," and she's like, "Oh my God!"

2. For some teenagers, a word spoken in between each word in a sentence.

Yeah, like, I think, like, 'N Sync is, like, sooooooo, like, cool and, like, dreamy.

like it ain't no thing

Something done easily.

I date three guys at once like it ain't no thing.

like it was my job

Engaging in an activity repeatedly and/or skillfully enough that it's as if you were getting paid to do so. Particularly applies to nonwork-related activities.

I drink like it was my job. Not to mention on the job.

like like

More than liking as a friend, and a step above a crush, and a step below love.

I do not like like David, I just like him.

like whoa

To the extreme.

I'm studying like whoa for this midterm tomorrow.

link up

To call someone.

Yo, link me up tonight.

linkophile

A person having an ardent interest in and enthusiasm for Internet sites, or "links."

Brad adds so many URLs to his blog, he's a total linkophile.

lip service

To just say something but not actually do it. To pretend that you believe a certain thing but not practice that belief.

The company pays lip service to equal rights but has only one woman working for them, and she's underpaid.

liquid

Money, cash flow, scrilla.

Yo, dawg, my liquid fit'na be flowin' like wata right now.

liquid bread

Could refer to any beer, but particularly apt for heavy, full-bodied beers like Guinness, which can be very filling.

I don't need lunch; I just had some liquid bread.

liquid courage

Any alcoholic beverage that turns a person mean, brave, or excited. An instant burst of courage (and often stupidity) comes from drinking it.

Before I stomp this dude's ass, I'ma need some liquid courage.

lit

So intoxicated that all a person can do is smile, so they look lit up like a light.

He's so lit he can't even talk.

literary masturbation

The act of using unnecessarily elaborate speech to convey a simple point, or speaking in a tone that would make you seem like a pompous dipshit.

I recently attended the queue at the food product facility, at which I purchased a deliciously decadent three-cheese lasagna and a bottle of Spumante.

live

Jumping, full of people, exciting. A happening event that is very enjoyable and has an intense vibe.

Yo, Angel's was live last Tuesday.

live in

To live in a fraternity or sorority house.

I love living in. Having all the girls around all the time is great for my gossip quotient.

llello

Spanish for "cocaine." Often spelled "yayo" because of the pronunciation.

I gotta go get some llello for tonight.

Man, we all got so llelled up last night!

llelled

The state of being high on cocaine.

Last night I got so llelled up, I felt like a god!

lmao

Acronym for "laughing my ass off." Used online.

Matt: Bill fell off the horse and injured his pelvis in six different places.
Joe: lmao!

loafing

To laze around and not have a care in the world.

Loafing does the body good.

loan shark

Term for a person, usually a member of organized crime, who offers loans without background checks, collateral, etc., but charges insanely high interest and has henchmen who will hurt or even kill those who do not repay the loan within a set time.

John got beat to shit by Loan Shark Tino's henchmen for not paying on time. If John doesn't pay Tino back by next week, they will kill him.

loc

1. Crazy. Short for the Spanish "loco."

Man, you know Mike-T is a loc-ass mutha. He shot, like, six cops in front of the police station.

2. Lock or locks of hair, like Jheri-curls, but always pronounced with the long "o" as in "go."

Check out the locs on that playa.

L

3. High on drugs.

Let's get loc'ed out on the balcony.

lockdown

1. Grounded. Can also be shortened to "lock."

I can't come out, I'm on lock(down).

2. A controlling relationship.

Yo, check it! Sista got Tyrese on mad lockdown again this weekend. Brotha won't be able to hang.

lol

Computer slang for "laughing out loud."

Jackie: Omigod! He is just so cute I want to take a bite out of him.
Brittany: lol!

loogie

A large slimy glob of spit mixed with nose snot. Cooks in restaurants are notorious for making secret loogie deposits on patrons' food.

I'll take a cheeseburger with french fries, hold the loogie.

look advantage

To stare at something you should naturally look quickly away from.

Comes from the saying "took advantage."

Girl 1: I was getting changed and was completely nude when some guy walked in on me.
Girl 2: Did he look advantage of you?
Girl 1: Yes, he stared at me, didn't say anything the whole time and wouldn't stop even after I covered up!

loopy

A state of goofiness usually occurring after a long night of partying or any other activity that provokes sleep deprivation.

I'm so loopy I just can't stop laughing!

loose rap

Telling lies or using corny pickup lines to impress a girl or guy to get their number, get them to fall for you, or get sex.

Charlie: Yo, what's up, shorrrrty, where your boyfriend at? I saw you across the room and, um . . . I was wondering if I could get your digits, cuz you look good. You know, I got a 2006 Cadillac fresh on 20-inch rims, I get mad dough, and I'll shower you with all the diamonds you want.
Ellen: Drop the loose rap, big boy! You had me at hello!

loosey
Single cigarette.

I smoked a loosey.

lop
1. Poorly executed; sloppy. Frequently used with job, as in "lop job."

Look at what a lop job that web developer did on his webpage.

2. A person who does a job carelessly; a stupid or lazy person; a person whose time and energy are misdirected.

That new intern's report was so full of errors I had him write it again, that lop.

low rider
A (usually customized) truck or utility with lowered springs from hydraulic pumps to give it a real pimpin' look.

That low rider is off da' hook and slammed to tha ground!

low talker
One whose volume of conversation is so low that you can barely hear them.

I think I'm engaged to a low talker, but I can't tell because when I proposed she just giggled and mumbled to herself.

lowdown
The truth. The skinny, or full disclosure of the situation.

Yo, slim, gimme the lowdown on the pig situation on my turf.

low-fi
Chilled out, relaxed, quiet, lazy, mellow.

Judging by how drunk I am now, tomorrow will be pretty low-fi.

low-key
Hidden, or on the downlow, so no one knows.

I was chillin' wit' the crew and shorty was lookin' good, but I already gotta shorty, so let's just make it low-key.

low-pro po
Short for "low-profile police." Undercover officers.

Those low-pro po's swear we can't spot them in Crown Vics with no plates and searchlights.

LSD
The most potent hallucinogen known to the public. In a chaotic environment such as a party, it can lead to a "bad trip," where the person under the influence gets

frightened and depressed. Also known as "acid."

Wow, that was some potent LSD. I was trippin' for two days.

lunch money

Describing the period of adolescence when kids get beaten up by bullies for their lunch money. Used to describe anything done poorly or not worth your time.

Dude, that was a lunch money party last night.

lurk

1. On an online message board, to browse the board often but never post anything.

That guy is always lurking, but he never posts.

2. To listen in on a conference call without announcing oneself.

Ron got mad at Don for lurking on the production call.

lylab

Acronym for "love you like a bro." Only to be used in a nonqueer fashion.

Aiyo, holmes, I'm out. lylab.

lylas

Acronym for "love you like a sister." Way to tag anything said to a close female friend so that one can say "I love you" without fear of being thought gay.

I have to go, but I'll see you at practice on Saturday. lylas!

urban

ma
Girl. Shorty.

Whaddup, ma? Can I get yo' number?

mack daddy
A pimpalicous man who gets anything he wants (e.g., sex, money, clothing, cars, etc.).

Dawg! Did you see that pimpalicous mack daddy? He's da man!

mack on
To flirt with or attempt to seduce someone.

I caught David macking on my wife.

mad
Extremely, very, a large quantity. Also "madd."

Yo, his car has pumpin' mad bass.

mad axes
Good hip-hop emceeing skills.

Yo, did you see that cat? He was throwing mad axes, son!

mad skills
Good skills. Usually used when people do something cool in a sport or a video game.

I've got mad skills, biotch!

mad-dog
To stare fixedly at someone in a hostile manner.

That guy was mad-dogging me after I got his girlfriend's number.

main

A person's number-one girl or guy, as opposed to the other partners they may have.

Yeah, man, I can't let my main find out about her because it's going to be a lot of trouble if she does!

maintain

To keep your composure even in the most adverse and drunken circumstance.

Dude, I need to maintain or I won't make it to the next bar.

makeout sess

A session where people (usually teens) make out.

Mallory and I had a makeout sess after band today.

mallcore

A modern form of music—influenced by but wholly separate from heavy metal—that incorporates rap, funk, simplified song structures, and subject matter geared toward the teens and youth of America, who spend far too much time at malls. Topics often include alienation, parental abuse, and "the pain inside." Early examples include Anthrax's "I'm the Man" as well as Faith No More's "Epic." Spinoffs like Korn soon began to take over the market with detuned and substandard products. As the style of music gained popularity, many bands, formerly true to heavy metal, began to lean toward mallcore. These bands, such as Metallica, In Flames, and others, made their sound more accessible by simplifying their work and adding aspects of electronica, whispered vocals, and simple chugging riffs, and by taking focus off of lead guitars.

The new In Flames album will definitely be mallcore.

malt

Short for "malt liquor," a cheap, sweet, slightly strong beer. Often found in 40-ounce bottles.

Let's go get some malt and chill.

malware

Short for "malicious software." A cousin of adware and spyware that usually downloads and installs itself on your PC without your permission. It often takes the form of programs called "porn dialers" that dial expensive or long distance numbers.

Stupid malware!

mami

Spanish slang for "baby" or "sexy."
Often short for "mamacita" or
"mamita."

*Ay, mami, tu tan caliente. (Oh, girl, you
so sexy.)*

mamma jamma

Person or thing that is considered
by many to be very sexy and/or
boss.

You peepin' at that hot mamma jamma?

Man, the

An unseen political force that
watches and oppresses everyday
people. Synonymous with "Big
Brother," as referenced in George
Orwell's novel *1984*.

It's just the Man trying to hold me down!

man crush

When a man has a crush on another
man without sexual attraction.
A form of hero worship, or the
desire to either be or emulate the
other man.

*Josh: Hey, Ted. I heard you spent the
night over at Dave's.
Ted: Yeah, we played Twister and
Scrabble, watched movies, and spent all
night talking, bizzatch.*

*Josh: Dude, you're 35, acting like you're
12, and you're using his language. You've
got a man crush.*

man purse

An over-the-shoulder bag used by
urban males. A common accessory
found on metrosexuals.

*Tad carries his papers to work in his
man purse.*

man boobs

Extra fat on a man's pecs that looks
like breasts. Contrary to popular
belief, not all man boobs are caused
by fat. Some men are naturally born
with higher amounts of estrogen
than others and once they hit puberty
start growing actual breast tissue.

*My friend Mark has amazing man boobs,
but he's not fat.*

man up

1. Brave it. Be daring.

*Jake: Hey, man, finish this bowl.
Ben: No, dude, I'm baked as it is.
Jake: Come on, man up.*

2. In basketball: get your man.

*Your guy is a shooter and he's wide open at
the three-point line. This is when you man
up—play tight defense.*

M

manky
Unclean.

You just did a crap and didn't wash your hands—ew, you're manky!

manscape
To remove excess body hair on a man via waxing, shaving, plucking, or other method. Common metrosexual activity.

When he took off his shirt, it looked like he was still wearing a sweater. I think a little manscaping is in order.

manual
To ride a bike with the front wheel off the ground. This term is also used in other sports with similar meaning.

That guy has mad skills; he can manual down the streets of San Francisco at 50 mph!

marinate
To sit on the couch and not accomplish anything. To loaf.

I was gonna go to class but I got high and decided to marinate instead.

mark-ass bitch
The worst type of bitch, one who is a "mark," which means that he/she is a target and is very vulnerable to attack from others, like a sitting duck. Calling someone this implies that you intend to murder them or do them harm in some way, or that you suspect someone else will, and that they deserve what's coming to them. Used in Tupac's song "Hit 'Em Up" to refer to Biggie Smalls and Junior Mafia.

Whoever keyed my car is one mark-ass bitch!

mash
1. To engage in sexual foreplay or heavy petting.

After you left the party, I ended up mashing with that chick from my chemistry class.

2. To travel at excessive speeds in a motor vehicle and/or use a lifted vehicle or four-wheel drive to traverse over obstacles.

Man, last night I was out in the car mashin' like no other.

mash note
A love letter, particularly a hot and steamy one.

He felt waves of jealousy when he discovered the mash notes to his wife from an old flame written 20 years ago, before they were married.

mashed

Seriously drunk or high on drugs.

I'm mashed off my face.

master of one's domain

The ability to go long periods of time without sexual self-gratification.

He is master of his domain; he can go for months at a time.

mate

1. A friend or companion.

This is my mate Eddie.

2. A sexual partner.

This is my mate Eddie.

max out

To take something to the extreme, sometimes causing overload or failure due to reaching the highest possible limit.

We smoked this blunt last night, and I maxed the hell out on Doritos, man.

Sir, I can't do P.E. today 'cause I've maxed out my ankle.

maxin' and relaxin'

Hanging out.

Guy 1: What up, homey?

Guy 2: Not much. Just maxin' and relaxin'.

McDonald's symptoms

Various symptoms of McDonald's overload. Signs that your state of health is not good. Can include: McStomachAche, McHeadache, McHeartburn, McCirrhosis, McTwitch, McDepression.

mean

So hot, sexy, and tight it defies description and boggles the mind.

That Escalade is one badass ride. I love the rims—they make that shit look mean.

mean-mug

To give someone a not-so-nice look.

Dude, that broad at the register totally mean-mugged you for buying those girl pants.

meatspace

The real, flesh-and-blood world. As opposed to "cyberspace."

I met a great girl online, and I'm flying to Idaho to see her in meatspace.

meaty

Good.

Hey! That new song is meaty!

meh

An interjection used to imply indifference toward a subject; "a verbal shrug." Mysteriously popular among teens. Synonymous with "bleh," "dah," and "mih." Usually pronounced without eye contact or body movement.

Kyla: You wanna go to the mall?
Sam: Meh, I have nothing to do for the rest of the day . . .

mental intercourse

The act of engaging in intelligent and interesting conversation. Topics range from sex to nerdy subjects.

I enjoyed our mental intercourse today. Perhaps we can do it again tomorrow?

merc

Short for "mercenary," a professional soldier hired for service in a foreign army. Used by urban geeks to describe the culprit in a fantasy ambush. Also refers to anyone who serves or works merely for monetary gain; a mugger.

Last night when I was walking home Jonn dropped down out of a tree and tried to merc me with some shurikens like he's a friggin' ghetto ninja!

metal

A type of music characterized by its cacophonous wall of sound and accelerated tempo achieved through distorted electric guitars playing fast-paced riffs, with the driving drumbeat often utilizing hypersonic double bass rhythms and emphasizing the continuous pumping action. The bass guitar is often playing similar to the guitar, but more with the drums, so as to add to the overall heaviness and depth. It can manifest in many different forms, and the spectrum of intensity is usually quite varied, from slow and heavy melodic grooves to complex and precise blinding rhythms, odd time changes, and sheer brutality. Vocals often deal with dark subject matter, anger, and aggression in the form of screaming, though melodic, smooth vocals are also accepted. Solos are also an integral part of metal music. Usually scales and arpeggios are played with some changes often in eighth, 16th, or 32nd notes, if only a few quick licks. Metal is progressive and dynamic, and usually provokes feelings that are therapeutic to the listener. Metal is rock music that has evolved.

Dude, this Slayer is some kickass metal!

meth

An abbreviation for methamphetamine, a drug that stimulates the central nervous system by causing it to release more dopamine, a neurotransmitter that gives someone a feeling of satisfaction.

Meth is a dangerous drug and should not be used by anyone.

metric shitload

A metric shitload is roughly 2.287 American measurement shitloads.

I've got a metric shitload of stuff to get done this weekend.

metrosexual

Modern enlightened, sort of Renaissance man. Secure and confident, capable and cool, typically well educated and stylish. Heterosexual with a twist, not gay by any means, but he probably has a few gay friends and can easily be mistaken for gay by rednecks and jock types. The only straight guy in a fabric store or antique shop who is not being dragged there by a woman. Often shortened to "metro."

Dan manicures his nails, wears designer suits, owns a lot of shoes, and takes an hour to do his hair, but he's not gay—he's metrosexual.

military precision

Perfect aim. Very professionally and calmly done.

He picked apart his opponents' argument with military precision.

mimbo

Male version of a bimbo. Made famous by an episode of the sitcom Seinfeld.

My girlfriend left me for that mimbo who drives the ice cream truck.

mind bullets

The ability to cause damage to someone or something using just one's mind.

In that picture, she looks like she's trying to kill you with mind bullets.

mindshare

Corporate speak for the estimated value of a product, artwork, or service as determined by its presence— or lack thereof—in the minds of the product's target audience.

He's not investing much advertising and promotion money in his enterprise; since he is a popular writer and designer, his name alone has mindshare value, because people tend to flock to his websites and pay attention to his blogs and editorials.

M

mint

Nice. Cool.

Man, that shit is mint. Gimme some.

miss me

Lose my number; don't call me; leave me alone.

You've cheated on me; now miss me.

Miss Thang

A person who thinks they are, like, so totally better than, like, you know, everyone else.

My sister, little Miss Thang, is getting on my nerves. She's such a brat!

mix

1. When a DJ plays sound from two sources together, whether those sources are turntables or CD players using a mixer. Often DJs will adjust the tempo of the two sound sources so they are exactly the same and flow together well rhythmically.

I was mixing pretty well.

2. A DJ's set or spiel.

Maybe I'll throw that beat into my mix.

mob

To take more than your fair share of something.

Dave: Can I have some of your pizza?
Matt: Sure, but don't mob on it or anything.

mockumentary

A fictional film in the style of a documentary. A mock documentary.

The mockumentary This Is Spinal Tap documents the fictional band Spinal Tap.

mojo

A charm or a spell. Often refers to sex appeal or talent.

I can get any girl if I just use a bit of the old mojo.

mom battle

Similar to a freestyle battle, except where a select portion of a sentence is integrated with the phrase "your mom" and repeats back and forth between two "your mom-ers" until one runs out of variations before the other.

Scott: That movie was dumb.
Drew: Your mom is dumb.
Scott: You are juvenile and ugly.
Drew: Your mom is juvenile and ugly.

money

1. Cool, sweet, banging.

*Girlfriend, that diamond ring your boo
bought for you is so money!*

2. A friend or acquaintance.

What up, money?

moon on a stick
Everything. Expression of the wish
to have it all.

*Would you like anything else? The moon
on a stick perhaps?*

mos' def
Short for "most definitely."

*Andre: Want a cig, man?
Jimmy: Mos' def!*

mourning
A typical greeting among goths.
Equivalent to "morning" but the
preferred usage is during nighttime.

*Coma: Mourning!
Keops: Goth day!
Coma: I feel miserable.*

mournography
The oversensationalizing and
dramatizing of tragic events (such
as the deaths of politicians or
celebrities), often to a titillating
degree, especially when employed in
journalistic practice.

*After Reagan died, the ensuing
mournography was obscene.*

mouth-breather
Idiotic and useless human being.
Suggests they aren't very evolved
because they breathe through their
mouths. An affinity for sexually
crude humor generally accompanies.

*My boyfriend's such a mouth-breather that
he can't walk and chew gum at the same
time. But I love him anyway.*

moxie
Sass, courage, spunk, determination,
attitude.

That girl's got moxie. I like her.

mp3
A format (MPEG) used in digital
compression of music that makes
entertainment industry executives
shit a brick because it makes it easier
for people to get music without
paying for it by easily trading it on
the Internet.

*Check out my mp3 collection. I heard it
gave the president of EMI an aneurysm.*

mug
1. To stare, gaze, gawk, look
intensely.

Yo, that chick was straight muggin' you. Go talk to her.

2. To stare at someone in a menacing or threatening way.

That cat's mugging. I think he wants to fight.

3. An idiot.

That mug went and got caught mugging some jogger. At least he looks good in his mugshots.

mullet

Any haircut that is significantly longer in the back than the front or sides.

He decided that a mullet was too much work to take care of, so he got it cut short.

munchies

The desire to consume copious amounts of carbohydrates and fats after inhaling the byproduct of combusting the hemp plant.

I ate chocolate ice cream on a blueberry bagel. I must have had some hardcore munchies.

muppet

A person who is ignorant and generally has no idea about anything.

Don't talk to me like ya know me, ya muppet.

Murphy's Law

The law that says anything that can go wrong, will go wrong.

I just won the lotto, but I lost the lotto ticket. Murphy's Law, man.

muscle

1. To dance by stretching out your arm, then flexing your biceps with one arm, then flexing the other. Seen in the Usher "Yeah!" video and in many hip-hop clubs.

Look at that baller in the trucker hat. He's doin' the muscle!

2. Someone paid or in service to protect and/or do the physical hardships of another.

Joe's got a hired muscle outside his bar.

my bad

A flippant apology. A way of saying "I did something bad, and I recognize that I did something bad, but there is nothing that can be done for it now, and there is really no reason to apologize for that error, so let's just assume that I won't do it again, get over it, and move on with our lives." Can be shortened to "my b."

Erica: You just spilled your beer on my term paper!
Sarah: My bad. You know, you can print another one.

my boy

A close guy friend, or a guy you really like. A homey.

John Kerry was my boy. I can't believe G.W. is going to be president for four more years.

n00b/noob

A newbie. An inexperienced, ignorant, or unskilled person. Especially used in computer games. Also "newb."

Ha ha! That n00b got pwned.

naff

Not very good, but not bad enough to warrant a passionate dismissal.

The White Horse, mate, nah, it's naff— you wanna get yourself down to the King's Arms—full of totty on a Friday night.

nagware

Software released as freeware or shareware that nags the user into purchasing, supporting, or upgrading on a regular basis.

Try downloading HTML-to-XYZ!

It's nagware, but it works great!

nah mean?

Know what I mean?

That shorty is bangin', nah mean?

Nancy

Mocking term for a man engaging in feminine activities or otherwise compromising his masculinity.

Come on, Nancy, you've been getting ready for an hour. We're late for the game.

nappy

Unkempt or messy. Often refers to hair.

That rastaman has some nappy dreadlocks.

nar

Short for "gnarly."

Did you catch that nar episode of
Barney?

narc

1. Short for "narcotics officer." A
member of law enforcement who
enforces drug laws.

Don't pull your stash out around Jake.
I think he's an undercover narc.

2. A person who is not a member of
law enforcement but turns you in to
police for doing or dealing drugs.

Ronnie is such a narc. He told the cops I
was smoking pot in the bathroom.

3. A person who turns you in to any
type of authority figure (parents,
teachers, boss) for something you
did wrong.

My little brother the narc told Mom about
the pornos under my bed.

4. The act of turning someone in
to law enforcement or authority
figures.

Don't narc on me, man. I'll give you a
couple buds if you keep your mouth shut.

narsty

Combination of "gnarly" and
"nasty." Something nasty that's
actually kind of cool or strange.
Also spelled "gnarsty."

That gal over there with the 5 o'clock
shadow sure is narsty.

nasty

Extremely.

Oh, man, that test question was nasty
hard. But the party we had after the test
was nasty awesome.

near beer

Nonalcoholic beer.

Near beer is the worst of both worlds: all
the shitty taste of beer, and none of the fun!

near-birth experience

When birth control fails but no
pregnancy results.

When the condom broke last month I had
a near-birth experience.

neener

An interjection typically used to
taunt, ridicule, or boast.

No thanks to you, but I was able to score
the last tickets to the show tonight, and
you're not going with me, so neener!

neg

Abbreviation for "negative."

Girl 1: You going to the party?
Girl 2: Neg. I have to work.

nerd

A person who is intensely interested in a particular hobby or topic. A geek with self-confidence. One whose IQ exceeds his weight.

Rich is quite a computer nerd.

network

To meet important contacts and opportunities at bars, clubs, and big events.

I was out all night, networking at the party.

never have I ever

A game (that can involve drinking) in which people go around in a circle saying things they have never done. Everyone starts with all 10 fingers up and puts a finger down if they have done that thing, and the first person with no fingers remaining wins (or loses, depending how you look at it). If it's played as a drinking game, everyone who has done the thing the person says must drink.

By the end of never have I ever, the guys thought the girls were a bunch of freaks.

new money

Someone who is rich but does not come from a wealthy background. The opposite of Paris Hilton.

She was new money after discovering the value of her blender on Antiques Roadshow.

new school

Contemporary. Opposite of "old school."

Alicia Keys, Amerie, and Nivea are new school.

New York minute

Very fast. From the general belief that everything in New York moves faster than it does in the rest of the world.

I'll get this job done in a New York minute.

newsertainment

Mindless information about an entertainer or show that is portrayed as news.

Anchorman: In our top story, Cody was voted off the island this week in a stunning upset during last night's episode of Survivor.

next shit

Anything that is completely fresh and new, and kicks the status quo's ass.

His lyrics are brilliant, and the beats are some next shit entirely.

nice ups

A way of throwing props to someone, saying thank you, or showing respect. Similar to "big ups."

Hey, Greg, nice ups for hooking me up with that Ice Cube seven-inch. It bumps.

nick

Mainly British slang.
1. A police station, jail, or prison.

I spent last night in the cells at the nick.

If they convict me, I could do five years at Wandsworth nick.

2. To steal. To pinch, tax, half-inch, lift, knock off.

The band's clothes look like they were nicked from the local Oxfam's reject pile.

nickel-and-dime

1. To provide people with small bags of marijuana.
2. To be extremely cheap with someone or demand every last dollar.

Thurgood: What up? You gonna nickel-and-dime me today as usual?
Samson: Aight, dawg, $15.
Thurgood: Sheeit, all I got is this $14. I'll get you the $1 later.
Samson: No can do. I need it all up front.
Thurgood: Man, why you gotta go and nickel-and-dime me like that?

nine

Refers to any pistol whose barrel's girth is nine millimeters.

I was packing my nine for protection.

nine nine

Close to but not quite perfect. Refers to 99 percent.

I had a real nine nine day today at work.

ninja skills

Ability to do something without being detected or suspected. "Ninja" refers to stealth and not being seen; "skills" refers to being unusually good at it, or being a natural at something.

Stroup: Hey, who just slapped me?
Taylor: I got mad ninja skills!

nip slip

When a braless female's nipple accidentally slips out from under a loose-fitting garment.

Hold up, pause it there. Yup, total nip slip on Tara Reid!

nip tuck

Plastic surgery.

That has to be a nip tuck—those breasts were huge!

Nipplegate

The scandal during the 2004 Superbowl halftime show in which Janet Jackson "accidentally" exposed her entire right breast.

Nipplegate provoked a media frenzy.

nipply

Cold (which makes your nipples stiffen).

It's really nipply today.

nitro

1. Short for "nitrous oxide," a gaseous compound used in car engines to make more oxygen available during combustion, thus allowing the car to inject more fuel, which makes the engine faster and more powerful.

He punched his nitro too much and too early, and his engine exploded.

2. Really cool. A person, place, or thing that is unequivocally, quintessentially spectacular.

Dude, you may be platinum in Quake, but I am nitro at sniping in America's Army.

no, I won't make out with you

A phrase that one person says to another loudly and in public to attempt to embarrass that person. Usually sarcastic and sometimes said to a complete stranger who wants to ask something simple. Used in the movie *Billy Madison*.

Girl: Excuse me, do you have a pen I could borrow?
Guy: No, I won't make out with you!

no big

Short for "no big deal."

Katie: Oops, I'm so sorry I stepped on your toe!
Maria: Hey, no big.

no deals

No way; I do not accept the charges.

No deals on the curry. It smells like ass.

no dice

No luck. Plans fell through. Not going to happen.

No dice on tonight. Everyone has to work.

no diggity

No doubt; for sure.

Guy 1: That girl knows how to work it!
Guy 2: No diggity!

no doubt

Interjection of agreement.

Muffy: That was a refreshing and invigorating game of squash.
Buffy: No doubt.

no homo

Interjection used to show that you aren't gay after saying something that sounded gay.

Hey, man, pass the nuts. No homo.

I cornered him in my room and nailed him with a board. No homo.

no love

To "get no love" is to receive no respect, recognition, kudos, or empathy from a crowd or audience.

Shaquille O'Neal gets no love when he travels with the LA Lakers to Orlando.

no wukkas

Abbreviation of "no wuckin' furries," which is a less vulgar derivative of "no fuckin' worries."

Rob: Can't make it out tonight—no money!
Mick: Ah, no wukkas, mate—I'll lend you a score.

noogie

A painful sensation caused by the rubbing of knuckles, fist, or hand to one's head, generally causing hair displacement and mild cursing.

Oh man, National Noogie Week is coming up! I'd better run so Sarah doesn't catch me in the middle of her mad noogie spree. Otherwise mass destruction of my hair follicles and/or scalp will occur!

nookie

A term for any kind of sexual activity.

You're not getting any nookie tonight!

nopers

No. Opposite of "yeppers," or "yes."

Saleskid: Would you like to purchase the extended warranty plan?
Me: The answer would be nopers. Sounds like a ripoff to me.

nose candy

Cocaine used for snorting.

I had three lines of nose candy.

not bitch

Phrase used to reserve any seat in a vehicle except the "bitch seat" in the middle. The first person to call "not bitch" gets the passenger seat; people after that get distributed around the car.

Person 1: Hey, there's Aaron's car.
Person 2: Not bitch!

not even

Expression of disagreement.

He said he was from Wanganui and I was like "not even"!

not in my book

Not true, according to my morals, principles, and beliefs.

Cop: Oh man, what a hard day of busting drug dealers it's been. A big fat J would really hit the spot right now. Can I borrow some papers?
Your square ass: Isn't smoking marijuana . . . um . . . illegal?
Cop: Not in my book.

not so much

Polite or watered-down way of saying "no."

Boy: I love that movie. Don't you?
Girl: Not so much.

nowt

Nothing, zero.

Lend us some money, mate. I ain't been paid yet, so I've got nowt.

NSA

Acronym for "no strings attached."

In the classifieds: Young blonde athletic cutie seeks NSA fun with equally cute female.

NSFW

Acronym for "not safe for work." Used to describe Internet content generally inappropriate for the typical workplace. Opposite of SFW, "safe for work."

I'd show you the pics from the party, but unfortunately they're all NSFW.

nublet

A person who is new who acts like they are not new at something. A newbie, newb, n00b, noob, nube, novice, amateur, rookie.

Stop being such a nublet and listen to the conversation before jumping in.

nugs

Good quality, hydroponically grown weed in nugget form.

Do you know where I can score some nugs?

number one

Yourself.

Gotsta look after number one.

number-four year

A year whose number is divisible by four in which most events that operate on a four-year cycle take place, such as leap year, summer Olympics, and the United States presidential election.

Y2K was one hectic number-four year.

nummers

Tasty, enjoyable.

M & M's Minis are nummers. So is their tube.

NutraSweet daddy

An older male with enough money to coax a girl into staying with him, but not enough to ensure the girl is pretty. Can't afford enough sugar to be a sugar daddy.

The NutraSweet daddy picked up his "participant button" bride from the discount strip club after she got off work.

nuts and a half

Something very extraordinary, mind-blowing, interesting, extreme, and often death-defying.

He jumped off the tower? He's nuts and a half, fo' sho.

N

O

OC

Short for "out of control." Crazy, extreme, frantic, or wild.

Man, that party was OC until the police came.

OD

Short for "overdose." Past the limit. Over the top.

That was OD when the police arrested Grandma for jaywalking.

o'dark hundred

The hours before the sun comes up. A play on military time.

Oh shit, I gotta wake up at o'dark hundred tomorrow morning.

off the grid

Unrecorded. Untraceable through normal means.

Amish people live off the grid.

off the heezy

Cool, hip, trendy. Bastardization of "off the hook." Also spelled "off the heezie."

Yo, that party was off the heezy. We need to do that again sometime.

off the hinges

Awesome. Unbelievably good. Wild. Cousin to "off the hook" and "off the chain."

Oh man, that party was off the hinges!

off the hook

Describes something so cool and in demand that it's busy all the time,

like a phone that's always occupied.
Out of control.

*Man, that cat was fighting six people and
he beat them all. It was off the hook—you
should have seen it!*

off the island
Out of line. Unpopular. Antisocial.
After the reality TV show *Survivor,*
where you get voted off the island
because no one likes you.

*Sadie forgot my birthday last week, even
after I reminded her five times. She is so
off the island.*

OG
Acronym for "original gangster."

Yo, dude, those wheels on your bike are OG.

oh, snap
Interjection conveying unpleasant
surprise. Popularized by Tracy
Morgan on the TV show *Saturday
Night Live.*

*Girl: Did you hear? The due date for our
chemistry projects got bumped up to today!
Guy: Oh, snap!*

oh-shit handle
The handle in most vehicles located
in the interior of the vehicle above
the door. Used in extreme driving
situations where passengers do
not wish to be thrown around the
interior of the vehicle. Situations
that warrant the usage of the "oh-
shit handle" include hard braking,
abrupt cornering, skidding, career-
ing off a bridge.

*Me: Mike, I'm going to take the 25 mph
turn at 55. Better grab the oh-shit handle!
Mike: I've been holding the oh-shit handle
since you started the car!*

okey-doke
1. Someone who has been tricked
or duped.

*Man, that okey-doke was easy prey.
We got his money and his car from him
without him even realizing.*

2. A trick.

They played an okey doke on you, Shad.

okies
Okay. Expression of agreement or
acknowledgment.

*Nancy: Meet you in town today.
Trina: Okies.*

old school
Anything that is from an earlier era
and looked upon with high regard
or respect. Can be used to refer to

music, clothing, language, or anything really.

My car is so old school it measures time with a sundial.

ollie

To jump over something with a skateboard. Usually accomplished by pushing on the tail of the board and jumping up with the board stuck to your feet. Any such jump.

Yo, dude, I straight ollied a 10-stair without breaking my legs!

OMG

Acronym for "oh my God."

OMG, you will never guess what happened last night!

omniphobia

The fear of everything.

Timmy was diagnosed with a severe case of omniphobia. He can't even leave the house without being heavily medicated with antianxiety drugs.

on and poppin'

Refers to something (such as a party) that's going to be fun and crazy, or something that's certain to happen.

This party is going to be on and poppin'!

on blast

To embarrass someone or make someone look stupid.

I heard you told Jay he had bad breath in front of the whole class. You really put him on blast.

on blocks

Messed up. Busted. Taken from the practice of leaving a car that has been stripped on concrete blocks.

I told you not to let anyone in—now my whole room's up on blocks!

on chill

Having a relaxed state of mind. In chill mode.

Caller: What's good, my nizzle?
Answerer: Ah, you know me, I am on chill, as always.

on crack

Describes someone whose actions are so stupid or messed up that one would suspect cocaine use.

Man, you're on crack! You will never get with that chick.

Dude, Ms. K's on crack! She gave me a C–!

on deck

An old shipping term for those who

were supposed to be on guard or doing duties. Later used in baseball to refer to the player batting next. Now applies to anyone who's next.

Let's get this line movin', people. Who's on deck?

on everything
Very serious. You swear on everything important in your life.

On everything, if he says one mo' thang about my momma, I'ma kill that boy.

on ice
Delayed or postponed.

We're gonna put the plans for the new place on ice for a little while.

on jump
Crazy. Crunk.

I was getting on jump at that party last night.

on lock
Figured out. Under control.

That boy's got the game on lock.

on point
Up to par. Ready to perform at optimum level.

Cops! Man, throw that weed outta the car and get on point.

on the B
Whack, lame, or otherwise secondary to something that is better. Refers to the B-side of a music single, which is not as good as the A-side.

Ghostbusters *was hot, while* Ghostbusters II *was totally on the B.*

on the boss
In all seriousness. For real.

On tha boss, man, I got that new Escalade!

on the bus
Barhopping without a plan, in search of something (or someone) better. Most often used derogatively, as this kind of night rarely turns out well.

We've already been to two bars. If you're going to be on the bus all night, then I'm going home.

on the cheap
Done inexpensively or on a tight budget.

When we went on vacation in Europe a few years ago, we did it on the cheap, staying in hostels and biking around wearing our backpacks.

on the creep

1. Cheating on one's significant other.
2. On top of a creepy person.

Don suspected his wife was on the creep with that crazy old bum who lived under the bridge. His suspicions were proven correct when he came home early from work one day to find the hobo's shopping cart parked outside and his wife in bed on the creep.

on the fly

As quickly as possible.

I need that chicken dish on the fly!

on the low

To keep something a secret. Also, "on the downlow."

He is hiding Mac-10s in his garage. That's on the low, so don't go telling everyone.

on the other side

1. Homosexual.
2. Very drunk, almost to the point of being torn down.

Sid: Aye, mon, did you see Betty making out with that girl last night? She must be on the other side.
Phil: Nah, man, it's not anything like that. She was just on the other side.

on the real

Expression of agreement.

Jack: That girl's body is nice.
Joe: That's on the real.

on the tip

On top of the situation. Doing well. Excellent.

Man, that was great. You're on the tip.

on your six

Directly behind you. From the military designation of location where 12:00 is directly in front of you, 3:00 is to your right, 9:00 is to your left, etc.

Hang on, we've got two Japanese Zeroes on our six! I'll try to shake them!

one

Goodbye. Shortened form of the Rastafarian concept of "one love."

I'm out. One.

one time

The police. So called because you can only look one time at them, since doing a double take might attract attention. Used in Sir Mix-A-Lot's song "One Time's Got No Case."

Oh, snap! Here comes one time, Jimmy.
Hide your weed.

one-cheek bench sneak

The easing out of flatulence gently,
usually when sitting down, so as not
to attract undue attention.

I was on a date, so I had to pull the
one-cheek bench sneak.

ones and twos

A set of turntables.

Yo, he's off the heezy on dem ones and
twos, son.

onion booty

Booty that looks so good it makes a
grown man want to cry.

Damn, man, that girl's got onion booty.

onstage

In Disney theme parks it is any area
to which guests have access. Cast
members must be on their best
behavior onstage and must display
good show (certain standards set
forth to them by the company).
Certain things not allowed onstage:
eating, drinking, smoking, talking on
the phone, talking about one's
personal life, using guest restrooms,
being unfriendly.

I need to get off the phone. I'm about to
walk onstage.

oogly

Really ugly. If "ugly" is defined as
"being hit with an ugly stick,"
"oogly" is "being beaten with an
ugly log."

Damn! Yo' girl's oogly!

oregano

A spice commonly sold as fake
marijuana.

That wanksta sold me a kilo of oregano
the other week. Now he's lyin' in chalk.

otaku

1. An extremely negative Japanese
term referring to a shut-in or
someone with no social life. It also
implies that the person's entire
life is molded around fictional
characters (usually animé and
manga characters).

God, that kid is such an otaku. He won't
leave the basement unless it's to buy new
Dragon Ball *fansubs.*

2. In America, the term has been
embraced by animé fans, who use
the word as a positive term for
fanboy/girl.

I, like, so totally love Sailor Moon!
Serena rawks! I am, like, the ultimate
Sailor Moon *otaku!*

otay
Okay.

Otay. I'll be right over.

out like the vapors
Leaving a place relatively quickly.

When Louie's beer shits started acting up in the middle of math class, he realized he'd better be out like the vapors to save himself from the biggest embarrassment of his life.

out of order
Crazy. So off the hook and out of control it should be broken.

Damn! We raised the roof of dat house last night. That party was out of order.

outta hand
Out-of-control crazy. Exceptionally cool.

That party was outta hand. The DJ was dope and there were hella fine girls there!

overflow mode
Used to describe the actions of a short-tempered female who always seems to be angry. Related to menstruation and PMS.

Damn, Alyssa is always in overflow mode.

overstenched
When someone wears too much perfume, cologne, or body spray to the point where it doesn't smell good anymore.

That kid wears way too much cologne—he's overstenched.

own
Also "pwn."
1. To kick someone's ass. To have total and undeniable dominance of a person, group of people, or situation so as to make them/it akin to one's bitch.

I will own you, newbie.

2. To make a fool of. To confound or prove wrong. To embarrass someone.

I owned you in Counter-Strike. You were owned at the party yesterday.

3. To rule over.

Enemy planes owned the skies.

urban

ox

A sharp blade or knife.

I'm gonna cut that foo' with mah ox.

oxygen thief

Someone so completely lazy or useless that their only effect on this earth is to use up oxygen that could otherwise have been consumed by someone who doesn't deserve a solid kick in the arse.

I work with an oxygen thief. She brings a pillow and blanket to work and sleeps through night shift.

PQ

pack heat
To carry a concealed firearm for protection, or to carry out violence.

Don't come to Brick City, unless yo' packing heat.

pack up
1. To put marijuana into a bong.

Can you pack me up a cone, dude?

2. To go for a chronic smoking session with friends.

Let's go home and pack up.

palmetto
A marijuana cigarette in which cigar paper is filled with cannibis, rolled, and smoked. Popular in urban, inner-city areas.

Yo, biyatch, cyph that palmetto!

pants
1. Short for "underpants." British slang.

I've been wandering around my flat all day in only my pants.

2. To pull down someone's pants, trousers, or skirt. Short for "depants." Also "debag."

While I was talking to some girls my so-called friend came up behind me and pantsed me.

3. To inflict a crushing defeat on someone.

Our team got pantsed again.

4. To crush someone with criticism.

Don't make silly comments in an Internet discussion group or you will be publicly pantsed.

5. Rubbish. Worthless. Nonsense. British slang.

Your opinion is pants. No one wants to hear it.

paper doll
A female who is only interested in money.

She only roll wit him cause of his phat ride . . . pure paper doll!

paper stack
Money.

I'm out of control now that I got my paper stack.

papers
Short for "rolling papers," thin sheets used to roll joints, generally of marijuana.

Mike, we need to get high! I got the dime sack, now where the papers at?

parade maker
A driver and/or car that goes consistently under the speed limit, causing a backup of many cars, a lot of frustration, and the inability to be where you want to be on time.

Gee, boss, I'm very sorry that I'm 10 minutes late, but I was in a long line of cars stuck behind this parade maker.

party favor
A girl who sleeps with a lot guys she meets at parties.

That party favor Jennifer slept with two guys at the same time after she had just met them at a party.

party foul
1. An action that goes against the feel of the party or bar atmosphere.

Going to a costume party with no costume—what a party foul.

2. To spill an alcoholic drink.

Shit, you got that all over me! Party foul.

PDA
Acronym for "public display of affection." Applies to couples who French-kiss and touch each other in front of friends and family.

I want to break up, Jeff. I can't handle it anymore—I don't do PDA and I'm not as into this as you are.

peace easy

A lovely combination of "peace out" and "take it easy" for all those too lazy or too busy to say both. Double the meaning, half the time.

Guy 1: Errights, man. I gotta bounce to class ultra quick-style.
Guy 2: Eh, no prob. Peace easy.

peace out

1. Goodbye.

Yeah, see you. Peace out.

2. To leave or retire.

Yo, I gotta peace out. I'm tired.

3. To kill.

I just peaced out that spider with my shoe.

peace pipe

Any pipe used to smoke marijuana.

Pass that peace pipe over here. I need another toke.

peach fuzz

Very short, soft hair on the face.

I don't need to shave yet—it's just a little peach fuzz.

peel out

To leave. To tap out.

Why must you peel out now? Stay longer.

peen

A derogatory term used to denote someone who is annoying. Short for "penis."

Joe always snores and keeps me up. He is a peen.

peep

Short for "people." Often used to refer to your regular group of friends, your crew.

How many peeps will be there?

peep game

Interjection meaning "check it out" or "lemme tell you something."

Peep game, this is how we gonna do this.

peep this

Check this out.

Yo, peep this. Maria looks fine in this picture.

pen15

Exclusive club for those in sixth and seventh grade. Only requirement to enter is to have the club's name written on one's body part, such as an arm or hand. (Actually, a way to write "penis" on things and trick people.)

Johnny, join the pen15 club! Alls ya need to do is let me write pen15 on your arm.

perma-fry
Refers to the ability of drugs to permanently affect the user, even after the user stops taking or doing them.

*Girl 1: I don't think weed perma-fries people, but cocaine will change someone for life.
Girl 2: I think you got it wrong. Have you seen the stoners who hang out at the car wash? They'll never function at full mental capacity.*

perp
Short for "perpetrator." One who is suspected of committing an act.

The perp exited the vehicle and made a furtive gesture as if to grab a weapon, whereupon I blew him away.

petro
Scared. Afraid. Short for "petrified."

He was mad petro when I was about to fight him. He almost ran away.

phat
Acronym for "pretty hot and tempting." Cool. Awesome. Great.

Dude, your new pink hair is totally phat.

phishing
Tricking people so you can steal their personal information; usually done over the Internet.

This is a clever phishing attempt by a couple of hooligans. I'm glad you didn't give them your password.

phone it in
To perform an act in a perfunctory, noncommittal manner, as if it didn't matter.

She sang the national anthem, but she was just phoning it in as far as I could tell.

phreaking
A form of hacking, as applied to telephone networks. Phone phreaks exploit weaknesses in the phone system to make long-distance calls for free, tap into others' calls, take control of lines, get free phone services, and the like.

I phreaked the PBX with my blue box.

pics or shens
A demand made on Internet forums to post images of a currently discussed topic. A lack of images is tantamount to a lack of proof;

P

hence the consequence is "shens," or "shenanigans." Roughly translated, it means "show images of said topic or I will consider your claim to be false."

Cantankerous: I'll be spending the weekend with my girlfriend.
Clyde77: Is she hot?
Wildfir3: I don't think she even exists. Pics or shens!

pid

Short for "stupid." Also "'pid."

That Prince Harry was so 'pid prancing around in a Nazi uniform.

pidittle

A car that drives with only one working headlight, or the game you play when you see one. When you spot a pidittle, you must punch the ceiling of your car and yell "pidittle!" The first person to do so gets one point. Seven points add one year to your sex life.

Girl: Dude, you totally ran into that tree and totaled your car.
Guy: Well, I might have seen it if we hadn't been playing pidittle for the last seven hours.

piece

1. A gun, knife, or other weapon.

This piece shoots nice and only costs $50.

2. Anything used for the smoking of various drugs, most commonly marijuana, most commonly a pipe.

Dude, nice piece! Let's smoke.

3. A graffiti mural.

Yo, I threw up a hot piece down near Second and Main.

4. A place.

Dude, I'ma bounce out this piece before drama goes down.

5. Short "piece of shit."

Dude, look at that car; what an ugly piece.

pig

1. Derogatory term for a police officer.

So then Ian started talking shit to the pigs, and they arrested him.

2. Derogatory term for a capitalist.

When the revolution comes the pigs are going to get it.

pig sty

A cop hang-out, like a doughnut shop or the police station.

You must be an idiot trying to rob a pig sty like Dunkin' Donuts. Have fun up north, bitch.

pimp

1. To make something look more flashy and showy. Usually applied to cars and homes.

Blake really pimped out that Escalade with those spinners, tinted windows, and 2,000-watt system.

2. To advertise (generally, in an enthusiastic sense) or to call attention in order to bring acclaim to something; to promote.

A friend of mine created a collage of Angelina Jolie's tattoos, and I pimped it on my website so people could see her work.

pimp juice

Anything that makes the opposite sex want you. Includes money, clothes, cars, and status.

See that shorty? She wants my pimp juice.

pimp the system

To get more out of a job than one is supposed to get.

Jon: Where'd you cop that grip?
Larry: I figured out how to pimp the system, G. Took it out the register on my break!

pimp tight

Ridiculously ill, the sweetest thing ever.

Ay, did you see dat Escalade on 24s wit dat crazy paint job bouncin' thru da hood? That shit was pimp tight!

pimped out

Having excessive embellishments or ornaments, particularly of the flashy kind, like feathers in fedoras, black canes with silver handles, multicolored mismatched shoes, and colorful crushed-velvet suits. Preferably all of the above worn at once.

By the amount of bling bling he was flashing, we knew he was pimped out.

pimpin'

1. To attract a member of the opposite sex.

Ricky is pimpin' with dem hoes.

2. An object of great appeal.

That Jaguar is pimpin'.

pimpstress

A female pimp.

Megan will sell your ass on the corner 'cause she's tha pimpstress.

ping me

To send a signal or make brief contact. Often, to call or message someone. Originally, in naval warfare, one ship sent a sound, or "ping," to measure the direction and delay in the "echo" of that sound off of another body (usually a submarine). More recently from computer networking, when one computer sends a quick, pointless query to another to find out if it is still online and see how long the response takes.

Julayne: Can we go to the movie tomorrow?
Trey: I don't know. . . . Ping me around eight and we'll see how things are going.

pirate juice

Poisonous liquid, called pirate juice because of the skull and crossbones drawn on the bottle.

Dude, did you just drink the pirate juice? Call 911!

piss off

1. Sarcastic response meaning "yeah, right" or "whatever."

George: Yeah, I dropped 20 hits of Ecstasy last night.
Jim: Piss off! You'd be dead now if you'd done that.

2. Interjection meaning "get lost" or "go away."

You'd better piss off outta here before the cops arrive.

3. To get someone mad.

You've gone and pissed off the IRS? You in sum shit now.

piss with the seat down

To mistakenly commit a foolish act under the influence of alcohol, which you will have to sort out afterward.

I'm sorry, sweetheart, I shouldn't have slept with your sister, but I was drunk. I guess I really pissed with the seat down.

pissing contest

Literally, a competition in which two or more people, usually (but not exclusively) male, urinate with the intention of producing the stream with the greatest distance. More often used figuratively to refer to a meaningless though nonetheless entertaining act in which people try to outdo one another in any way.

The conversation between the two men was merely a pissing contest. Both were trying to impress the attractive woman standing nearby with their wit and intelligence.

pitch a bitch
To throw a fit.

She pitched a bitch when she caught him cheating!

pitching wedge
Someone who only looks good from far away.

Dude, I saw her the other day. You don't know. She's a pitching wedge.

pity party
A party you throw for yourself after something bad has happened to you.

After Donny broke up with me I threw myself a little pity party with some vodka.

pixel pusher
One who moves pixels on the screen to make graphics. Any kind of computer graphics designer who makes things look pretty. A graphics jockey of sorts.

Rodney is the resident pixel pusher here who will design all your graphics and make your ideas look pretty.

plastic
A credit card.

I borrowed my dad's plastic and bought an aircraft carrier on eBay.

play
1. To cheat on or use someone.

My friend told me you were at the mall playin' on me with some skeez.

2. Hella game from the opposite or same sex.

I had much play up in the club 'cuz I was mad blingin'.

play hooky
To be absent without leave. Truant.

All John does is play hooky from school and stay home and do drugs.

play it off
To do something embarrassing in front of other people and then act like you meant to do it.

I leaned out of the car to wave at Sam, but Sam was not there, so I played it off by sticking my hands on top of the car.

played out
Used too much. Worn out. Old.

Damn, that Civic is so played out—everybody got it.

player
Someone who uses someone else for sex or other favors, usually by

charming the victim until they fall in love with them. Can be shortened to "playa."

Lamar's such a playa. I seen him with Nikki last night but I know he's with Amber, and Latasha thinks she's his girl. He's playin' them all.

player hater

Derogatory term for a person who openly criticizes a playa or attempts to sabotage a playa's game. Playa haters hate only because they're jealous—they wish they could be as successful, or that they could be with the playa. Can be shortened to "playa hater."

I was trying to talk to this girl, but she was hanging out with this dude who's a total playa hater. Everything I said, he tried to turn it around to make me an asshole.

playette

A girl player. Plays the same games that guys play but plays them better. She doesn't have to have sex with guys to get them to be with her; basically she plays guys like video games.

Brittany always has more than one man. She's a total playette, and she always gets what she wants.

plead the second

To whip out a gun. Similar to "plead the fifth" (remain silent), except this refers to the Second Amendment to the U.S. Constitution (right to bear arms).

When my P.O. was sweatin' me about why my whiz test turned up positive for coke, heroin, and seven varieties of elephant tranquilizer, I had no choice but to plead the second and put his narc ass in his place.

plumbing

The reproductive system (gender neutral).

She went to the ob-gyn to have her plumbing checked out.

PLUR

Acronym for the lifestyle concept of "peace, love, unity, and respect." Popular in the rave community, it's a loosely defined dogma of camaraderie among all humanity.

We as a community need to observe PLUR in our everyday lives; the reason we love the people around us is because we all love the music, and so we should try to reach beyond that and embrace our fellow man.

po'

1. Short for "poor."

Yo' mama so po' she can't afford the "or."

2. Short for "police." Also "po po."

Watch your back. Po' on your six.

pocket rockets

A pair of aces in your hand in a game of Texas Hold 'Em poker.

In the movie Rounders, *Teddy KGB was dealt pocket rockets, with which he took down Mike McDermott.*

podestrian

A person who wears the iconic white standard iPod earbuds in their ears.

I saw three podestrians just waiting for a bus. They're everywhere!

poindexter

One who looks and acts like a nerd but does not possess the supernatural intelligence of a nerd.

Stop playing Dungeons and Dragons, poindexter.

pokey

Slang for "jail" or "prison."

I almost took a trip down to pokey town last night!

polar

Beyond cool. Colder than ice.

That jacket is so polar, Shannon! Where'd you get it?

poof

British slang for a homosexual.

I'm starting to think that guy is a poof. His porn collection is entirely homoerotic.

poor man's

A knockoff of inferior quality, or something similar to something else but not as good.

Jared was horrified when he remembered going home wasted with a Jessica Alba look-alike, then woke up the next morning naked next to the poor man's Rosie O'Donnell.

P

pop a cap

To discharge a firearm, usually a handgun.

Fool, if you don't scram, I will pop a cap in your ass.

pop a seat

Sit down.

Hey, you! Pop a seat!

pop and lock

A style of break dancing that involves short, rapid movement of the arms and legs (popping), combined with brief pauses between movements. Sometimes accompanied by subtle foot movements known as "gliding," in which the breaker appears to move around the floor without using/ lifting their legs.

Me: Yo! Check it out! There's some b-boys poppin' and lockin' over there!
You: Hot damn! Let's go scope it out!

pop the collar

To fold the collar up, which is a sign that one is a straight-up pimp.

He popped the collar on his green polo shirt and walked over to flirt unsuccessfully with the ladies.

popper

A break dancer who does "pop and lock" moves. Can also describe, but not as often, a raver's "popping" type of dance where they bounce on the balls of their toes.

That guy in the Black Eyed Peas is an ill popper.

poppin'

Started. Happening. Going on.

Is this a party or not? Let's get this shit poppin'!

porkchop

Police helicopter.

The porkchop is hunting perps tonight.

porn storm

Surfing for porn and getting bombarded with pop-up windows.

I tried to mouse off last night, but I kept getting caught in a porn storm.

porno-styling

A descriptor for things that are super cool and especially that you might find in a porno.

Your new place is totally porno-styling. You are going to get massive play here.

POS

1. Acronym for "piece of shit."
2. Acronym some companies use for "positively outstanding service."

If you would clean that POS off the floor, that would really be a demonstration of POS. Hell, I'd promote you!

3. Chat lingo for "parent over shoulder."

Me: hey, 'sup?

You: nm.
Me: g2g pos ttyl
You: k lata buhbye

poser

A person who attempts to blend into a specific social group. Also "poseur."

Justin is a poser goth. He comes to school in all black, but he doesn't even know who Edgar Allan Poe is.

posse out

Expression used when your crew peaces out.

Yo, posse out. Later.

post

To stay where you are. To hang out. Also, "post up."

Hey, Rob, I'm just going to post here tonight.

postal

Crazy or insane; irrational. Came into use after a number of workplace shootings by disgruntled U.S. post office workers.

Tina tore up her homework, yelled at her mom, and slapped her little brother! She's gone postal!

pot

Marijuana.

Let's smoke some pot.

potatoes

Vodka. After the common substance used in making vodka.

Let's go drink some potatoes.

pothead

A person who smokes a lot of marijuana.

Damn, look at that pothead. His eyes are almost shut.

pound

To consume large amounts of alcohol in a limited amount of time.

Yo, let's pound these brews before going in.

pour one for my homies

To pour liquid (usually an alcoholic beverage) on the ground as a sign of reverence for friends or relatives who have passed away. In many cases, a 40-ounce bottle of liquor is used.

Yo, man, I just heard Mista Rogaz died, dawg. I'ma pour one for my homies.

power hour

An hour in which you drink 60 beer

shots, one per minute. A lightweight alternative to the Century Club.

Guy 1: Last night was really lame. I went over to Dee's house, we did a couple power hours, then I drove home.
Guy 2: Dee who?
Guy 1: Deez nutz!

pregame
To drink before going to a party.

We really need to pregame tonight before we go out.

preggers
Pregnant. Also "preggo."

I shouldn't have slept around. I got preggers.

preppy
Specifically, one who goes to a preparatory or "prep" school (typically on the east coast), or a school with the intent of preparing its students for college (often Ivy League and in New England). Generally, one who exhibits similar characteristics. Often wears Polo, Lilly, Brooks Brothers, Lacoste, L.L.Bean, ribbon belts, prints (e.g., embroidered animals, palm trees, etc.), sweaters tied around the neck, collar popped, hair ribbons or ribbon headbands, pearls, and other classic jewelry. Partial to monogrammed and engraved items. Preppies may not always match exactly, but they are always well put together. They are confident and unafraid to express their own styles and be daring in their fashions.

Les whispered to Tyler that Linds looked very preppy with her pink popped Pulitzer, cable-knit cardigan, and pearls.

press
To try to scare someone.

We was getting on the bus and she came up to me trying to press me.

press the flesh
To shake hands; to meet and greet.

The politicians were very tired after a long day on the campaign trail, kissing babies and pressing the flesh with their constituents.

press up
Trying to impress or court the opposite sex with smooth talk and flattery.

Jonathan tried to press up on Tina while she was waiting for her ride home.

prevert
A softcore pervert. Someone who is in the early stages of perversion.

He was drawing naked women on his school homework, the little prevert.

primary digits
The phone number a person expects friends and family to use.

I need to make sure you have my primary digits.

pro status
Carrying something out with perfection. Of high quality.

I hit that shit pro status.

pro-ho
A girl who has mastered the "game."
Not to be confused with a slut or a whore. Female version of "pimp."

Libby's got mad game. Those haters are just jealous 'cuz she's a pro-ho.

problem solver
A gun.

I'll bring my problem solver, 'cause you never know when shit might get live.

probs
Short for "problems."

Ron: Can I come along?
Tia: No probs.

procrastination
What you're probably doing right now.

I meant to do my paper but went procrastinating at urbandictionary.com instead.

profanity loophole
An exploitation of the limited ability of software to prevent profane content from getting through to users.

My mom: What are all these e-mails for pr0n about?
Me: Oh, just a profanity loophole.

professional student
Person who receives multiple degrees and keeps taking courses instead of holding a profession related to the degrees earned. Can be a compliment or an insult.

Hey, Jack, won't you get a real job and quit being a professional student?

profile
To show off. To be seen by all at your best.

I was just profilin' at da club wit' my niggas and hoes.

props
Short for "proper recognition."

I had to give him props for sleeping with that smokin' hot girl, Vanessa, even though she's my girlfriend.

prostitot

A young girl (10–16) who dresses slutty and tries to be a prostitute but does not act actually perform prostitutional activities.

That girl is such a prostitot!

prosumer

Of a quality often acceptable to both professional and consumer users. Especially refers to electronic equipment.

I wanted something nicer than a $500 consumer camcorder, but I couldn't afford a $50,000 professional camcorder, so I bought a $2,000 prosumer camcorder.

psyched

To be excited or pumped up about something.

I'm so psyched about the party!

puff puff give

To take two distinct drags off of a joint and give it to the next person in the rotation. Acceptable smoking protocol. Also "puff puff pass."

Don't bogart that tulip, man. Puff puff

give. In some circles, you could really get messed up if you screw up the rotation.

pull

1. To successfully attract a person to such an extent that you would be able to snog or perhaps have sex with them if you so desired.

With the help of my lucky Y-fronts I should pull tonight.

I pulled this hot chick last night.

2. To "have pull" is to be attractive.

That hot chick has some mad pull, brotha.

3. In Ultimate Frisbee, the throw that starts play at the start of the game or after a goal has been scored. Also, to make such a throw.

That was a nice pull.

Okay, who's gonna pull?

pull the trigger

To force oneself to puke by sticking a finger down the throat. Used more in the drinking sense than in the bulimic sense.

When we got to the 150th minute of trying to join the Bicentennial Club, I realized I might have to pull the trigger if I wanted to stay in the game.

pump

1. A pump-action shotgun.

I got a pump in the trunk, cuz!

2. To sell drugs.

I'm always pumpin' crack, cuz!

pumped

All fired up. Ready to kick ass. Exhilarated.

Man, I'm feelin' pumped about the rally!

punch drunk

A term derived from boxing where a boxer gets hit by his opponent so many times that his disorientation is similar to being drunk.

I stopped the sparring match when I saw that he was punch drunk.

punk

1. Lifestyle that involves thinking what you like, doing what you like, doing it when you like, and not caring about very much at all. Punk music has a lot of subgenres, including pop-punk, and tends to be very fast, sometimes repetitive (the shit bands, anyway), and the lyrics are often very offensive. People often mistakenly think that punks want to kill themselves or everyone around them, but that is not true.

The Clash was a punk band that helped create the punk scene.

2. To rip someone off, trick someone, or tease someone.

I heard that boy gon' get jumped for punkin' that guy.

purple haze

Extremely potent marijuana, specifically marijuana buds that have a purple hue to them. Also accompanied by a fragrant, usually fruity smell and mad perma-grin. Also just "purple."

Yo, you gotta come over and smoke, boy! I got the purple haze!

purse out

For males: to not do something because of a girly reason, to wuss out.

Tim was going to go to the bar with us tonight, but he pursed out because he had to get up early tomorrow.

push up on

An attempt by a male to get into a woman's pants.

'Sup playa—mind if I push up on your old honey?

put in print

To kill. To put someone in the obituaries.

Step up off me, boy, or I'll put you in print.

putty exam

An exam the teacher makes so difficult that the entire class fails. He can then "resculpt" the class to give the kids he likes the higher grades and the kids he dislikes the lower grades, according to a bell curve.

I better start kissing up after that putty exam.

pwn

1. An intentional misspelling of the word "own," with a similar meaning: to dominate an opponent. Especially used in online games.

He totally got pwned by the other team. What a noob.

2. To be great or ingenious.

This strategy pwns!

quack

To talk rubbish or drive a point home unnecessarily.

Stop quacking about it! No one wants to hear you.

quarter to eight

A BMW 745i sedan.

You see my boy kickin' it in the new quarter to eight?

quarter-life crisis

Refers to the numerous personal crises brought on by entering adulthood and being expected to become a responsible, productive member of society. Characterized by first gray hairs/wrinkles, excessive drinking, hanging out with people who are younger in order to feel younger again only to end up looking creepy, extreme fear of all of these things. Also a "mid-youth crisis."

Wow, paying back these student loans is really a bitch. They are not helping my quarter-life crisis one bit. . . . Time to put on my tie and go sit in my cube and play solitaire—I mean, work.

quarters

A drinking game in which players try to bounce quarters off the table and into a short cup (either empty or filled with beer). If the quarter goes in, everyone else must take a drink.

It would take about 50 games of quarters before I'd even consider takin' her home.

queerbait

Derogatory term for a man who attracts gay men or a man who claims to be straight but acts gay.

Guy 1: Dude, Ryan just said that guy over there was hot!
Guy 2: Oh my God! I knew it! He's such a queerbait.

quote unquote

Synonymous with "supposedly," "presumably." Used in conversation to indicate that quotes should be placed around the following word or phrase. For example: quote unquote work = "work."

I quote unquote work on Fridays.

Q

R

rack

Breasts.

She has a nice rack.

rad

Short for "radical." Popularized by the Teenage Mutant Ninja Turtles and still primarily used by people on the west coast who find words like "cool," "awesome," and "tight" to be tired and overused; "rad" is generally considered to be a much higher praise.

Those are some rad shoes.

radcore

Totally awesome.

Holy crap! That's so radcore to the fully full on hardcore max extreme.

rail

1. A line of any power drug, including cocaine, crystal meth, special K, and crushed-up prescription pills, among others.

Blow that phat rail, man.

2. To ride in, drive, or pilot a vehicle in a fast and precise manner down a twisty road. To go fast or haul ass.

I was railing down Highway 1 until that highway patrolman caught me.

raise

Parent or parents; the people who raised you.

I am having Thanksgiving dinner with the raise this year.

urban

ralph

To throw up. To lurch.

Watching the professional eater on The Daily Show *tonight made me want to ralph!*

random

1. Completely haphazard. Out of context. Having nothing to do with what you are currently doing or talking about.

Girl: So what do you want to do today?
Guy: I can burn through my ears.
Girl: Dude, that was random!

2. Someone you don't know but either hang out with or hook up with one time.

Who was that random I hooked up with last night? Did anyone get her name?

rank

Horrible, disgusting, sick.

Arhh, mate, your socks are rank!

rate

To think something is sick, cool, good, or hot.

I really rate that new girl at work.

raunchy

Sexually exciting and/or explicit.

That was a very raunchy movie.

rave

A large, almost always underground party that includes excessive drinking, many sexual activities, loud electronic music, a lot of lighting effects (strobes, lasers), and often fog machines. There is no definite form of dancing and no dress code, but most ravers wear jelly bracelets, necklaces, and sticks that glow.

Person 1: Dude, I went to this rave, and I lost hearing in my left ear, 'cuz dem music is all loud!
Person 2: Dude, that's so pro!
Person 1: Whaaaaaaa?

real the deal

The opposite of "fake the deal." To be honest and not put up a front.

She finally decided to real the deal and confessed to Jimmy her boobs were fake, but the penis she'd been hiding from him was very real.

red state

A state that has recently gone Republican and is shown on the political maps as red; opposite of "blue state."

You'll never carry a red state with a pro—gun control candidate.

red-flag

To stop or be stopped. Derived from the racing flag that is used to stop a race because of unsafe conditions.

We're red-flagged at this gas station because it's snowing too hard for us to go on.

red-light district

A place where prostitution is common.

Guy 1: Hey, have you ever visited Kabukicho, Japan; Patpong, Thailand; Wanchai, Hong Kong; and Sunset Boulevard, Hollywood, California? I sure did for the last couple of years, and all were awesome!
Guy 2: Well . . . all of the places you've visited are red-light districts, so I'm sure you did have a real good time.

reefer

Marijuana. Weed, bud, kill, grass, trees, smoke, cheeba. Refers to any form: joint, bowl, plant, or sack.

All these damn kids care about anymore is drinking their booze and smoking the reefer.

regulate

To lay down the law. To begin controlling shit, often by physical force or restraint.

If he pulls that shit again, I'm gonna have to regulate that mutha.

rellies

Relatives.

I had to put up with the missus's rellies all weekend, mate.

renob

"Boner" spelled backward. A less derogatory way to call someone a boner.

Justin is a total renob today.

rent-a-cop

Security guards, usually unarmed, who are hired by companies and rented out to agencies for things such as concerts or school security.

My school is full of rent-a-cops, armed with nothing tougher than their cell phones. Safe, it ain't!

'rents

Parents or caretakers.

The 'rents are home this weekend, so the party can't be here.

uRban

rep

1. To represent.

I be repping Brick City.

2. Reputation.

That fool has a bad rep.

respect

Interjection used to indicate your admiration or respect for someone.

Jeff: I drank a whole case of beer last night. Todd: Respect!

retrosexual

A retrosexual is the opposite of a metrosexual. He is a man who spends as little time and money as possible on his appearance.

Normally a very fastidious woman, Mary was shocked to realize she was overcome by his raw retrosexual appeal.

re-up

Sign up again. People in the armed services who are coming to the end of their term of enlistment need to decide if they will sign for another term—in other words, if they will re–sign up or "re-up." Recently crept into the mainstream meaning anything extended or renegotiated, like a contract or term of office.

Shaquille O'Neal re-upped his contract.

revolving door

Any company that has a high turnover rate, meaning employees are quitting almost as fast as others are hired.

Damn, this place is becoming a revolving door. We've gone through four guys in that position this quarter. . . .

rewind

In the drum and bass scene, the DJ's practice of replaying a record that has been enthusiastically received by the audience. Spectators "call for a rewind" by holding cigarette lighters in the air; if there is enough demand, the DJ will spin the record backward and play it from the beginning.

The crowd loved that track so much that I had to do three rewinds.

riced-out

A car used for street racing that has been modified with many parts imported from Japan.

Lingling has the most kick-ass riced-out Honda.

ricockulous

Something (an idea, person, object, etc.) that is beyond ridiculous.

The amount of reading my professors have assigned this quarter is ricockulous!

ride on dubs

To drive a car with 20-inch or larger rims. Also "roll on dubs."

He's so pimp'n riding on his new dubs.

ride the edge

To be ahead in a certain skill or profession, to be on the cutting edge and take all the risks of being the first and leading the others.

A recent graduate in quantum physics, Amalia now rides the edge of nanotechnology.

ride the girl bike

To lose amazingly badly. To suck hard at any activity.

Cullen was riding the girl bike when Aaron played him on the PS2.

ridic

Short for "ridiculous" but means extraordinary or remarkable.

Look at those tig ol' bitties! Her body is ridic!

ridonkulous

Completely absurd and laughable. Term popularized by the fictional character Seth Cohen on the TV show *The O.C.*
1. Significantly more absurd than ridiculous; without possibility of serious consideration.

That was the funniest movie I've seen. It was consistently ridonkulous. Absolutely hilarious!

2. Fitted to excite absolute ridicule; intentionally crazy and silly; completely absurd and laughable.

I can't believe that jackass tried to steal a police car. That's ridonkulous!

right and proper

Completely, utterly, totally.

I'm screwed, right and proper.

right on

Yeah, whatever.

Person 1: Wanna go to Denny's?
Person 2: Right on.

righteous

The best possible.

Oh man, that lasagna was righteous!

uRbaN

rigid

A motorcycle with no rear suspension, or a frame for such a motorcycle.

He had to be hardcore to ride that rigid all the way from New York to LA.

rims

The visible part of a car wheel. Often highly customized by people who want to show off their car—like jewelry for a car. Can be various colors, but are usually gold or silver. Some have special spinners that spin even when the car is not moving. Many people want nice rims and will go to great lengths to acquire them, even stealing them, carjacking people to get them, or killing people over them.

Man, check out those pimped-out rims! Those are the sickest rims I've ever seen!

ringtonc DJ

An annoying person who shuffles through all their ringtones incessantly.

Jordan: Aye, ringtone DJ, I don't wanna hear your tones. Stop showing off, you turd.
Ringtone DJ: Do you like this one?
Jordan: Arrrrrrrggggg!

rip

1. To inhale a hit of marijuana.

Can I have a rip off that doobie?

2. To use software to turn songs on a CD into mp3s ready for download.

Mike ripped the whole Ludacris CD and put it on Kazaa before it came out in stores.

3. To bad-mouth, dis, or burn someone or something.

Stop ripping me about my new haircut.

rip a fart

To expel gaseous materials from one's anus.

My roommate had to rip a fart, so I got the hell out of there.

ripped

1. Having an unusual amount of body muscle.

Damn, she's ripped. She could crush me!

2. Intoxicated.

I just smoked 14 joints and drank 67 beers. I am ripped!

rippers

Amphetamines.

He is speeding off them rippers.

road snot

The oil and rubber that rises to the surface on roads when the first rain of the year comes. It makes the roads slippery as hell.

Well, it's November 1 and the first rain of the year hit the roads of Los Angeles. Fresh road snot rose to the surface and caused 100 accidents today.

road warrior

A traveling businessperson who spends much of their time on the road, often driving between meetings or presentations.

Sahda's a serious road warrior. She's clocked 12,000 miles on her car just driving to give presentations.

ROAR

Acronym for "right of admission reserved." Typically seen on clubbing/rave tickets, it means that if you're a drunk/tripping fool, the bouncers will kick your ass out.

This is an alcohol- and drug-free event. ROAR.

robosexual

Someone whose primary sexual orientation is toward robots. Inspired by Bender from the TV show *Futurama*.

A robosexual person is likely to have a job that involves computers.

rock

1. To use. To make do with, usually to great effect.

You don't need to make up the guest bed; we can rock the couch.

2. Streetball term for a basketball.

The way Joe handled that rock it made the whole crowd stand still.

3. A form of cocaine.

Yo, I'ma buy a rock. You want anything?

rock it

Interjection meaning "okay!"

*Johnny: Let's go see a movie.
Stanley: Rock it!*

rock on

A phrase rockers use to greet each other, say goodbye, or just say when something is cool.

Later, dude. Rock on!

rock out

To be compelled by the total arse-kickingness of a song (mainly rock and metal) to go ballistic. This can include air-guitaring, showing the horns, and generally making an ass out of yourself.

urban

Dude, he's rocking out to some hardcore metal.

rock up
To arrive.

I rocked up at about 11 p.m., when the party was just getting crunk.

roffle
To roll on the floor laughing. From the Internet chat acronym ROFL (roll on floor laughing).

It was so funny I roffled for about 10 minutes!

ROFLMAO
Acronym for "rolling on floor laughing my ass off." Indicates more laughter than "ROFL."

The chicken crossed the road to get to the other side? ROFLMAO!

roid rage
Unwarranted rage resulting from intense steriod use; juice-raging.

I get roid rage from sticking too many needles in my ass.

roll
1. Ecstasy. From the fact that people used to sneak Ecstasy into clubs by melting a Tootsie Roll and sticking a pill into it.

Shizz, that roll was nice.

2. To take a hit of Ecstasy.

C'mon, roll with me.

3. To jump and/or rob a helpless or unsuspecting person.

You better put those Benjamins away 'fore you get rolled up in this mug.

roll call
When a person gives shout-outs to different people from their crew and hood.

Roll call! I wanna give a big shout-out to my crew, to my job for giving me a raise, and to Hennessy for keeping it crunk.

roll deep
Going somewhere with a large amount of people. Also "roll thick."

We rollin' 20 deep in da club.

roll out
To leave.

We got what we wanted, so let's roll out.

roll up
1. To have sex.

2. To arrive.

3. To smoke weed.

Me and my girl rolled up last night after me and my crew rolled up at her place and we all rolled up and got high.

rolled

Busted by the police or other authority, usually for minor incidents like noise violations at parties or small amounts of drugs.

We got rolled at the park for smoking our weed that we just rolled.

rollin'

On a roll. When everything is going smoothly and perfectly and you feel invincible.

Tapped some girl I met at the club last night, woke up this morning, and she was still looking hot. Boss called and gave me a promotion and raise. Then I won 200 bones at the casino. I'd say I'm rollin'.

roofies

Street name for the common date-rape drug Rohypnol. Has an incapacitating effect similar to but stronger, faster-acting, and more durable than alcohol. Also "rufies."

The sick bastard slipped her some roofies. It's the only way he could ever

hope to score with a woman.

root

To have sex.

If ya wanna root, just ask!

rotate some tires

To go for a drive with some friends and try to pick up chicks.

Let's go rotate some tires, man!

round file

The trash can, where you throw useless documents.

Wife: What did you do with the bill?
Husband: I put it in the round file.

rubber band

Tire with a narrow sidewall. Usually for large rims. As wheels get bigger, the tires on them have to get smaller to still fit in the wheel well. Usually used in reference to tires on 20-inch and larger wheel sizes.

That boy Jim is riding on some rubber bands.

ruca

Spanish term for girlfriend, homegirl, or wifey.

I asked her to be my ruca and she gave me the "let's just be friends" speech.

run digits

To place a phone call.

Run my digits when you get done with your ruca.

run the table

To keep winning a game so that you stay on the table and opponents keep coming like lambs to the slaughter.

Last night Simon and I ran the beirut table and groupies were eyeing us like kids in a candy store.

run up

1. To suddenly approach someone.

I ran up on Eminem in Detroit and got his autograph.

2. To ambulate quickly across an inclined surface.

After I increased the incline on the treadmill, I really had to run up.

3. To accumulate.

You took your girl to Wendy's for your one-year anniversary? Dang, man, better not run up too much money on the ol' credit card bills.

If you run up too big a debt to that loan shark, he'll probably run up on you. If I were you, I'd run up into the hills and not come back for a while. Cracka.

rush

1. To hurry.

You ain't from Russia, so why you rushin'?

2. To check out different fraternities or sororities and decide which one you want to pledge.

Ryan was wasted off his ass during frat rush, so we breathalyzed him and it was off the charts!

3. The early part of a high, especially a cocaine high.

Guy 1: Man, that rush from those caffeine pills was intense.
Guy 2: No, it wasn't. Shut up.

4. Mr. Limbaugh.

We were jammin' to Rush Limbaugh in the car and a cop pulled us over.

5. Short for "Russian."

That guy's either a Polack or a Rush.

You'd better rush so we can go to the frat rush party on time and snort coke and get a rush while listening to Rush or Rush Limbaugh, you Rush.

rust bucket

An ancient car or ship, covered in rust.

Look at that rust bucket! I'm surprised the thing holds together.

S

sack up

To gather up one's courage for a daunting task.

David: I'd like to ask Jane out, but . . .
Chris: Oh, sack up and ask her, will you?

sack-tap

A trick played on a fellow athlete where the open hand smacks the target's testicles with the knuckles in a sharp, wrist-flicking motion.

Dude, I sack-tapped Brandon, and now he has the whole team trying to sack-tap me.

safe

Cool, good, nice, sweet.

Dude, those new shoes are safe as hell.

sailing with the Captain

To drink large quantities of Captain Morgan's rum, usually with a group and, hopefully, to the point of oblivion.

That girl I hooked up with was so fugly that I had to go sailing with the Captain before I could take her home.

salted over

Similar to "screwed over" but in a more disdainful respect.

She said she'd call me back in a minute, but after three hours I realized I'd been salted over.

salty

Unusually grumpy or cross. In a bad mood. Unfriendly or hostile.

URBAN

Aaron is salty tonight; he isn't getting along with anyone.

sammich
A sandwich, with connotations of extra goodness. For example, if you pour gravy on a roast beef sandwich, you then have a roast beef sammich.

Subway sells sandwiches, but I'd rather go home and make a sammich.

sap
1. A person whose character has a spiritually debilitating effect on others. Typically an unhappy person who perenially moans to others but can also be someone who exhibits annoying behavior.

Mike drones on and on about conspiracy theories—what a sap!

2. A fool; someone who is prone to being taken advantage of.

This is the third time Joe bought vanishing cream on the Internet; what a sap!

sauce
Very good. Amazing.

The TV show Friends *is sauce.*

sauced
Drunk, plastered, hammered, trashed.

My mom was sauced after that party.

saucy
Hot, with a little attitude, but not too much.

She's a saucy little number, isn't she?

sausage fest
When the number of males overwhelmingly exceeds the amount of females present.

This party is a total sausage fest! Let's call Sarah and have her bring some of her girlfriends over.

savage
Bad-ass. Cool. Violent.

That's a savage drink you just made. Thanks, bro.

saw the elephant
Saw the main attraction (like in the circus) and can now go home.

Maria, this museum sucks. We saw the elephant. Let's book.

scab
1. To obtain something from someone with no promise of repayment.

Don't invite Rob to the party; he'll just scab drinks off everyone.

2. A person who frequently obtains goods/money from others in such a manner. Also "tightarse."

That guy is such a scab! Don't let him know you got paid today.

scam
To make out with or have sexual relations with someone you are not in a relationship with.

Me and that really hot chick from the bar scammed last night . . . it was pretty great.

scan
To observe, peruse, check out.

Wow! Scan that hot babe over there!

scandalous
Bad. Raunchy. Out of control.

That guy's scandalous; he stole his own mama's TV.

scatter
Someone who is messy or disorganized.

Oh, look at Christine—she's such a scatter!

scene
A term often used to define the type of music one listens to, the clothes one wears, and the group one hangs out with.
Examples of common scenes: indie, emo, punk, straight edge, etc.

Man, I can't believe you're a Republican! It's so against your scene!

scenic route
The long way, or sometimes the wrong way.

We were supposed to turn on 13th Street to get to the Capitol, but I guess we can take the scenic route . . . through Virginia.

school
To do well, so that you are, in effect, teaching others or teaching them a lesson.

I got schooled by that big guy while playing basketball.

school of hard knocks
Life.

You can learn more common sense from the school of hard knocks than you can from most any university.

schwag/swag
1. Weak or impotent cannabis or dirt weed.

Tom refuses to buy or smoke schwag weed—he only likes kind bud.

2. Something of exceptionally poor or low quality that is generally looked down upon.

The people joked that Tom has a schwag car, but little do they know he is planning on buying a new Audi next week.

schwing

Interjection used by males when they see a beautiful woman. Onomatopoeia describing the sound of a sword being unsheathed. Phallic connotation.

Woowee, look at her! Schwing!

science

In hip-hop culture: knowledge or street smarts.

That nigga was tight; he dropped science on the mic.

scooped up

In a relationship. Taken.

Jon: Look at Tonya over there; she's lookin' fine.
Bobby: Don't bother. She got scooped up just last week.

scope

To look at someone, think about how fit they are, and think about being with them. To check someone out.

Yo, she is scoping you, man.

score

1. To get, receive, purchase, steal, or have. Synonym of "cop."

Yo, I'm about to score a case of beer, want some?

2. To succeed in seducing someone sexually.

Did you score with Tina last night?

scratch

To create musical noise by moving a piece of vinyl back and forth in a rhythmic fashion under a needle on a phonographic turntable.

He scratches at his friend Mike's club down on 9th and Broadway.

screamo

An obscure subgenre of emo (short for "emotional hardcore") best characterized by the intense use of screaming. While all emo bands must scream at least once to be officially "emo," screamo bands must be screaming the majority of the time. Examples include: Joshua Fit for Battle, Envy, and Bucket Full of Teeth.

I'm too afraid to go in the pit of a screamo band.

screen shopping

Shopping on the Internet without intending to purchase anything. Window shopping on the Internet.

I'm screen shopping on eBay.

screw the pooch

To make a major mistake.

Man, I really screwed the pooch when I talked to my boss while I was drunk last night.

scrilla

Money.

Yo, she's got mad scrilla. We're gonna rock the mall later.

script kiddie

An inexperienced computer user who uses premade tools (scripts) to take control of computers on the Internet. Script kiddies don't understand or respect the tools they use. Used in a derogatory way, similar to "newbie."

He's not a hacker. He's just a script kiddie.

scrub

An inferior person.

Come here, scrub! Take your beating!

scut

Short for "scutwork," the work of a useless person. Used frequently in teaching hospitals by junior residents and medical students to describe mindless and thankless errands, such as chasing down radiology reports, drawing blood, and staying on hold with the health department— anything that is heavy on the service and light on the education.

I don't know if I'll survive grand rounds today. I was up all night running scut.

scuzbucket

A scumbag.

That guy is a complete scuzbucket.

seafood problems

Crabs.

That boy is scratching so hard down there, I think he has seafood problems.

seal the deal

To reach the point where it is a virtual certainty that a given thing will happen. Often used in a sexual sense.

The first five drinks that Ron bought the girl at the bar definitely improved his chances, but the roofies he slipped in the sixth drink really sealed the deal.

search engine

Shamelessly endorses other websites by letting people add their sites to a great big list of sites.

I searched "ancient Egyptian remains" on the search engine and got 14,000 results, mainly consisting of pornography.

seat check

Interjection announcing that you are reserving your spot when you have to get up and get something.

I'm gonna get a beer. Seat check.

seeds

Children.

My seeds are with their mom now.

seen

Expression of agreement.

Guy: Smoke this sensi and you'll get lifted—no joke. Don't check it with no lightweight stuff. Seen?
Girl: True, true. Yeah, man. Seen.

self-first

The rule you use to get out of the "bros before hoes" rule. Only to be used when there is more than an 80 percent chance of you getting laid.

I know our rule is bros befo' hoes, but you
see that girl all up on me? It's self-first tonight. Sorry, playa.

sell popcorn

To stand by and do nothing to change events.

I was getting the crap kicked out of me, and my buddy Mike was just standing around selling popcorn.

sellout

One who betrays a cause for personal advancement. Anyone who sacrifices artistic integrity in an effort to become more successful or popular (generally in music); someone who forgets their roots.

It's the American dream to be a sellout.

serve

To make a fool of someone.

Oh, shit, he served them suckas in that rap battle.

set

1. Crowd. Gang. Unit.

I stay holdin' it down for my set.

2. Surfer slang for several big waves breaking one after another.

Oy! There's sets comin'! Go, go, go!

sex up

To embellish or exaggerate.

Tony Blair was accused of sexing up reports of weapons of mass destruction in Iraq.

sex without the X

Dull, lifeless, boring, unexciting lovemaking, as in non-X-rated sex.

A day without sunshine is like sex without the X.

sexcellent

So amazing and exceptional that it's comparable to sex. Does not necessarily refer to a sexual experience.

That was some sexcellent parallel parking. You will pass your driver's test even if they blindfold you.

sexile

To banish a roommate from the room/dorm/apartment for the purpose of engaging in intimate relations with one's significant other/sex partner.

Man, I'm sexiled for the whole night. Can I crash at your place?

sexpot

An attractive young woman who is usually horny and promiscuous.

My new roommate, Amber, is a total sexpot.

SFW

Acronym for "safe for work." Used to describe Internet content that could be viewed in the presence of your boss and colleagues (as opposed to NSFW, "not safe for work").

My boss checks my browser history, so only show me your party pics if they're SFW.

shady

Suspicious; can also be an activity bordering on criminal.

That shady guy over there is seriously creeping me out.

shaft

To screw someone over.

I got shafted on an eBay transaction— they never sent my stuff.

shag

1. To have sexual intercourse.

I would really like to shag Samantha.

2. A form of rough pipe tobacco.

I'm going down to the shop for some shag.

urban

shake

1. The cruddy end bits of a large bag of weed.

I bought a dime and got some extra shake.

2. The last girls to leave the bar at closing time.

We got so desperate we went trolling for shake outside the college bar at 3 A.M.

shakedown

Cops raiding yo' house, person, or car illegally to find drugs, cash money, or guns.

The cops busted a shakedown on Jimmy's weed house.

shank

1. A homemade knife.

I heard he got hit with a rusty shank.

2. To stab someone with a homemade knife.

John got shanked and it took twenty stitches to close him up.

shark

To engage in overt attempts at procuring a partner of the opposite sex. You can accuse someone of sharking by putting your upright, straight hand up to and at right angles to your nose and forehead, and weaving your head from side to side, as if you were a shark in the murky depths.

I stopped sharking a minute to get chips and drinks.

sharp

Good or sleek.

Yo, that was a sharp throw, man!

shart

Blend of "shit" and "fart." A small, unintended defecation that occurs when one relaxes to fart.

I sharted at the party last night and went home pronto to change my clothes.

shattered

Drunk.

Ian was so shattered he had to call his mum to pick him up at 3 A.M.

shazbot

An exclamation used to express a negative feeling, such as disappointment or mild annoyance.

Shazbot, I missed again!

sheeple

People who are unable to think for

themselves. Followers. Lemmings.

All the teens were wearing bell-bottoms because they were sheeple.

sheila
A female.

She was a spunky sheila.

shibby
Great. Really good. Cool.

This beer is so shibby!

shields up
To cover your face with the collar of your T-shirt in order to avoid the smell of flatulence.

Geez, Jimmy. That smells atomic. Shields up, everyone.

shine
1. Jewelry. Bling.

Best give up yo' shine, playa.

2. To insult someone in front of other people.

Damn, that girl was shining on yo' ass and you didn't say nothin' to hit her back.

shiny
Cool, nifty, awesome, pretty, amazing, wonderful, great, remarkable.

Girl 1: Hey, what do you think of my new car?
Girl 2: Shiny.

ship
1. Short for "romantic relationship"; popularized in fanfiction circles.

I see a ship developing between Hermione Granger and Ron Weasley.

2. To endorse a romantic relationship.

I ship Ron and Hermione.

shit, dawg
Interjection meaning "oh my goodness!"

Shit, dawg, that is the biggest house I ever seen!

shit hit the fan
An idiomatic expression used to convey that something disastrous has occurred.

I told this guy at my school how his girlfriend was a good lay, then the shit hit the fan.

shitballs
Expletive conveying great frustration or fright.

As Dan was smoking a fat marijuana joint he saw his father enter the house and exclaimed, "Oh, shitballs!"

shiznit

The greatest, in a certain category or universally. Phenomenal, biotch! Also "shiznat."

Damn, Tony! Your new ride is the shiznit! Lemme borrow it to drive by Mya's.

shizzam

Interjection used when doing or having done something extraordinary. Equivalent to "ta-da!" or "voila!"

Shizzam! Your gold watch is now in my pocket.

shomance

A "show romance" that develops between reality-show contestants or participants, especially one that ends as soon as the show is over. Often a ploy to gain more camera time.

I thought Nick and Amy shared a real romance on The Apprentice, *but their immediate breakup proves it was just a showmance.*

shook

Scared, afraid, hesitant. Used in

Mobb Deep's song "Shook Ones."

Fear of STDs got him shook like a leaf.

shoop

To have sex.

Fact is, your girl already thinks you want to shoop with me, so let's get it on.

shoot the shit

To chat idly about things that neither person involved in the conversation will be likely to remember.

John: We shot the shit for a while.
Jeff: Oh yeah? What'd you talk about?
John: I don't remember.

shorty

Also "shawty" in the American South. Can be shortened to "shawt" or "shawtdawg."
1. Affectionate term for a girlfriend, attractive female, or concubine.

What up, shorty? You lookin' straight! What's your number?

2. A girl on the side, separate from your main piece or boo.

I had to be careful 'cause I was out with shorty and I didn't want to get caught.

3. A younger friend, sibling, or offspring.

You'll get there soon, shorty. Keep your head up.

shotgun

The front right seat of a car. Comes from the Americans' fascination with the Old West, when the person sitting next to the coach driver carried a shotgun to fend off robbers or Indians. Sometimes shortened to "shotty." The seat behind the shotgun is "cobain," since music legend Kurt Cobain was behind a shotgun when he died.

He drove to Vegas with Mallory riding shotgun and the hitchhiker in cobain.

shout-out

To acknowledge someone on a radio station or television show. Popular on MTV's *Total Request Live.* Also a part of a rap album in which the artists thank their family and crew.

Shout-outs to my boys in the ATX, and to all my peeps holding it down in DC.

show weight

Your ideal weight for appearance in public (e.g., on a TV show, high school reunion) or to fit into a particular outfit.

Martha only has two weeks before her reunion to get down to her show weight.

shower in a can

Deodorant, which is used when time is short or the showers aren't working. Usually in a post-sport setting.

Hey, Grant, got any shower in a can? Can't be arsed having a shower. Need a beer instead.

shred

In snowboarding, surfing, and kayaking: to ride with speed, style, and skill.

Check out Chris shredding the hill with perfect heelside turns. Good form!

'shroom

Short for "mushroom." In drug culture, refers to the psilocybe mushroom or "magic" mushroom. When ingested, produces a hallucinogenic high and may lead to bad trips, similar to LSD.

'Shrooms are grown in cow crap!

shut down

To reject or decline, especially when someone's hopes are up.

I asked out this guy but he shut me down.

shysexual

Someone who doesn't seem to show

an interest in either gender. They're just not openly sexual. Usually it's just because they're incredibly shy.

I wonder if Andy likes anybody. I can't tell because he's such a shysexual!

sick

Interesting, cool, new.

That rave was sick. You shoulda been there.

"sick day"

When a person working at an office takes a day off because they are "sick." Usually they participate in an activity that is nowhere near their daily work-related tasks.

I've been doing a lot of work lately. I gotta take a "sick day" next week.

sign scramblers

A group of enthusiasts who rearrange the plastic letters found on signs outside of businesses and schools alike, often forming vulgar phrases.

Those pesky sign scramblers hit my sign again. They changed it from PRUNING LILACS—BRING TOOLS—$5 FEE to LOCAL SLUT IS BRINGING PORN—$5 FEE.

sike

Interjection meaning "false!" or "just kidding!" Also "psych."

Yo' mamma look like Dumbo on speed— sike!

silent but deadly

A creeper, a floating air biscuit. A fart that cannot be heard but can sure as hell be smelled. Don't ever recognize this type of fart out loud, lest you fall into the rule of "Whoever smelt it dealt it." Sometimes referred to by the acronym "SBD."

Dayum, someone done let loose a silent but deadly.

silly juice

Alcohol. Drinking enough silly juice will cause you to get silly, and drinking even more will usually cause you to go home with a weather-beaten skank.

Dude, I don't understand you at all! Are you on some silly juice?

silverware

Bling made of silver. Could be rims, silver chains, etc.

You trying to jack mah silverware? I'll kill you!

sista

A female friend who is more than one's best friend.

You are more than that—you're my sista.

sixer

A six-pack of beer.

To start the morning off right, I downed a sixer.

skank

1. To dance to ska music by kicking your legs and moving your arms.

My friends and I went to a ska concert and we were totally skankin'!

2. A young female (or sometimes a male) with poor hygienic habits who wears very little clothing and is probably sexually "easy."

She, like, never bathes or takes showers! And she'll have sex with any guy who walks by! She's such a skank!

skater

Person who considers skateboarding a way of life. Often erroneously classified as "punks" who like to cause trouble, possibly because street skating sometimes causes damage to property. There are vert skaters and street skaters. Vert skaters skate in halfpipes. Street skaters skate stairs and ledges and such.

I'm a real skater. I do it for the right reasons—not to get girls or cash.

skeevy

Creepy, sneaky, sketchy, or nasty, especially when applied to wannabe pick-up artists.

Some really skeevy guy tried to pick me up last night.

skeezy

A combination of "sketchy" (dubious) and "sleazy" (dirty or vulgar).

That middle-aged man hanging outside the high school parking lot was majorly skeezy.

sketch

Uncertain or potentially bad, like a party that is to happen in the future but there are rumors of the cops already knowing about it.

I don't wanna go if it's gonna be sketch.

sketchy

Disgusting or very strange.

That girl with the green hair and boogers all over her face is uber-sketchy.

skid mark

Poo-poo stain in the seat of one's underpants.

I don't wipe; I've learned to live with the skid mark.

skillets

Closest friends.

Yo, I just be chillin' wit my skillets in my crib.

skills

Proficiency in a field of sports or everyday life. When one is very good at what they do.

Yo, Tracy McGrady has tight ballin' skills.

skin me

Interjection meaning "give me some skin" or "give me a high five."

Skin me!

skinny

The scoop. The details.

What's the skinny on your mom? Is she single?

skrilla

Money. Especially U.S. paper currency. Sometimes shortened to "skrill."

Shit, even with this job, I need mo' skrilla.

skunk

To beat badly, as in a race or sport.

The Cowboys got skunked last night.

skunk weed

Either a crossbreed of marijuana varieties (like sativa or indica) or just strong-smelling pot. Sativa is the more traditionally smoked outdoor-grown variety that occurs naturally in places like Colombia, Mexico, Thailand, and Africa; indica is a shorter, bushier variety found in Afghanistan.

This skunk is some evil shit. Where can I get some?

slag

1. An individual who cares not for relationships beyond the realm of the sexual. These people sleep with many partners, not caring about anything save for the moment of climax.

She slept with John, Rick, Tom, and Peter, and that was before breakfast. She's such a slag.

2. Rubbish that is not worth the time or effort of paying attention to it, but nonetheless draws one in. Used to describe unpleasant situations.

Lost your job, huh? Damn, man, that's some cold hard slag.

3. Physical trash, often scrap metals.

Don't forget to get the slag off the yard. The city is threatening to fine us!

slam

1. To verbally insult, dis(respect), or burn someone.

We should slam him 'bout having no game.

2. To mainline or inject drugs.

I got the crystal, you bring the rigs, and let's slam; I'm ready to party tonight.

slammer

Prison. Jail. The pen. The can.

Zach went to the slammer for robbin' a bank.

slang

The ever-evolving bastardization of the written and spoken language as a result of social and cultural idolization of celebrities.

Aw, snap, son. Check out the fine-ass sho-tee rockin' all dat ice. (Translation: Hello, my good sir. Take a gander at the beautiful woman wearing the expensive jewels.)

slanguage

Combination of "slang" and "language."

Slanguage is still used on CB in some places.

slashdotted

When a website becomes virtually unreachable because too many people are trying to access it. The term was born at the Slashdot nerd news service (slashdot.org), where users post comments and links to sites they recommend.

I can't load the page; the site must be slashdotted.

slay

To be really good.

Dude, that new Nevermore album slays!

sleep debt

Something you accumulate whenever you don't sleep an adequate amount on a given night.

If sleep debt was dollars, yo' mama would be a rich bitch.

sleep drunk

So tired your inhibitions and thought processes are lowered due to lack of sleep. Very similar to being drunk.

I pulled an all-nighter last night and had to run straight to class. I stumbled in so sleep drunk that now I'm worried about what I may have said aloud during discussion.

slice

An eighth of an ounce of marijuana. Derived from the fact that a slice is an eighth of a pizza.

I'm swinging slices for 50 bills.

slicey

A friend. A homey, home slice, or pal.

Me and my slicey went to the pizza joint last night and held the cashier up.

slick

Perfect in manner; sharp, attentive, having perfect answers for virtually all questions, and, of course, large amounts of gel in the hair.

That's why they call me slick.

slide

A person you mess around with outside of a relationship but are not serious about.

Nah, son, she ain't my girl—she's just a slide.

sling

To sell drugs. Also "slang."

I slang a 20 rock the other day.

sloppy seconds

1. What you get when you kiss, date, or have sex with someone right after someone else did. When you take someone's leftovers.

When the fraternity entered the bar the brothers were allowed to pick dates first, while the pledges got sloppy seconds.

2. Any decrease in the quality of available goods or people. What's left after the best choices are gone.

They were giving away free stuff, but Jenny got there first, so I got her sloppy seconds.

slore

Cross between "slut" and "whore." A woman who indiscriminately shares a bed with anyone who shows interest, often without protection and/or discretion.

Person 1: They're saying that chick who sued him was also with other guys that night.
Person 2: What a slore.

slow your roll

1. Slow down. Be calm.

Slow your roll, homey! I'm tryin' to relax up in this mutha.

2. Slow down your game. Stop coming on so strong to a female.

You'd better slow your roll, junior player. You'll just get shut down going like that.

slug bug

A game where you slug someone and yell "slug bug" when you see a Volkswagen Beetle.

Slug bug! No backsies!

slut

A derogatory term for a sexually promiscuous person (usually female) or a woman who wears skimpy or tasteless clothing.

That slut has slept with every man in this room!

smack

Drugs in general, but often specifically refers to heroin.

Guy 1: Dude, get off your ass and get a job.
Guy 2: Can't. I'm addicted to smack.

smarmy

Having a smug attitude, often accompanied by a squinty look and a superior smile that makes you instantly hate a person.

He's so smarmy I want to punch him in the face.

smash

To insult and/or punk someone, usually embarrassing them in the process.

Miguel smashed on James in class today. We were crackin' up.

smoke

1. To discipline through extreme physical exercise or activity; often done by a drill sergeant during basic training.

D.S. McCarthy smoked the whole platoon because one soldier's canteen was not full of water.

2. To blow someone away in competition. To soundly defeat someone.

My PowerBook smoked your G4 in those performance benchmarks!

3. To light up a cigarette or similar instrument, sometimes packed with drugs, then stick it in your mouth and inhale.

4. The gray debris that results from burning something.

5. To kill, generally with a gun.

The guy was smoking some smokes, which was too much smoke next to the NO SMOKING sign, so I pulled out my gun and smoked him.

smokey bear

Trucker-speak for a state trooper/highway patrolman. Mostly shortened to just "smokey" or "bear."

My dad was the first trucker to ever overtake an Ohio smokey bear on the highway without getting a ticket; he's a living legend among truckers.

SMS

Acronym for "short message service," a text-messaging service on mobile phones. Used in verb form: to send a text message over a mobile phone.

I spent my office hours SMSing everyone in my address book.

snafu

Acronym for "situation normal all fucked up." Used to describe a less than desirable scenario when everything seems to have gone wrong. Common military phrase.

Ashlee Simpson's band had a major snafu last night on Saturday Night Live *when they started playing the wrong song and she canceled the performance.*

snap

Interjection used to express a feeling of excitement, surprise, disappointment, or extreme satisfaction, depending on the context.
Alternative to "aw, damn," "aw, shit."

Oh, snap, the engine's on fire!

Check out the jelly shakin' on her as she drops it to the floor. Snap!

I was like "snap" when I saw them rolling this way.

snaps

1. Money.

Yo, you got some snaps for the movie?

2. Skills.

Damn! Homey got all the snaps on the mic.

3. Praise for a job well done.

Snaps for reeling in your man!

snarf

When one is eating or drinking and is provoked by something funny that causes them to laugh and expel food or drink out of nasal passages or mouth.

Dude, I was eating my lunch at school and this chick said something hilarious and I totally snarfed sandwich all over the place.

S

snark

Combination of "snide" and "remark." Sarcastic comment(s).

His commentary was rife with snark.

Her snarky remarks had half the room on the floor laughing and the other half ready to walk out.

"Your boundless ineptitude is astounding," she snarkily declared.

snipe

To bid on an eBay auction minutes before it ends, hoping that others will not be able to place a higher bid in time.

Damn! I thought I won that item, but somebody sniped it!

snog

To passionately kiss.

The world melts away into a clutter of noise and shadow when we're snogging.

snot rocket

When you plug one nostril with your finger and blow out of the other nostril with everything you have, sending a snot projectile out of the nose.

Without tissue, all I could do to clear my nose was to blow a snot rocket.

snow job

An effort to deceive, overwhelm, or persuade with insincere talk, especially flattery.

The entire presentation was a complete snow job.

snuff

1. To kill, assassinate, destroy, murder.

A lot of people get mugged and snuffed here.

2. Films in which participants are actually murdered, killed, or mutilated on camera.

The police raided his house and found a snuff film of a guy getting tortured with a razor blade.

3. Very fine tobacco used for snorting.

The sign of a true gentleman is that he does not sneeze when he takes his snuff.

SO

Acronym for "significant other." One's romantic partner.

My SO can't join us for drinks later.

so

Word used to make a point or

emphasize a statement. Often used on television shows like *Friends,* then quickly adopted by females and gay men.

You're so not going there.

I'm so not interested.

so over

Finished. Completely done. Kaput.

I am so over people who call mashed potatoes "smashed potatoes."

so yesterday

Something that was once popular, until it went uber-mainstream, and has now become passé.

Grunge is so yesterday. Get over it.

SOB

Acronym for "son of a bitch." A jerk or a bad person.

Get back here, you SOB!

SoCo

Short for "Southern Comfort" liquor.

Girl: What's up?
Guy: Nothin'. Just drinkin' on some SoCo.

soft crust

Not cool, no fun, boring, loserish. Opposite of "hardcore."

That bitch is soft crust, man! Who would ever wanna hang out with a loser like that?

solid

1. Interjection of approval, confirmation, or congratulations.

Me: Where's the beer?
Joe: I got 10 40s.
Me: Solid.

2. A favor done for someone.

Do me a solid and hand me that hammer.

some else

Shortened form of "someone else," "somewhere else," or "something else," depending on the context of the conversation.

Man, this party really blows. Let's go some else.

Dude, I really don't like that chick. I like some else.

Naw, man, I don't want to go play pool tonight. Let's do some else.

son

Informal interjection used to refer

to a man (whether it's a close friend or someone you don't know) when you're in a conversation with him.

Wassup, son?

son of a

Exclamation of surprise or pain. Short for "son of a bitch."

Dad: Says here you failed the 12th grade.
Kid: Son of a!

SOP

Acronym for "standard operating procedure."

Pee in the cup, soldier! It's SOP!

soup to nuts

Start to finish.

Riley: Did you watch the State of the Union address last night?
Mandy: Soup to nuts.

soymanella

Food poisoning acquired by eating contaminated fake meat.

I was puking all night. I bet it was that nasty-ass six-month-old soymanella-infested tofurkey.

spacin' g's

To willingly waste time, as though

you were floating in the zero gravity of space without a care in your mind and nothing to do.

Shit, sweetback, we've been spacin' g's all day today. . . . Nothing can beat this.

spaghetti code

In computer programming, code that flagrantly violates the principles of structured, procedural programming, is almost impossible to debug and maintain, and rarely works well. Suggests the tangled and arbitrary nature of the program.

You want me to work on this freaking spaghetti code? Please tell me you're kidding.

spam

1. When capitalized: extremely cheap American canned meat.

Who wants some Spam in a can?!

Yay, more Spam!

2. When not capitalized: unsolicited mail/e-mail sent out in mass quantities. Usually not even addressed by name to the person who receives it. Short for "stupid, pointless, annoying message."

Damn it, more spam!

3. In gaming, refers to either throwing grenades indiscriminately, many at a time, or any overused gun/combo/move/tactic.

Way to spam the room, buddy. You throw enough 'nades that time?

Spanglish
A mixture of English and Spanish used in an attempt to show one's diverse nature and willingness to adapt to local customs and language (or lack thereof). The sentence usually starts in Spanish but deteriorates into English with a Spanish accent.

Que pasa, me homey? Mes amigos and me are gonna kick the frijoles out of jou tf jou don shutcho taco hole. Comprende?

speculate to accumulate
Variation of "spend money to make money," though open to different contexts. A phrase used by potential profiteers to remind prospective investors that returns can only come from good investment.

We invested in some drinks for the ladies at the bar, under the rule of speculate to accumulate.

speed
Amphetamine.

Look at that paranoid pale-faced bloke talking bollocks who looks like he's been awake for two weeks! He must be on speed.

speed date
An organized social event to facilitate meeting new people, usually for heterosexuals wishing to meet new potential partners. Equal numbers of both sexes pay to spend about three minutes talking to each member of the oppposite sex. At the end of the evening everyone marks on a card who they would like to date again and who they wouldn't. The organizers then swap contact information between matches.

I went on a speed date and met Katrina. Our speed relationship's already over.

spew
Vomit.

He spewed all over the floor. Nasty!

spiff
1. Followed by "up": to dress up, especially stylishly.

You're all spiffed up today.

2. Similar to "nifty" or "cool." Also "spifftastic" or "muy spiffendo."

You won the contest? Spiff!

spike

To add alcohol to something.

OMG! Someone spiked the punch!

spill

To take a bad fall while attempting a great feat.

Dude-man, I totally spilled while attempting the 900.

spin

1. Public relations term meaning to slightly alter facts to shape a more desirable version of a story.

We put a different spin on our massive lay-offs; we called it a "corporate restructuring."

2. What a DJ does to records.

DJ Feist-E spins better than any other.

spin doctor

1. Public relations expert who ensures that the public understands things from a certain perspective.

We think that the spin doctors at the local TV station helped the mayor win the election.

2. A DJ or MC at a club or event.

The Club Boom anniversary party spin doctor was awesome!

spinners

Tire rims with additional rims that spin freely even after the car stops.

Look at dem spinners on that nice ride.

spit

To speak. Usually used in reference to hip-hop, rap, or poetry.

Let me spit this rhyme for y'all.

spit game

To flirt with or mack on somebody, but usually not very seriously.

I think I'll go out and spit game at some ladies tonight, but I'm not looking to take any home.

spliff

A marijuana joint. Specifically, a cone-shaped joint that is somewhat large and impressively rolled.

That party was wack 'til my dog busted out a fatty spliff!

sploser

Combination of "spaz" and "loser."

Dane is such a sploser that he writes himself pretend letters from his pretend girlfriend.

spoonerism

A word or phrase created by swapping the initial letters (or first consonant sounds) of two words or syllables to get a new word or phrase.

"peas and carrots" and "keys and parrots"
"tea bags" and "bee tags"
"trail mix" and "mail tricks"
"save the whales" and "wave the sails"

spork

A cross between a spoon and a fork. The god of silverware.

Use sporks instead of forks and spoons. You'll end up saving table space.

sporn

Combination of "spam" and "porn." What fills most e-mail in-boxes.

Matt anxiously checked his Hotmail inbox for relevant e-mail from his honey, but alas, it was filled to the brim with unncessary sporn.

sport

The name you call someone to make them feel like a total loser. Often used by fathers to refer to their sons. Also "champ" or "chief."

Dad: Hey, sport, whaddaya say your old man teaches you to throw the ol' ball around today?

You: Dad, I'm an All-American pitcher at U of Texas.

spot on

Well done, perfect, right on, bang on.

The food in England might not always be so good, but the brew in the pubs is spot on every time.

spray

To use a car with a nitrous oxide injection system in a drag race. Makes it go faster.

That 'Vette was pullin' on me, but I sprayed him and won by a length.

spring fever

A subtle, nonoffensive way of suggesting that someone is horny.

Jeez, Bob, quit staring at those girls. You must have a pretty bad case of spring fever.

sprung

Very attracted to a person, with an obsession often mistaken for love.

I know we've only been talking for two hours, but you've got me sprung.

spun

Under the influence of methamphetamine. Also "spun up."

Wow! You look really spun. Lay off the speed.

spyware

A program stealthily installed onto your computer that tracks what websites you visit. Often bundled with freeware.

I clicked on the link for "free money" and in an instant I was infected with spyware that changed my homepage and bookmarks.

square

A tobacco cigarette.

You got a spare square I can bum off you?

squeeze

A girl, or guy, who is not one's girlfriend but often has sexual relations with that person anyway.

Nah, man. She's not my girl, she's just a squeeze.

stag

1. A male-only social gathering.

I can't wait to go to Paddy's stag.

2. A man who attends a social gathering without his partner.

Paddy's going stag to the wedding in Newcastle.

staircase wit

Thinking of the right answer too late; the perfect, usually piercing riposte that you conceive only when replaying a verbal exchange later in your head. From the French "l'esprit d'escalier," the witty repartee you think of as you're going downstairs to leave.

My coworker Ann had taken to calling me "Markus," which I hate. I told her I hated it, and her response was, "It's a term of affection." I muttered something like, "Well, it's not." What I should have said was, "Okay, to cement this 'affectionate' relationship, I'll call you An(n)us."

stank

1. Nasty.

Why you wit that stank ho? You can do better!

2. Brutish emphasis; typically used in the phrase "put some stank on it."

Can you do it again? An' this time put some stank on it!

starter marriage

Exclusively refers to a couple's initial marriage, probably at age 24 or less, involving partners with little income and assets. Subsequent marriages are usually to partners higher up the socioeconomic scale.

All she got was an '84 Subaru and some crummy dishes. No jewels, no real estate, nothing really to split; it was a classic starter marriage.

static
Violence, trouble.

Those muthas be startin' some static!

stealth bomber
Someone who breaks wind silently, then moves out of the room before anyone notices.

What the . . . ? Oh my God, do you smell that? Who's the stealth bomber?!

steel
1. Any form of transport with a metal surface that can be used as a canvas by a graffiti artist.

Man, I painted some steel last night.

2. A handgun.

You carryin' steel?

steez
Style with ease. A person's unique style. How an individual carries himself.

You know I don't get down like that. You know my steez.

step
1. To leave, usually at someone's request or as part of a threat.

You'd best get to steppin'.

2. Rush, bring drama or violence to.

Don't step to me or you'll get whacked.

step it up
Take things up a notch.

Boy, you need to step it up, get big.

step off
Back off. Used as a threat.

You'd best step off!

step out
1. To go out for a night of fun (clubbing, pubbing, or whatever suits your fancy) with friends or a girlfriend/boyfriend.

We're stepping out tonight. It's gonna get crunk.

2. Followed by "on": to cheat on one's significant other.

Girl, don't get loud about this, but I'm stepping out on my man this weekend with that hottie I met at the club.

step your game up

To improve your skills or talents.

You gotta step your game up to make it in the rap biz.

stick-icky-icky

Highly potent marijuana.

That is some fine stick-icky-icky doja, man.

stitch up

A setup, a trick. If someone stitches you up, then they're playing you for a fool. It's often used when framing someone for a crime.

I don't believe it, Dave! I was at home all night, I swear! I'm being stitched up!

stoked

Really happy or excited.

When Billy got a shiny new bike for Christmas, he was stoked.

stone fox

One who is so awesome that not only are they foxy, they are also solid. The most perfect compliment for any lady.

You can get any woman to go out with you by whispering "You're a stone fox" in her ear.

stoner

Someone who smokes a lot of weed or considers marijuana a lifestyle.

Just because I enjoy a nice spliff every afternoon, my friends call me a stoner.

stoner's Graceland

Another name for Wendy's. The late hours, stoner-friendly food, and 99-cent value menu are the main reasons. Dave Thomas is to stoners what Elvis is to your grandma.

Wendy's employee: How may I help you tonight, sir?
Johnny Potsmoker: Just give me the 420 meal. You know the drill.

stop short

To brake suddenly in order to cop a feel while "restraining" your passenger from being thrown forward. Popularized by the sitcom *Seinfeld*.

Vince slammed on the brakes and stopped short, opening an opportunity for him to cop a feel.

straight

Okay with how things are going.

Guy 1: You want a piece?
Guy 2: No, man, I'm straight.

urban

straight edge

Punk lifestyle that involves keeping a clear mind and a clean body, refusing to use drugs, drink, smoke, or have promiscuous sex. A phrase from a Minor Threat song glorifying the lifestyle. Abbreviated as "sXe."

I am proud to be set apart from the crowd, based on my lifestyle choices. I am clean, I am coherent, I am straight edge.

strapped

1. Low on a particular resource.

I'm strapped for booty.

2. Equipped with something, usually firearms.

Don't mess with me. I'm strapped.

street

Of or pertaining to the urban "street" culture, undergound, based around the core of hip-hop, skateboarding, BMX, etc.

Yo, that dude was fly and dressed so street!

street cred

Grassroots credibility earned through major accomplishments in the face of adversity. For example, a playa who has a rough childhood and tough upbringing but managed to make something respectable out of his life has street cred because he knows firsthand what it takes to be successful in this tough world.

She has mad street cred because she's been in the slammer.

street meat

1. Any variety of meat sold by a street vendor. This includes hot dogs, sausages, kebab, steak sandwiches, etc.

Let's pick up some street meat.

2. A streetwalking prostitute.

Let's pick up some street meat.

street pharmacist

Drug dealer.

Cal: Yo, you heard Jay started slangin' crack?
Luis: He gon' get shot by the hood's street pharmacist.

street sweeper

A 12-round revolver-style shotgun designed for destruction, or a number of shotguns converted to 10-plus round capacity.

Let's see how this bulletproof glass stands up to my street sweeper.

streetball

Basketball played outdoors on a blacktop and with fewer rules (no blood, no foul).

I'll beat you in streetball any day, homey! I got $100 on it! No refs and no crying.

strewth

Interjection of affirmation meaning "It's the truth."

Strewth, that was a hard day. Toss me a Foster's, mate!

strong

Having a lot of people in the same place at the same time; very crowded.

Shamiqua: Damn! Tonight the place is packed.
Latisha: I know. It must be 700 strong!

Strong Island

What people from Long Island, New York, proudly call their place of residence.

Yeah, you know where we from—Strong Island!

studio gangster

An insult that refers to somebody who raps about gang lifestyle in hip-hop but has never lived it. Also refers to being a wannabe gangster.

Jo: You hear MC BangBang's and DJ Killalot's new tracks about them robbing a liquor store?
D: Man, them fools ain't nothing but studio gangsters.

stunna

A person who drives around town in nice cars, on dubz, showing off their ice and bling.

I'm the numba-one stunna up in this, beeyatch, an' don't forget it, ho!

stunt

To floss or to show off.

You can stunt if you want, but your ass'll get rolled on.

stunters

A community of riders who enjoy performing stunts or extremely dangerous tricks on their lightweight sportbikes or motorcycles, often on public roads or highways. Sometimes shortened to "stuntas."

Look at those stunters, pulling wheelies on the 401. . . . These idiots are the reason I have to pay $3,000 a year to insure one motorcycle.

stupid

Can be used just like "mad" or

"hella" to amplify positive words.

Dude, that hot dog was stupid good! And your mom is mad stupid hot, yo!

styles

In street basketball, the keen ability to control the ball via various dribbling moves and tricks. Akin to "skills."

See that boy dribble? He has mad styles!

stylin'

Looking good; usually reserved for people or clothing.

I'd look stylin' in that jacket!

sub

Abbreviation for "subwoofer," a type of loudspeaker that plays bass.

Damn, how many subs you got in that car? I heard it two blocks away.

suburbia

The white ghetto. The bane of urban existence and just plain evil.

You just survive in the city, but you know you're alive. Move to suburbia and you just exist.

suck

To be really, really crappy. "Sucks" is sometimes written as "sux."

That team last night really sucked. They just plain sucked. I've seen teams suck before, but they were the suckiest buncha sucks that ever sucked.

suck ass

To be of such inferior quality as to boggle the mind.

This is an awesome song! It's too bad the station sucks ass to the max!

suck wind

1. To be left in the dust, as in a race or other competition.

That last hill on the cross-country course left me sucking wind as I watched everybody pass me.

2. To suck or to lose really badly. Worse than "to suck."

This traffic sucks wind.

3. A negative dismissal in the tradition of "go to hell."

Oh yeah? Well, tell them to go suck wind.

sucka MC

A person with poor lyrical ability. A non-originator or innovator of hip-hop, utilizing the same old gangsta clichés. Opposite of "dope MC."

This sucka MC wishes he could keep up with me.

suckage

1. Total state of sucking. The worst.

Giant robots crushed the casinos and mooshed the brothels and started fires that burned things and left ruin and suckage behind.

2. The amount that something does suck.

When you first encounter Diablo, you truly test your degree of suckage at D1.

suckin' diesel

Expression meaning things are going exceptionally well. Sometimes used when a bad situation gains hope.

I thought my computer was broken, but Gina fixed it by plugging it in. Now we're suckin' diesel!

sucks to be you

A phrase that expresses mild sympathy for the plight of another while implying greater relief that those circumstances have befallen someone other than the speaker. The American equivalent of the German "schadenfreude," which denotes actual pleasure in the suffering of another.

Wow, dude, she gave you herpes? Sucks to be you. . . .

sugar baby

A woman who provides companionship and/or sexual relations for a wealthy, older man in exchange for expensive gifts and/or money; a "gold digger."

If you're a rich man and your woman pays attention to you only when she wants your credit card, you're bein' played by a sugar baby!

sugar daddy

A man (often an older man) who provides money or other favors in exchange for sexual relations.

All she wants is a sugar daddy.

sugar momma

A woman (often an older woman) who provides money or other favors in exchange for a sexual relationship.

I got that new sports car from my sugar momma.

suicide doors

Suicide doors refer to car doors that open in the opposite of the regular direction—hinges are at the back, and the front of the door opens. Many cars before WWII had those and now it is a popular conversion on tuned trucks. Suicide doors are considered far more dangerous than normal doors because of the possiblity of opening during movement.

I am thinking of converting my truck to suicide doors so I can take stuff in and out easier.

suit

Slang for a businessman or any authority figure (e.g., manager, boss, supervisor) who normally wears a suit.

Those suits have been riding my ass all day.

summer school

A nickname for a person (usually a girl) who exhibits no class (hence, summer school).

Whatever you say, summer school.

s'up

A contraction of "what's up?"

Jack: Hey, s'up?
Jill: Not much.

super fly

Awesome, great, cool, hot.

Damn, girl, you super fly.

surfie

A person who is identified by the fact that they surf.

I'm a surfie girl at heart, so I hit the beaches as much as possible when I'm not working.

suss

Short for "suspect" or "suspicious."
1. Someone suspicious or unlikable. A suspect person.

He's a suss. I don't trust him.

2. Suspicious or out of place, like you might attract unwanted attention at a bad time, like when committing a crime.

Stop looking so suss.

3. To betray or "dog" someone.

Yeah, he sussed me with that money he was supposed to pay me back.

4. Watch closely, surveil; sometimes followed by "out."

That cop is sussing us out.

5. To know something well. To plan ahead. Also often followed by "out."

I had the whole plan sussed out.

6. Filthy, disgusting, or revolting.

Dude, you look suss. Take a shower.

7. A filthy, disgusting or revolting person.

Those susses just got out of jail.

swag

Acronym for "stuff we all get." Freebies, giveaway stuff, usually cheap and intended for promotional purposes. Sometimes spelled "schwag" or "shwag."

I went to the convention and picked up all kinds of swag.

I picked up some great swag at the concert last night.

swank

Extremely cool. Dope. Kickass.

Man, that car is so swank.

sweat

1. To like or adore.

J: That guy is so hot.
A: You sweat him so hard!

2. To copy or imitate.

I painted my room purple. The girl down the hall came in and said she painted her room purple too. My response: "Yeah, you sweat me."

3. To idolize.

Jessica Simpson is so awesome. I sweat her.

sweet

Great. Cool. Awesome. Can be used alone as an interjection.

Oh, man, that concert was so sweet!

Hey, I just got the last tickets to the concert. Sweet!

sweet as

As great as anything one can think of.

That bitch was sweet as.

swing

To have open promiscuity with a select group of partners who "swing" each other.

If you don't swing, don't ring!

swizzle

Snoop Doggified version of "sweet."

That's a swizzle rizzle.

swole

Extremely muscular or buff.

Craig: Yo, Ray-Ray, have you seen Trey lately? He's been hittin' the weights, hasn't he? He's swole, dawg.

T

tab

Single dose of LSD on paper squares. Also known as a "blotter."

I took seven tabs last night and I'm still semi tripping.

table muscle

A huge belly.

You see Bronco Def's table muscle? I bet he weigh 350 and could stay at the buffet all day long!

tadow

Combination of "tada" and "wow." Amazingly great or awesome.

Dayam! Did you see the new Rolling Stones cover with Britney Spears on it? She was tadow!

tag

To create graffiti. Usually implies vandalism with spray paint, but can be any graffiti.

Get up, man, we're going tagging tonight.

take it to the bank

Verify it and find it to be true. A way to say, "What was said is the absolute truth and can be verified."

Mount Everest is the tallest geographical point on this planet, and you can take that to the bank.

take names

To take control. Usually used in reference to military actions.

Marines: Kick ass and take names!

take off

To initiate a fight. To throw the first punch.

If that bitch keeps talking shit, you better take off on his ass.

take out the trash

To date someone who someone else tossed out like the trash.

I dumped Susanna last month and now Benji is with her. That garbage man is always taking out my trash.

take the L

Short for "take the loss." Frequently used to describe flunking a test, being dumped, being stood up, being beaten up or robbed, or losing one's money in the stock market, gambling, or through exploitative business schemes.

I really took the L on that history exam.

take to school

To beat someone in a competition, prove someone wrong, or otherwise show them how it's done.

Well, Quentin, you beat him 5–0, you really took him to school.

talk shit

1. To say something untruthful, uncalled-for, or rude, often with the intent of instigating a strong (possibly negative) reaction.

Jeff: Ted, you suck so much that David Oreck is having a tough time outmatching you!
Ted: Don't talk shit to me, playa. Keep talking and I'll deck you.

2. To make empty threats.

Tom: I'm gonna break your kneecaps open and make you drink the fluid.
Drake: Yeah, right. You're just talking shit.

talk to the hand

A saying used to ignore and disregard a comment or an insult when you can't think of a way to counter it. When this phrase is used, it is customary to raise your hand, palm facing out, and place it almost touching your adversary's face. This can make even the most civil person raging mad. Another variation is "talk to the hand 'cause the face don't give a damn."

Misty: Kylee, you a nasty, ugly, stupid—
Kylee: Talk to the hand. (raises hand to Misty's face)

tanked

Intoxicated with alcohol.

He got tanked at the party on Saturday and spent all day Sunday praying to the porcelain god.

tanorexic

A widespread disease: No matter how tan you are, you never think you are tan enough.

Leigh Anne: Melissa, sweetie, I think you've had enough sun today.
Melissa: No, no, I must get a tan.
Leigh Anne: You've been at the beach all day. I think you are tanorexic.

tap

To gain access to something, usually sexual relations with a female. An "untapped resource" is someone who hasn't been with anyone yet, or someone with a lot of potential whom not many people rate or notice.

That new girl in my tutorial is an untapped resource. Everyone thinks she's a nerd . . . but I just know it can be tapped!

tap out

To get out; to peel out; to leave quickly.

I need to tap out in 10 minutes.

tapped

1. Exhausted. Tired.

I was tapped after working that 12-hour shift.

2. Broke.

Buying all those shots at the bar left me tapped by last call.

target practice

Placing a flushable object in a toilet (like a small piece of toilet paper), then urinating on it. Usually done by males.

I'm bored and sober. So I'm doing target practice in the bathroom.

tasty beverage

A drink that contains alcohol.

Let's hit up Riley's for a tasty beverage.

tat

Short for "tattoo."

Check out my new tat.

technical difficulties

Signs of intoxication, including slurred speech and wobbly movement.

Sorry I couldn't show up to your gig, mate. I was having a few technical difficulties.

T

techno

A type of electronic music typically characterized by a medium to very fast tempo, synthesized instruments, heavy bass, and sometimes exotic and strange instruments, drums, and sound effects. Sometimes mixed with other genres such as jazz, rock, hip-hop, and various ethnic genres to create different results. Variations of techno include: acid, rave, synth, gabba/gabber, goa, trance, trip-hop, house, jungle, industrial, old-skool techno, ambient, hardcore, nu NRG, speedcore, deathcore, experimental, club, punkcore, space funk, electro, ghetto tech, euro, new-skool rap, booty house, acid jazz, garage, etc.

I just downloaded some tiiiiiiiiiight acid techno tracks off the net!

technosexual

A dandyish narcissist in love with not only himself, but also his urban lifestyle and gadgets; a straight man who is in touch with his feminine side and has an extreme fondness for electronics such as cell phones, PDAs, computers, software, and the web.

You'd never believe it to look at him, but he's a technosexual!

teledump

Being dumped over the telephone.

The only worse way to break up is to be cyberdumped via e-mail or instant messenger.

I just got teledumped; how much worse could it be? Oh yeah, well at least I didn't get cyberdumped. That'd be too harsh.

telly

Television.

I need to go watch the soccer game on my new flatscreen telly.

Texas tea

Crude oil.

They struck the ol' Texas tea . . . lucky sumbitches movin' on to Dallas.

Texas two-step

When you are driving and want to change lanes, but there is someone in the other lane, you quickly jerk the wheel into that lane but stay in your lane. This panics the driver, and as they hit the brakes you get the room you need to safely move into that lane.

This car will not let me over; time to do the Texas two-step.

text

To send an SMS message from one person to another via mobile phone.

Have you texted James about tonight?

text talk
A language used in SMS messages to make them easier, and quicker, to write. Also "txt tlk" or "thumbtext."

A: i (L)d it but evry1 startd sayin tht i cut maself n evrythng wen it woz ma falt!! so i aint nomor! but it woz wkd!!
B: Save the text talk for cell phones. Write me a real letter.

thang
Thing.

Hit that thang!

that guy
The person everyone loves to hate and never wants to become. The guy who makes an ass of himself and embarrasses everyone who knows him.

I was driving in heavy traffic and got stuck in the middle of the intersection just as the light turned red. Because of me, no one could get by. Suddenly I became "that guy."

that's butt
Short for "that's butt ugly." Nasty.

Anquan: Yo, you see that girl ova there?
Shawan: Naw, man, that's butt.

that's hot
Interjection of approval. Often used on *The Simple Life* reality series by Paris Hilton in her monotone voice when referring to almost anything.

Paris: Where are you from?
Me: Columbia.
Paris: That's hot.

Paris: What color is your shirt?
Me: Green.
Pari : That's hot.

that's how we do
A substitute for the phrase "yeah, man, that's how we do (or say) things" or "that's how we act 'round here, brotha." Can also mean "that's a good girl/boy" or "that's mah girl/boy/boi." Also "that's how I roll."

Yeah, man, that's how we do.

that's my word
Interjection used to reinforce a statement.

Person 1: Ew, stay away from that one—she's a skank.
Person 2: No shit?
Person 1: That's my word!

that's what I'm talking about
Statement of agreement. Used even

if you've never talked about the subject before.

Dude #1: Look at that chick!
Dude #2: That's what I'm talkin' about!

the block is hot

Statement meaning the police are on the block.

The block is hot! Better run for cover.

the bomb

Really cool.

Einstein is the bomb!

the bomb diggity

The greatest thing ever.

You might hear the following in Philly:
The Phillies are the bomb diggity. In fact,
this cheesesteak is the bomb diggity.

the breaks

Bad luck, a damn shame, or an unfortunate occurrence.

Doc: What up, dawg.
Timmy: Nothing much. I lost a quarter
under the washing machine a couple
minutes ago.
Doc: That's the breaks.
(A week later)
Doc: What up, dawg.
Timmy: Didn't you hear? I lost my job

and my wife left me for the mailman.
Doc: That's the breaks.

the falling leaf

Basic snowboarding move. When someone is first learning and is scared to attempt carving, they go all the way down the slope on their heelside by first heading downhill with their dominant foot, and then their other foot, imitating the motion of a falling leaf.

Sarah was tired of falling on her ass every
time she tried to carve, so she just did the
falling leaf all the way down the slope.

the fear

A state of intense, drug-induced paranoia.

Where's my knife? . . . The fear's got me
bad, man.

the jacket

The fuzz. The five-O. The police.

I'm tired of the jacket taking my stash.

the kid

A way to refer to yourself in the third person. Often used by G-Unit members 50 Cent and Lloyd Banks.

Bag lady: Paper or plastic?
Wanksta: Aaaawwww pleez, bitch! You

know what the kid be all about. Da paper, ho! Now wrap dem groceries up good, baby. You know how I roll.
Bag lady: Here you go, sir.
Wanksta: And while yo' at it, throw in this here 50-pack of jimmy hats, 'cuz you know the kid be hittin' it all night, baby! Yeah, beee-otch!
Bag lady: Thank you for shopping. Have a nice day.
Wanksta: Peace! The kid be out! (leaves)
Bag lady: What was up with that dumb white kid?

the red button
Nuclear button.

During the Cold War there was much fear about whether or not we'd really have to use the red button.

the shit
The best. Without "the," it has the opposite meaning. "My teacher is shit" = bad teacher. "My teacher is the shit" = the greatest teacher.

Man, this weed is the shit! I can barely feel my feet!

Man, this weed is shit. It tastes like oregano.

thick
1. Crowded. Full of people, usually at a party or club.

Your party was gettin thick 'til the five-O showed up. Everybody rolled out then.

2. Having a nice butt, nice legs, not skinny, with meat on your bones. Thickness is the shit.

Damn, that girl is thick, yo!

threads
Fancy clothes.

Hey, don't touch the threads.

thrift score
Finding something of value in a cheap store or yard sale. Does not apply to the Internet.

Check this thrift score: leopard print platform shoes for $5!

throw
To engage in a fistfight.

Are you talking to me? You wanna throw? Let's throw!

throw 'bows
To dance, as in the "Southern Hospitality" video when rapper Ludacris holds up his fists and looks like he's punching the sky, throwing up his elbows (hence "'bows").

T

We hit up that new club on Friday. I was throwin' 'bows the whole night!

throw down

1. To do a DJ set or mix.

I threw down a set last night at this party and rocked the spot.

2. To fight.

Some boys were all up in our faces, so we had ta throw down ta represent.

3. To have a large party.

He threw down hardcore last weekend.

throw salt

To purposely try to foul up someone's mack game and keep them from getting sex.

Why are you throwing salt in my game? I oughta punch your lights out.

throw under the bus

To reveal information damaging to another's character, as to a boss or girlfriend.

Yo, Ben, thanks for throwing me under the bus with that remark about those girls.

throw up

A quick graffiti bomb. Usually not the writer's full name. An unfilled throw up (outline only) is a "hollow." A filled throw up is usually a "crack-fill" (quick back and forth strokes with a fill color). Also called a "throwie" or "throw."

You know that kid who throws up NE? What do they write?

throwback

Old-school or retro person or thing.

That Larry Byrd jersey is a throwback.

throwed

1. Magnificent. Pleasing to the eye.

The club was throwed tonight. You shoulda been there.

2. Intoxicated or high.

He was too throwed to notice his drawers were around his ankles.

3. Out of style.

It was so embarrassing to see her wear those throwed-ass shoes.

thug

1. A person, usually a man, who has taken to a life of violent crime. Usually raised in a hostile, deprived environment. They differ from gangsters in the respect that they are

not into organized crime. A thug could graduate into a gangster and may work for one, while still doing spontaneous muggings or dealing. When in gangs they can be proprietary about their turf.

You see that thug over there selling rocks?

2. To act like a thug.

Tupac admits to thuggin' since elementary school.

thugged out

Appearing to be a member of urban ghetto culture through affected attitudes, mannerisms, language, or dress.

Ah, man, you are looking especially thugged out today with them suede pleats and that bowler hat.

tick

1. Bloodsucking parasite who takes over your life, bleeds you dry, and is hard to get rid of.

I spent the better part of the morning in downtown's Third Circuit Court having a tick removed.

2. To get some playing time in a sports game.

That dude is garbage. He gets no tick.

3. Buff, fit, good-looking.

When he wore his Armani suit he looked tick.

tig ol' bitties

A spoonerism for "big ol' titties," meaning large breasts. Often used as code, or the slurring language of a drunk, while in the presence of a buxom woman.

Yar! Let us drink to the queer old dean *hic* and let's 'ave somma thum tig ol' bitties.

tight

1. Close (when referring to a friend).

We been tight since middle school.

2. Cool, stylin' (when referring to an object).

The chromed-out rims on his new car are tight.

tighten it up

To get one's shit together.

After he broke his sobriety and drank, Amy told John to tighten it up.

timin'

A cooler way to say "happenin'."

What's timin'?!

tin

A badge carried by law enforcement officials.

Officer Fox had to turn in his tin and weapon back at the station.

tips

Short for "tipsy." Slightly drunk.

We all had a good drunken time down at the bars, and Susie got especially tips.

tired

Boring. Old. Overused.

That song is tired. Change CDs.

tits

Good, tight, cool, awesome.

Yo, I just picked up that new game— shit is tits!

TMI

1. Acronym for Three Mile Island, a nuclear power plant near Harrisburg, Pennsylvania, that leaked radiation in 1979 but is still operational.
2. Acronym for "too much information."

Tex: So how's that job at TMI going?
Billy Bob: Pretty good, at least since that accident way back, which made me grow a third ear on my ass.
Tex: Damn, dawg, TMI!

TNT

Incredibly awesome. Alternative to saying "it's the bomb."

Dude, this song is the TNT.

to the dome

To the head. Often used in reference to taking a large quantity of intoxicant in a short time so that it goes straight "to the head," or to refer to taking a blow/bullet to the head.

Dude! Did you just see that? John just took a half-ounce to the dome! He'll be lucky if he doesn't pass out cold.

toast

1. Guns.

We gonna ride up with tha toast and just bust slugs.

2. Destroyed, terminated, ceased functioning, ended abruptly by external forces.

My car was toast after I hit that wall.

toasted

Extremely intoxicated by alcohol or other drugs.

We got kicked out of home economics 'cause we would always show up toasted and eat all the cookies.

toe up

Wasted beyond belief by an illegal substance of some sort or by alcohol. Also "tore up."

Yo, man, I'm gonna go to that party tonight and get so toe up you won't recognize me!

toke

To inhale marijuana smoke.

Hand that peace pipe over here. I need another toke.

told

Put in one's place, whether in the form of a humiliating insult, beating, or other form of defeat.

Oh, you came in here all arrogant, but you got told!

tool

1. Someone who tries too hard. A poser.

People who wear huge logos on their shirts are tools.

2. An idiot who doesn't realize they're being used by other people.

Someone who can't think for themselves.

Kip: Dude, I need a ride to the party.
Rico: Ask Napoleon. He's a tool.

toolish

Out of character and/or done to suck up to another.

Ted, it was toolish of you to pick up the boss's laundry after he made you work the weekend.

tool box

A mega tool; a boy who thinks girls worship him when they really want to vomit on his shoes. Also "tool kit."

Matt is not just a tool—he's the whole box of tools, a complete tool box.

toppin some Gs

Making some money. Working.

Dawg, I gotta top some Gs tomorrow.

tore down

Extremely drunk. Wasted, smashed, or plastered.

Your sister: Hey, baby, wanna get it on?
Nick: No. I drank too much. Can't you see I'm puking here?
Your sister: I don't mind a little puke.

You know where to find me, big boy. I'll be waiting for you.
Nick: In your dreams, ho. I may be tore down, but that doesn't change the fact that you're straight tore up.

tore up

Extremely ugly, busted, broke down, and haggard. "Straight tore up" is the superlative form.

As Kelly fell out of the ugly tree and hit successive branches on the way down, she went from nothing to write home about to ugly to broke down to busted to straight tore up!

totty

1. An attractive or sexy person. Usually refers to women, but sometimes used for men.

Bill thought Jim was a good bit of a totty.

2. To be unsteady on one's feet, usually as a result of intoxication.

After five pints Bill was very totty.

touch

1. To kill.

Your boy got touched.

2. To beat.

Touch him up.

3. To rob.

That store needs to be touched.

tow

To give someone the boot. To dump one's significant other.

If he doesn't call me by Friday, he's getting towed.

toy

A graffiti artist's term for a novice. More experienced graffiti artists will often write "toy" next to the tag or graf of the novice.

That toy threw up some shitty tag over my graf.

TPS reports

Pointless busywork assigned to you by your boss. From the movie *Office Space*.

Sure I'll make the coffee and rearchive all of the company's files from the last ten years so that they are organized by account number instead of the customer's last name, even though we don't really use those files anymore. And I'll get those TPS reports to you first thing.

tracers

The blurry lines you see as things move around after consumption of too much alcohol and/or too much drugs.

Oh, man, I'm so messed up I'm seeing tracers.

trade junk
To have casual sex.

I invited my friend over to watch movies and trade junk.

tranny
1. Transvestite or transsexual.

Jon is a tranny. Check out his girly clothes.

2. A vehicle's transmission.

Pull that tranny so we can overhaul it.

3. In snowboarding, the transition between the table and the landing jump.

Some idiot skier hit me on the tranny.

transcriptrix
A kinky-sounding name for the woman who records meeting minutes.

The association was getting a little stodgy, so this year instead of electing a secretary, we changed the name to transcriptrix.

treat
To show someone how terrible they really are at something.

Our volleyball team beat the other team badly. Man, they got treated!

trees
Marijuana, THC, shwag, or nugs (kind bud).

Them trees got me higher than a mutha.

trendsbian
Any female engaging in same-sex interaction for the purpose of obtaining attention or popularity.

She is such a trendsbian.

trick out
1. In the car tuning scene: to modify a vehicle with as many types of aftermarket parts as are supported by that certain vehicle.

As soon as I get my settlement check, I'm gonna trick out my ride.

2. Heavily accessorized with premium or above-average modifications.

At her coronation, the Queen was all tricked out in brocade, ermine, and the crown jewels.

Mike tricked out his new apartment with a sweet surround-sound system.

T

trifling

Lazy, pathetic, worthless.

Man, you didn't take a shower after being with that girl?! You just triflin'!

trip

1. To act whack; to overreact or to lose yo' cool.

Yo, homey, don't trip. We'll get dem bitches next time.

2. A single complete experience of using acid (LSD) or any other powerful hallucinogenic drug.

That trip was crazy last night. I'm never taking the brown stuff again.

3. Something crazy, chaotic, or cool.

Wow, that ride is a real trip!

trip-hop

A blend of electronica and downtempo hip-hop, urban and ethereal, street and ambience. Thoughtprovoking, sensual, and deep. Often features string section and/or brass section. Can be either instrumental or with female vocals. Occasionally with rap. Trancy and smooth. Often jazzy. Sometimes features turntablism/scratching. It's head-nodding music and chillout music.

Portishead, Massive Attack, DJ Shadow, Goldfrapp, Lamb, Morcheeba, Smith & Mighty, Alpha, Björk, Earthling, Hooverphonic, Mono, Smoke City, and Zero 7 are a few exemplary trip-hop groups.

trip out

To lose your mind on drugs.

That acid made me trip out bad.

triple-dog dare

The ultimate dare one can issue to another. You cannot back down from a triple-dog dare; the dare must be implemented or carried out.

I triple-dog dare you to put your tongue on that frozen light post.

trippy

Crazy or weird.

I fell off the roof. Yeah, it was pretty trippy.

Trojan

A piece of software to gain access to a computing system while the owner isn't aware of its existence. Often introduced in a system hidden in an appealing-looking free package or game. Works on the same principle as the Trojan horse Odysseus used to conquer Troy in Homer's *Iliad*.

Guy 1: I planted a Trojan in her system—
I even have access to her webcam now!
Guy 2: You really should get a life, dude!

troll
One who posts a deliberately provocative message to a newsgroup or message board with the intention of causing maximum disruption and argument.

Oh no, not another troll making racist and homophobic posts . . .

trucker cap
A $40 hat worn by sorostitutes because "white trash is soooo cool this year!"

Oh my God, Christy! You have to see this great trucker hat I got at American Eagle yesterday! It's soooooo much like a real trucker hat, only I paid $40 for it! Aren't I cool?!

true that
Interjection of agreement. Means "ditto."

Guy 1: Man, that show last night was the bomb.
Guy 2: True that.

trust-fund baby
One who lives off their parents.

Jerry's parents pay for everything and he doesn't do shit. He's such a trust-fund baby.

TS
Acronym for "tough shit."

Man 1: Dude, I just broke my leg. I can't make it.
Man 2: TS.

tubular
Used mostly in the '80s, or by people mocking the '80s to describe something awesome or excellent.

That's totally tubular, dudette—way to go!

tulip
A special type of joint made famous by the Dutch that looks like a regular joint with a tulip-shaped sack of marijuana on the end of it. It looks like a tulip with a long stem hanging from your mouth.

Guy 1: How much weed we got left?
Guy 2: Quite a bit. Definitely enough for a tulip.

tunnel runner
An individual who runs through a city's underground tunnels with the intent of exploration, tagging, or escape, often while dodging security patrols or trains.

The police have been arresting any tunnel runners they catch trespassing in the subway system.

turf
To trip and fall on the ground.

I was running around outside of the bar and I turfed—scratched up my arm pretty good.

turkey drop
This happens when a dating couple try the long-distance relationship thing when they go off to college in September. Typically, when Thanksgiving rolls around and everyone goes home for the holiday, someone gets dumped. Hence the "turkey drop."

I hope Bob and I make it past the turkey drop.

turntablist
One who uses turntables in the spirit of an instrument; whereas ordinary DJs simply stand there and play two records, a turntablist scratches and manipulates his vinyl, and supplements it with breakbeats and samples.

DJ Premier, Alchemist, and Eric Barrier are all true turntablists.

tweek
To be under the influence of methamphetamine. Also "tweak."

Man, I got all tweaked two days ago and I'm still awake.

tweeker
A methamphetamine user. Can be recognized by their extreme paranoia and flagrant dishonesty.

If you let those damned tweekers come to your party, don't expect to have your stereo in the morning.

tweenager
A person who has entered the "in between" years of 10 to 12. These children display common traits, interests, and developing psychologies separate from those in younger, and older, age brackets. Commonly abbreviated to "tween." Usually in relation to consumption and marketing.

Those Mary-Kate and Ashley clothing products are specifically marketed to tweenagers.

twig and two berries
The male genitalia, collectively.

Foul! You hit me in the twig and two berries.

twist off

To consume alcoholic beverages, but usually beer. The term comes from twist-off beer bottles. Used in country singer Tracy Byrd's song "Drinkin' Bone."

Sam is such an alcoholic that he has to wake up every couple of hours during the night to twist off because he starts to get too much blood in his alcohol stream.

twist up your fingers

To display a gang sign or be in a gang.

Little Johnny used to play soccer and go to Boy Scout meetings, but now he twists up his fingers and slangs crack rock on the corner.

twisted

1. Very drunk.

Yo, we got twisted before we went to dat party!

2. Mixed up, confused.

Don't get it twisted. Just 'cuz she slept with the whole block don't mean she's a ho—she's just friendly.

3. Crazy, wild.

That guy is into some twisted shit. He wanted me to tie him up.

twitterpated

Complete and immediate infatuation with someone or something that occurs with the onset of spring; giddy excitement rooted in the physical. From the Walt Disney movie *Bambi*.

Ask Marie about her new army boy. She's so twitterpated she can barely talk.

two-comma kid

A kid whose parents are very rich (two commas implying a seven-figure income or net worth).

Yo, Cam is a total two-comma kid . . . wouldn't be anywhere without his dad.

twomp

1. The amount of marijuana that can be bought for $20.

He just sold me a twomp!

2. A $20 bill.

I threw down a twomp.

T

U

uber
When used before a word, magnifies that word. Indicates the ultimate, above all, best, top. Also "über."

I'm uber-confused. Can you explain it just one more time?

UDI
Acronym for "unidentified drinking injury." Random bruises, aches, and pains one picks up when one is drunk but can't remember exactly how they happened.

My boyfriend: I'm pretty sure I broke a finger playing cards last night.
Me: Whatever. Sounds more like a UDI.

ug
Short for "ugly." Reserved for a person who is so ugly they don't deserve the second syllable.

Ew, did you see her? She was an ug!

uglify
To make very ugly.

The company really uglified their shoes this season.

unco
1. Short for "uncoordinated."

You're too unco to play soccer.

2. Being otherwise clumsy in any respect.

You're so unco, you can't even beat Tetris.

underground
Art, opinion, or organization that

exists outside of mainstream society or culture. Also known as "independent" or sometimes "counterculture."

Giff preferred the underground music scene in her area to the bland stuff that played on most radio stations.

unflushable
The girlfriend or boyfriend who simply will not be dumped. Unable to get rid of.

Beth is maddeningly unflushable; I broke up with her again last night and we still ended up at her place.

ungood
Surfer term for "bad." Also used in George Orwell's novel *1984*.

Dude, that wipeout was totally ungood.

ungoogleable
To be effectively anonymous on the Internet because a Google search for your name returns an overwhelming number of results about someone else with the same name.

Honey, let's name him James Smith so he'll be ungoogleable when he grows up.

unholla
Interjection of disappointment or disagreement.

Dave P: Hey, did you see that girl back there?
A Dizzle: The one with a mustache?
Dave P: I thought it was a shadow, but she looked pretty good.
A Dizzle: Unholla—that bitch was grimy!

units
Short for "parental unit." Your parents.

God, the units are cramping my style.

unleash the fury
To be particularly violent. To open a can of whoopass. To attack animalistically.

He was like all in my face, until I got to a point I had to unleash the fury.

up against it
In trouble. Used in a situation in which the deck is stacked against you.

We're really up against it now!

up in my Kool-Aid
Someone's personal business. Used in the deepest parts of the hood.

You best be steppin' off! Why you all up in my Kool-Aid?

up north

In jail (mostly used in hip-hop music).

Drew: I'm gonna take these drugs up north and smuggle them into Canada. But first I gotta stop at Dunkin' Donuts. I'm mad jonesing for one of those.
Jason: Damn right you gonna be heading up north, cracka. Dunkin' Donuts is a pig sty. Them po-pos gonna arrest yo' white ass.

up on dat

Knowledgeable. To know something or have current information. Mostly used to brag or tell someone they don't know something.

I been seein' your girl for months now, you jus' wasn't up on dat.

upchuck

To throw up.

I upchucked my lunch.

upriver

In prison.

I got sent upriver.

upstate

Jail. The same thing as "up north" or "upriver." Comes from New York, where thugs get sent to the penitentiary upstate of the city.

My boy upstate finally got up out the joint.

urban exploration

Going places you're not supposed to go in a city. Often the act of urban exploration is illegal, as trespassing is usually necessary. However, the majority of urban explorers do not vandalize property. One of the cardinal rules of urban exploration is "take only photographs, leave only footprints." Also known as "urban adventure" and "UE."

There's an abandoned factory. Are you up for some urban exploration?

urbanup

To look something up on urbandictionary.com.

Dude, you don't know what "1337" means? Urbanup!

urch

To throw up, be sick, vomit.

That guy at the party was urchin' everywhere!

urban

va va voom

The feeling you get when you're filled with inspiration or full of excitement and energy.

She got her va va voom back when she realized that she had not missed the deadline for the contest.

value add

A business euphemism for "the reason I'd like you to think I'm useful."

My value add on this project is to leverage best-known-methods (BKMs) to focus on strategies leveraging core competencies moving forward synergistically to achieve our mutual business objectives.

vaporware

Usually software, but can be anything that is promoted and marketed without ever actually being produced. All hype but no substance.

I'm going to upgrade, but the manufacturer's promised upgrade is six years late—it's total vaporware.

V-card

Virginity. All virgins have a "V-card" until they "cash it in" for sex.

Guy 1: Jason spent the night at some girl's place.
Guy 2: Did he cash in his V-card?

V-Dub

A Volkswagen product.

That V-Dub is slammed.

veg out

To be an (often stoned) couch potato.

I just vegged out on Friday night!

verbal diarrhea

When someone is just talking so much shit it's like it spews from their mouth in a disgusting and uncontrollable way.

Jeff has so much verbal diarrhea that he's going to get his ass kicked.

vest

A bulletproof vest. Most typically a Kevlar vest worn by police officers. Term popularized by rapper 50 Cent, who wears one all the time.

Playa's got some enemies, so he's been sportin' a vest.

vet

A gang veteran who has seen many street wars. Also a veteran of the drug game.

He's a vet. Been running drugs for ages.

Viagrate

To imbue with lasting vigor.

Revenues are slumping; therefore, we must Viagrate our sales force.

vibe

A distinctive emotional atmosphere sensed intuitively.

It gave me a nostalgic vibe.

violent

Bad-ass. Cool. Savage.

That's a violent drink you just made. Thanks, man.

viral

Short for "viral marketing." An online marketing strategy that encourages people to pass on a marketing message. Often amusing and low-budget, a good Internet viral campaign (like "Terry Tate: Office Linebacker") will get surfers forwarding the ad to all of their friends, who e-mail it to more friends, and so on, giving the company great word of mouth.

FWD: Check out this hilarious viral from Hyundai!

virus

A harmful computer program that spreads itself to other computers once contracted, somewhat like its biological counterpart.

I just installed Windows Vista, and before I could even update I got a virus.

vom

So disgustingly repulsive it makes you want to vomit.

The food in the dining hall tonight is vom!

vomit comet

1. Multi-engine jet plane capable of sustaining dives long enough to simulate weightlessness; primarily used for astronaut training and films like *Apollo 13*.

I didn't realize my flight to JFK was on the vomit comet until the captain invited us to unbuckle our seatbelts and float freely about the cabin.

2. The late-night bus you have to take home after the subway stops running. So named because all the patrons on it are drunks from the bar, and alcohol-induced vomiting is a common occurrence.

I hate taking the vomit comet home. You meet the drunkest weirdos on it.

VPL

Acronym for "visible panty line."

Before thong underwear became all the rage, VPLs were considered the ultimate in undergarment sexiness.

V-plates

A label given to a person who has not experienced sexual intercourse; a virgin. Derived from L-plates, square white signs with red letter "Ls" on them that are displayed on the back and front of a vehicle driven by a person who is learning to drive in the U.K. L-plates are removed from the vehicle once the person is a qualified driver.

John lost his V-plates at the party last night.

vurp

A burp laced with a little vomit; usually occurs when you've had one too many and it has become difficult to distinguish between the two.

I made it through the whole night without vomiting, not including vurps, of course.

W

wa gwan

Interjection meaning "What's up?" or "How's it going?"

Yo, wa gwan, Starr?

wack

Not cool, sorry, sad, pathetic; also "whack."

He's wack as hell!

waffle-crapper

A chick so hot that you wouldn't care if she walked up and crapped on your waffle. In fact, you would probably welcome it.

She's no waffle-crapper, but I'd hit it.

wake and bake

Waking up and, while in bed, immediately smoking the "prepacked" bong that is sitting ready to smoke on your bedside table. Can be used to describe any situation where someone smokes within one hour of waking up.

I'm becomin' a bit chronic these days, like wake and bake every day and shit.

walk of shame

When a woman leaves the home of a man (quite possibly one she met the night before) in the early morning hours—hair sticking out in all directions, makeup half gone, with her undies in a pocket or her purse.

After a night of partying and excessive drinking, Cheryl woke up God-knows-where with an unknown man beside her. In a fit of regret, she gathered her belong-

ings as quickly and quietly as possible and crept from the man's home to do the walk of shame.

walk-and-talk

To call someone on a cell phone while doing errands. Considered the lowest form of telephone communication.

I was gonna kill that bitch when she did a walk-and-talk.

wambulance

A fictional ambulance or rescue squad for someone who cries or whines, most often without provocation. A way to insult someone who often cries for no apparent reason; a crybaby, a brat, or someone suffering from hypochondria.

Kid: Waaa, waaa, I want a cookie, waaaa, waaaa, waaaaa!
Mom: Did someone call the wambulance?

wang chung

Going out and having fun, in a vague, undefined kind of way (since no one ever really knew what "Everybody Wang Chung Tonight" meant in the band Wang Chung's song).

Let's go get a couple of 40s and wang chung down by the river.

wanger

Polite way of saying "wanker" if there are old people, ladies, or children present.

Oh yeah, Matthew is a right wanger. Sorry, Grandma!

wank

1. British slang for masturbation.

There was a guy in the park having a wank in the bushes.

2. A discussion without purpose or substance that often involves pretension and bullshit.

Then the entire conversation degenerated into complete wank.

wanker

A British term for one who masturbates. Commonly used as a general insult.

That wanker cut me off in traffic!

wanksta

A contraction of "wanker" and "gangsta" used pejoratively to label those who purport themselves to be gangstas but who are simply posing as such.

I saw Baz wearing all his bling yesterday and his most thuggin' gear, threatening to

W

duff people up. He really is a total wanksta.

wannabe

A faker, a poser. Someone trying too hard to fit in with a specific crowd. They usually change the way they act, dress, and/or talk, but people see past that.

Gangster wannabes act tough and hard, but when in a dangerous situation they piss themselves and run home.

wapanese

A derogatory term used to describe anyone who is a fanatical follower of Japanese culture. Often finds the Japanese culture to be superior to any other culture and takes great pride in showing off a new word or new words learned from animé or manga he/she has translated. The term "wapanese" is often misapplied to any person who watches animé, or Japanese cartoons.

Wapanese munch on imported Pocky and wash it down with a bottle of Pocari Sweat.

war

A way of teaching dumb-ass Americans about geography.

A: Say, where the hell is Peru anyway?

B: I don't know, Mr. President. Let's go to war to find out.
A: Yeee haaw! Hot diggidy, I'm gonna shoot me some Perus.
B: Peruvians, sir.
A: Whatever. Get the nukes warmed, will ya?

war in

Opposite of "peace out." Said when leaving people you don't like.

That's it, I'm outta here! War in!

wardrobe malfunction

An accidental or supposedly accidental failure of clothing to cover parts of the body intended to be covered. Made famous by Justin Timberlake during a Super Bowl halftime show when he tore off Janet Jackson's clothes.

Hit the five-second rewind button! Her name ain't baby, it's Janet, and things just got nasty. She just had a wardrobe malfunction!

warehouse

To store not-yet-drunk beer or other alcohol on the side during a drinking game, as opposed to actually drinking it.

After Grilled Cheese won the beirut tournament, his trophy was taken away when Bobby pointed out that he had warehoused enough beer to feed a family of four for a week.

warez

Computer software illegally distributed over the Internet without the publisher's consent.

Jon: How could you afford that expensive software?
Al: I can't. It's warez.

Warhol moment

The 15 minutes of fame that, if Andy Warhol is to be believed, we are all entitled to have.

When Mary was selected to appear on Big Brother, *she knew this was her Warhol moment.*

warm it up

To start it up. To get something going.

Warm it up, Chris. Let's go!

wash out

To lose traction, usually while going around a turn. Used in many contexts, including cycling and motorsports.

Snowflake washed out around that last hairy turn and plowed into a tree.

waste

To beat someone up in a fight or decisively win a contest against another person/team.

Chuck is going to waste Timmy after school today.

waste your flavor

To cramp your style or disrespect someone, making the person look like a little bitch, or anything less than a pimp.

Kenny: . . . and then I was jockin' all the fly bitches and deez hoes were all up on my nuts and I was like "Which one of you ladies is gonna get on the old Ken-meister Express?" Hellllz, yeah!
Steve: Shut up, man, you're all talk.
Kenny: Sheeeeeiiit, man, why you always gotta be wastin' my flava? Beeeotch, I oughta blast gats on yo' ass!

wax

To kill or murder.

Yo, let's wax that mutha.

wax idiotic

To talk about things that are boring, mundane, or annoying.

I had to sit there while they waxed idiotic about Britney Spears and Hilary Duff.

weak sauce

Weak. Insignificant; calling one "weak sauce" compares said individual to the "mild" sauce at Taco Bell—attempting to be like the other hot sauces, but not living up to expectations.

Damn, that fool at the gym was weak sauce.

weapons grade

Better than the rest. Of higher quality.

Usually my weed connection is okay, but last time, that shit was weapons grade.

wear dark blue

To be a member of the Crips gang.

Snoop Dogg claims to wear dark blue.

wedgie

The act of grabbing a person's underpants and lifting them high above their head while that person is still wearing them.

That last wedgie really damaged me. I'm telling Dad!

weed

Marijuana, pot, dope, grass, Mary Jane, chronic, hash, reefer, ganja.

Yo, you know the song about weed? It goes

"Roll, roll, roll a joint / twist it at the end / take a puff, that's enough / pass it to a friend."

weight

Term used to describe large shipments of drugs, usually illegal.

There's a pretty good amount of weight waiting to be picked up down by the dock.

westside

The west coast, where the real Gs are from, especially Los Angeles.

Hell, yeah, I'm just bangin' on the westside right now. I'll hit ya back.

wet-paint syndrome

Urge that possesses people to do the secret little things they do when they think others aren't looking or when their curiosity is aroused by a sign that is posted telling them not to do something. Inspired by the corridor you walk down for twenty years without touching the walls, until one day you smell fresh paint and the corridor has been roped off with signs that say DON'T TOUCH—WET PAINT. An overwhelming urge comes over you to touch the wall.

Dave's wet-paint sydrome compelled him to feed the zoo monkeys right in front of the DO NOT FEED THE ANIMALS sign.

whack

1. To kill. To assassinate.

You want we should whack that barking dog?

2. Appalling. Unconventional. Also spelled "wack."

Yo, that's whack. I don't want none of that.

what it do?

Interjection meaning "What's happening?" or "How are you?"

Bob: Hey, what it do?
Joe: Chillin'.

what the shit?

Alternative to "what the hell?"

Did he just do what I think he did? What the shit?

whateves/whatevs

A noncommittal, nonchalant answer to practically any question, usually accompanied by a shrug of the shoulders.

Sarah: Do you want to go out with me tonight?
Margaret: Whateves.

what's good?

Another way of saying "How are you?" or "What's happening?"

Bob: What's good?
Me: I'm cool, man.

wheels

Bodybuilder jargon for legs.

You got some big-ass wheels, mate. You must squat 200 kg, right?!

wheels fell off the wagon

A phrase used to indicate that something suddenly went very wrong, like when a romantic or sexual relationship takes a bad turn.

Her incessant screwing around on him made the wheels fall off the wagon, and he dumped her.

wheels of steel

Record turntables, often specifically (but not necessarily) Technics SL1200 series turntables, noted for their steel platters.

This is DJ Hyper manning the wheels of steel tonight.

whilin'

Too harsh in manner, tone, or behavior.

She be whilin' and she don't understand why no one likes her.

W

whip

1. Someone who has their significant other under their thumb/control.

Jonno couldn't make it—he's out with his whip!

2. An expensive, stylish automobile or motorcycle.

My dad let me drive the whip so I can take my girl out tonight.

whipped

Completely controlled by a significant other, but usually refers to a guy being completely controlled by his woman.

Damn! Joe is whipped!

white hat

A computer expert, usually a former hacker, who now uses his or her skills for legitimate causes.

That guy who wrote the OMG0RZ virus? He's a white hat now, works for Sun Microsystems.

whoadie

A friend, particularly someone from the same area of the city as you.

Wassup, whoadie? You got that new CD?

whoop it up

1. To have a good time; to participate in a wild and exciting event.

Man, I can't wait for the party tonight. . . . We are going to whoop it up! Oh yeah!

2. Interjection of agreement or acceptance. Also used as a form of acceptance.

Guy 1: Do you want a beer?
Guy 2: Yeah, guy, whoop it up.

whoop whoop

A warning of approaching police cars.

Whoop, whoop! Go, man, go—clear out!

whoopass

Punishment via beating.

Am I gonna have to open a 2,000-year-old can of Chinese whoopass on you?!

whyle out

Also spelled "wile out." Sometimes shortened to whyle/wile.
1. To act the fool; go crazy.

Man, when Tisha found out he was cheatin', she was whylin' out!

2. To overreact.

It wasn't that bad; she was just whylin' for attention.

wicked

1. Great. Cool.
2. Adjective used to intensify any adjective that follows it.

That wicked cool car is wicked fast, but it's owned by that wicked old guy, who drives it wicked slow, which makes me wicked sad 'cause I'm wicked broke and I got to walk a wicked long way when it's wicked hot out.

wife beater

Form-fitting white ribbed tank top worn by men; looks good on well-built fellas, pathetic on skinny fellas, and disgusting on fat beer-bellied fellas.

Brad Pitt looks damn good in a wife beater.

wig

To worry or be frustrated.

Kev's wiggin' about the game this weekend.

wig out

To throw a huge fit.

When Ko called Johnny a bitch, Johnny completely wigged out.

wig split

To get shot or hit hard in the head.

Darren got his wig split by his ho after she

caught him in bed with another ho.

wigger

A pejorative term for a Caucasian kid who mimics the language, dress, and mannerisms of black ghetto kids.

Wigger: Yo, bizzle, you best step off mah bread!
Suburban white girl: Didn't you get that do-rag at Hot Topic? And why are you wearing a FUBU shirt?
Wigger: Yeah, well . . . you know that's how we do. . . .

wingman

Someone who goes along with their friend on a date so that when their friend picks up the hot girl the wingman gets stuck with her ugly friend. A very noble job, and guys usually switch off wingmen at different clubs.

Aight, man, I'll be wingman this time and fall on the grenade, but you owe me big time.

wiped

Short for "wiped out"; really exhausted, to the point of not being able to move or function.

I spent too long at that party last night—man, am I wiped.

wired

Jittery, like after you drink too much coffee, or otherwise hyper and excited.

I sat in the Waffle House for four hours and left the place completely wired.

woose

A lightweight, a coward, a big girl's blouse. Worse than a wuss.

If your mate is too scared to do something dangerous, like doing that big surfboard jump, stay out late 'cause he has to be home for his bird girlfriend, or talk to a girl in a bar, then you shouldn't hang out with such a woose.

word

Interjection of agreement; sometimes also used as a greeting. Also "word up."

Chris: Yo, you goin' to that rocks tonight?
Barrett: Word.

word is bond

A way of stating that your word is beyond reproach. Often used by rappers.

My word is bond.

word is born

Bastardization of "word is bond," or "my word is my bond." Has become common use, and is even a Run-D.M.C. song title. Has come to mean "the truth is manifest."

Yo, word is born, the government keeps screwing us.

word life

Interjection meaning "I swear to you on my life what I tell you is true." It was used by rappers in the early '90s to mean "I promise."

I'ma send you cryin' to yo' mama after I mess you up! Word life!

work it

To show people how attractive and talented you are.

She's workin' it, dude!

worked

Getting beaten very, very badly in a competition of skill.

If you went one-on-one with LeBron you would get worked.

working girl

Euphemism for a prostitute. Often preferred by the sex workers themselves.

I don't like being called a whore or a prostitute. I'm a working girl.

wrecked

Extremely ugly, beat, busted, broke down, or tore up.

When Tony realized the girl he met over the Internet looked nothing like the Cindy Crawford picture she'd sent him and was actually totally wrecked, he realized he had no choice but to tell her he had a bad case of the beer shits and sneak out the bathroom window.

WTF

The universal interrogative. Used to abbreviate "What the fuck?" When used with an exclamation point instead of a question mark, it becomes an exclamation of amazement, confusion, disbelief, etc. Both forms are often accentuated with "mate" or preceded by "dude."

Dude, WTF are you on?

WWJD

Stands for "What would Jesus do?" Often printed on cheap bracelets or along the length of lanyards. Articles with "WWJD?" are worn by Christians to promote and/or reflect the idea that in times of conflict or moral dilemma, one should speculate (based on the teachings and behaviors described in the Gospels) what Jesus would probably have done in the given situation.

WWJD? Well, for starters, he probably wouldn't purchase and wear tacky jewelry.

W

dictionary

XY

X
The drug Ecstasy.

They went to a rave but didn't do any X.

XYZ
An abbreviation for "examine your zipper." Used when someone's fly is down.

Hey, guy with the purple satin underwear—XYZ!

ya heard?
Interjection meaning "You know what I'm saying?"

I'm the greatest, most awesomest person who ever lived. Ya heard?

ya smell me?
Variation of "Ya feel me?" which is a derivative of "You know what I am saying?" which is short for "Do you understand what I am trying to explain?"

I'm just tryin' to come up in da game. Ya smell me?

yada yada yada
Conversation glosser-over, similar to "blah, blah, blah."

Yeah. I met this lawyer, we went out to

dinner, I had the lobster bisque, we went back to my place, yada yada yada, I never heard from him again.

yak
1. To vomit.

Hey, man, I gotta yak.

2. Cognac. Used by hip-hop/rap artists.

I'm just sippin' yak.

y'all'd
"You all would," to a redneck.

If y'all'd round up them there pigs for me, I reckon I'd give you a quarter.

Yank
1. A term used by the British to describe all Americans.

The Yank just asked me if London was near England. Bloody education in the States!

2. A term used by American Southerners to describe Americans from non-Southern States.

John Boy: He called you a Yank, Billy Bob!
Billy Bob: Nobody calls me a Yank! I'm gonna shoot the limey bastard!

yard
Prison. Refers to prison yards in correctional facilities.

I was a lyrical genius when I performed on the yard up north.

yard sale
1. The evidence or remains of a catastrophic accident or wipeout, in which the victim's belongings are scattered or spread out across a large area (resembling a traditional yard sale).

The U-Haul trailer fishtailed into the oncoming semi, then the median strip was a yard sale.

2. To fall while skiing or snow-boarding and leave a trail of gear behind.

That two-planker is having a yard sale down there.

yellow fever
A mental disease that afflicts wapanese, fanboys/fangirls, and otaku. Symptoms include:
a) A sexual obsession toward females of Asian descent.
b) An obsession toward Asian media and entertainment, primarily animé, hentai, manga, and other Japanese media.

dictionary

c) A sudden urge to imitate anything from Asia, for instance, learning Japanese and eating sushi just for the sheer sake of trying to be "Asian."
d) Thinking that one knows more about Japan than the Japanese themselves, despite never setting foot in that country or even reading about it.

An Asian-American girl was harassed by some psycho who had a bad case of yellow fever. Fortunately, she had a can of pepper spray in her purse and did not hesitate to use it on him.

yellow-card
To punish someone who does something stupid.

Shirley got caught smoking in the girls' loos, and the principal yellow-carded her sorry ass.

yes man
Someone who always agrees with authority and does what he's told.

I've worked here longer, but Jim got promoted because he's a brown-nosing yes man.

yestrosexual
A formerly homosexual person (usually male; for females "hasbian" is preferred) who is currently in a relationship with a member of the opposite sex.

Allen: Knut used to be dating Brad, but now he's dating Liz.
Derek: Sounds like he's another yestrosexual.

yo
1. When followed by an apostrophe (yo'): Short for "you" or "your."

How's yo' momma?

2. An informal address or title to one whose name is not known; can be used as an interrogative address.

Hey, yo! What's up, yo?

3. A declarative or imperative exclamation, whether alone or within a sentence.

Yo! What the hell do you think you are doing?! Yo, just do your job!

yo' momma
The answer to any question, when the correct answer isn't known.

Teacher: Please tell us who the first president of the USA was?
Kid: Yo' momma.

yogasm
An orgasm achieved during yoga, since certain yoga positions can be extremely physical and get the mus-

cles going and the blood flowing.

I had a major yogasm today after class. I wish I could go every day. . . .

yoink!

An exclamation that, when uttered in conjunction with taking an object, immediately transfers ownership from the original owner to the person using the word regardless of previous property rights.

Though I cherished my automobile, I had to purchase a new one when my second cousin came up from behind me and politely exclaimed, "yoink!" while taking my car keys.

you and your mama!

Used to intensify an insult.

Shut up! You and your mama!

you dig?

Shortened form of "Can you dig it?" meaning "Do you understand?"

The chick's not a man, so stop calling her "man," you dig?!

you know how I do

Interjection used to acknowledge someone's approval. Also used to express that a present state or action is so oft-repeated it is as habit to the speaker. Similar to "That's how I roll" and "That's how I do."

G1: You got with dem 22s on yo' ride, man? That's gangsta.
G2: Act like you know, man. You know how I do.

you know it

Interjection of agreement.

Brad: That's a massive spliff you just rolled.
Kris: You know it.

young

Describes an article of clothing that is too small.

I must have gained ten pounds—these pants are hella young!

your face!

Short for "In your face!" Interjection used to gloat over someone else's misfortune.

Your face! Sucks to be you!

your hotness

Formal title given to a male or female who is sexy, well-dressed, and has much charisma.

(to a lady entering the club) Woo, make way for your hotness, coming through!

your mom

An abstract concept loosely affiliated with notions of the intended audience's maternal figure. Normally expressed as an intended slight on said maternal figure. Often serves as indication of the end of a conversation.

X: That is one very fat farm animal.
Y: You're a fat farm animal.
X: I'll show you a fat farm animal.
Y: Your mom is a fat farm animal.

your move

Whenever you deliver a witty remark to someone and completely burn them, you say "Your move, sir/ma'am" to rub it in, suggesting they can't top that.

Your mama is so stupid, when she threw a rock at the ground, she missed! Your move, dude.

yum

Expression of approval.

That ass looks good. Yum.

yuppie food stamps

The ubiquitous $20 bills spewed out of ATMs everywhere. Often used when trying to split the bill after a meal.

We owe $8 each, but all anybody's got are yuppie food stamps.

Y2K bug

Short for "Year 2000 bug."
1. A software bug caused by the use of two-digit numbers to represent the 20th-century year. When the date became 2000, some software thought it was actually 1900.

I have to fix the Y2K bug in this old Cobol program.

2. A bunch of bullcrap made up by paranoid doom-saying wackos and the computer-ignorant media.

When the Y2K bug hits, planes are going to be dropping out of the sky!

urban

Z

zero day

The distribution or release of digital media (such as software, video, or music) before it is sold in stores or before it hits the street. Zero-day releases may be pirated or stolen and may break the law, but not all zero-day releases are obtained illegally.

I own a zero-day copy of the next version of Windows—two years before its official release date.

zero hour

When a countdown is scheduled to end. Alternatively, a deadline.

It's zero hour and my dissertation is due. I hope no one actually reads these things.

zero tolerance

1. A "get tough" policy of making no exceptions to the law, born as a response to a general sense of uneven application of rules and punishments. To react to something with absolute prejudice and without considering mitigating circumstances.

I don't care if you've got glaucoma, we have a zero-tolerance policy to drugs, including marijuana.

We will react to sexism and racism with zero tolerance.

2. An excuse for people of limited intelligence not to have to think.

We have a zero-tolerance policy on tardiness, so even though you were robbed at gunpoint on your way to work, you're fired.

dictionary

zine

An independent publication (usually mass-produced by photocopying and in some cases, scanned, put on the Internet, or copied via fax). Can be on any range of topics and is usually a labor of love for the producers, rather than a way to make money. A means of telling one's story, sharing thoughts, and/or artwork/comics/doodles with all who read it.

Have you seen Jared's new zine? He did a really cool interview with the mailman.

zing!

An interjection commonly used after making a witty joke at someone else's expense while they are present.

Person 1: Your room smells like ass.
Person 2: That's because you're in it. Zing!

zipper-spark

To dry-hump while clothed.

Oh man, John wanted to zipper-spark with Susie so bad behind the bleachers at the junior high school.

zonk

To crash into a deep sleep after being extremely tired or inebriated. Often followed by "out."

After I got home from the strip club, I zonked out on the couch.

urban

Photo: Hope Harris Photography

Aaron Peckham was a computer science student when he launched Urban Dictionary, a parody of dictionary.com with a twist: users wrote the definitions. Soon Urban Dictionary garnered hits—and new definitions—from around the world. Its millions of visitors and authors made Urban Dictionary into the world's dictionary, with more than 1.3 million definitions describing current events, pop culture, and the newest slang.

Urban Dictionary has become a handy reference for media consumers and creators alike. Rush Limbaugh cited Urban Dictionary to define "jackball"; MSNBC used Urban Dictionary to help explain the "man crush"; and a UK judge used Urban Dictionary to translate rap lyrics in a court case.

In his spare time Aaron rides his bike, juggles, listens to *Loveline,* and keeps on top of pop culture by reading new Urban Dictionary definitions. He loves the power of technology to spread humor and understanding. He lives in San Luis Obispo, California.

PUBLIC LIBRARY OF JOHNSTON COUNTY
AND SMITHFIELD-SMITHFIELD, NC